Artificial Intelligence for Design and Process Science

Sang C. Suh
Editor

Artificial Intelligence for Design and Process Science

Springer

Editor
Sang C. Suh
East Texas A&M University
Commerce, TX, USA

ISBN 978-3-031-67885-1 ISBN 978-3-031-67886-8 (eBook)
https://doi.org/10.1007/978-3-031-67886-8

This Springer imprint is published by the registered company Springer Nature Switzerland AG
The registered company address is: Gewerbestrasse 11, 6330 Cham, Switzerland

Foreword

It is indeed a great pleasure to write a foreword for this book dedicated to Professor Murat Tanik and Professor Bernd Kraemer, my two great friends. This book, the result of a one-day workshop in Hawaii in January 2024, touches upon a variety of topics yet consistently highlights three crucial concepts: artificial intelligence (AI), transdisciplinary thinking, and human responsibility. The convergence of these concepts creates a prime *solution space* for solving the truly tough economic, environmental, and social planetary problems.

The leveraged power of transdisciplinary thinking, when supported and augmented by AI, increases the likelihood that humanity will develop solutions to the numerous existential crises currently looming. A deep commitment to human responsibility can guide the development of those solutions along moral and ethical pathways.

The Proper Use of AI

With massive processing power, continuous learning, and access to large datasets, AI can elevate rather than replace humans in problem-solving and decision-making. In arenas where human judgment and ethical considerations are paramount, as with healthcare and public policy, AI enhancement can prevent problems such as cognitive bias and decision fatigue. AI should remain in a supportive role bounded by ethical guardrails, which involves creating and using AI systems that are fair, transparent, and accountable. This includes considerations like avoiding bias in AI algorithms, ensuring AI decisions are explainable, and respecting user privacy.

The Importance of Transdisciplinary Thinking

Transdisciplinary approaches involve a rich interplay of technology and diverse fields of expertise, such as computer science, biology, economics, and social sciences. Collaborative environments where specialists from different disciplines work together can lead to innovative solutions that might not emerge within the silos of individual disciplines. AI can process and analyze the vast amounts of data that such collaborations generate, identifying patterns and insights that are not obvious. This broad integrated perspective helps in developing more robust, adaptable, and effective solutions.

Human Responsibility

While much attention is focused on developing ethical AI, human responsibility has far more significant implications. The blunt fact is that we have become an irresponsible society on a global level. Perverse societal incentives drive deeply damaging acts, such as the burning of the Amazonian rainforest or dumping of toxic waste in the poorest parts of the globe by multinational companies. In many countries, consumers carefully sort plastic recyclables, only to have those plastics either burned or dumped into the ocean, which has contributed to the formation of the Great Pacific Garbage Patch, a vast area of floating debris twice as large as the state of Texas.

The previous examples highlight the fact that today's tough problems do not fall under the jurisdiction of any single country or region, which makes them the responsibility of all humanity. As these problems are complex and subject to dramatic changes over time, a *solution space* that also changes, in response to conditions, is ideal. For instance, on a small scale the Kapi'olani Medical Center for Women & Children in Honolulu, Hawaii, is a responsive solution space. Care teams are transdisciplinary, comprised of members from various specialties and areas of expertise, and combining conventional medical treatments with alternative therapies. The medical center is supported by cutting-edge technology and equipment, and both the care teams and technology can be upgraded over time in response to need.

Reviewing this book has been a truly rewarding experience. I wholeheartedly recommend it to anyone eager to tackle the tough societal problems of today and tomorrow!

Ukiah, CA, USA
May 2024

Raymond Yeh
Chairman, SDPS Advisory Board

Preface

The rapid development of generative AI will have a significant impact on the design processes of emerging intelligent systems. Debates surrounding these topics of current interest must focus on collaborative human-AI decision-making, human-computer interaction, and the related improvements to design and process science. This collection of selected papers provides a focused overview of what role AI plays in the future of design and process of system development with perspectives on making it more relevant and beneficial for our society. It covers such topics as large language models, generative AI, Intelligenticism, communication dynamics representation, feature selection, smart design, and social goodness and demonstrates the general applicability of AI to various problems in transdisciplinary domains.

Yu Chen, Heather Macias, Gabriel Granco, Yunfei Hou, and Frank A. Gomez discuss how AI will impact education and open opportunities to educate the next generation of students from various disciplines to be capable of practical AI skills while having the awareness and confidence to innovatively contribute to their communities. They present a special project called AI for Social Good (AI4SG) that aims to teach AI through the lens of social good to students of multiple disciplines. The impact of AI4SG is illustrated by deploying the special curriculum among 514 undergraduate students in management information systems, geography, and computer science at three universities and evidenced by the report showing increased level of interest and curiosity in learning AI among the students, appreciation for project-based learning, and development of learning space within and beyond the classroom.

Lurong Pan, Frank M. Skidmore, Serkan Güldal, and Murat M. Tanik bring into light another aspect of communication dynamics by proposing a new theoretical framework and delving into the inherent role of energy within the proposed framework. This draws inspiration from Shannon's communication theory and explores the centrality of energy in varying computational models, from classical mechanics to quantum mechanics. In it, the confluence of information and energy revealed that information transfer necessitates energy interactions.

Morteza Zangeneh Soroush, Md. Sakib Ullah Sourav, and Yong Zeng present the concept of creativity supported by AI as an effective tool to complex cognitive processes. Creativity assessment, human-AI co-creation, and team creativity enhancement are presented as examples of AI applications to creativity with shortcomings and open questions.

Sang Suh and Swetha Reddy Pathuri introduce an interactive chatbot called CSACbot (Computer Science as Career bot) developed using neural networks, sentence transformers, and PyTorch. This chatbot serves as an innovative solution to provide comprehensive information about the field of computer science, guiding students and parents in making informed decisions about courses, majors, and potential careers. The CSACbot aims to bridge the information gap, empowering students to embark on successful academic journeys in computer science.

Cristiane Chaves Gattaz, Fuad Gattaz Sobrinho, Joaquim Roberto Neves Campos, Oscar Ivan Palma Pacheco, and Quymã da S. Viana introduce an AI framework for a Business Value-Centric Living Laboratory (BVLL), leveraging Semantic Modeling for Big Data Analytics, emphasizing the contextual nature of data analysis, and recognizing the importance of AI technologies such as machine learning and natural language processing in unlocking business potential sustainability. The PRIMETHOD methodology is presented with P3Tech Architecture Model showcasing how AI integration revolutionizes process management, value realization, and operational excellence in line with ESG and SDG principles.

Michael P. Papazoglou, Bernd J. Krämer, and Amal Elgammal present a proven digital twin-driven manufacturing approach—called manufacturing blueprints. This includes a novel manufacturing knowledge model and a programming approach to rethink and redesign the whole product customization and development process. Manufacturing blueprints promises to realize the vision of smart manufacturing by fully digitizing all physical assets and processes, connecting factory sites and plants to customize outputs, and allocating resources to provide a logical shift between the digital and physical realms of product customization.

Ray A. Gonzalez and Julia Rayz investigate the ability of transformer encoder models to discern and interpret the distinct meanings of compositional compound nouns, crucial for tasks such as semantic analysis and information retrieval. They uncover insights into the models' capabilities to comprehend the semantic depth of these expressions by conducting a systematic comparison of similarity scores among compound nouns and exploring the effects of modifier and head-noun manipulation. They highlight the potential of these models to advance our understanding and processing of natural language, promising significant improvements in search technologies and the broader domain of NLP.

Raghav Vadhera and Manfred Huber propose an approach to a network optimization policy on an abstract problem and architecture embedding those transfers across problems and thus permitting the optimization of networks for new problems without excessive additional training in a reinforcement learning framework.

Geetanjali Bihani and Julia Rayz provide a concise survey of relevant research on large language models (LLMs) resorting to shortcuts when performing tasks, creating an illusion of enhanced performance while lacking generalizability in their decision rules, and presenting challenges in accurately assessing natural language understanding in LLMs. They urge more research efforts to be put toward deepening the comprehension of shortcut learning, contributing to the development of more robust language models, and raising the standards of NLU evaluation in real-world scenarios.

Francis Joseph Costello and Kung Chang Lee propose the novel philosophical concept of "Intelligenticism" as a response to the recent impressive developments in AI and the proliferation of large language models. They propose and define that Intelligenticism consist of four philosophical components such as Anthroposia, Telopolarity, Virtuodymica, and Temporal Bifusion, delving into the effects of AI's widespread adoption, specifically as they pertain to IS/IT study. A conceptual framework that accounts for the unique challenges and issues of deploying and supervising intelligent devices that communicate with humans is also addressed in the study.

Clement Ting, Patrick Then, and Man Lau introduce an automated Feature Selection before Propositionalization (FSbP) and compare its characteristics with traditional feature selection techniques. They provide a use case for FSbP in KDD for oil drilling data, where FSbP is vital for timely project completion, discussing the implementation of FSbP algorithms for the oil drilling use case, areas for improvement, and limitations of FSbP.

Overall, this book is a source of inspiration for everyone in the academia and research sectors working on the vision of creating a strong, fruitful, and creative community of design and process science for social good through evolving and generative AI.

Commerce, TX, USA
May 2024

Sang C. Suh

Introductory Address

Dear Members of the Society for Design and Process Science and colleagues:

I'd like to share some thoughts I've had recently about the importance of imagination and wishful thinking in the creative process. They seem relevant to your theme of Convergence, and to share in its spirit.

In recent years, there have been several spectacular success stories in machine learning. Checkers, chess, and now the deep and ancient game Go have been conquered, in the sense that computers are now the best players. What does it teach us?

Perhaps ironically, one big takeaway is the value of a quintessentially human characteristic: imagination. At first that conclusion might sound strange. Do computers really have imagination? But, on deeper reflection, I think it's compelling. To choose their moves, the computers spin out and examine many alternative possibilities, before settling on the most promising. And what is imagination, but the ability to consider what is not, but might be?

Many creative people, including many physicists, have testified to the value of imagination in their work. In one of his most famous quotes, Albert Einstein said: "Imagination is more important than knowledge. Knowledge is limited. Imagination encircles the world."

The great quantum physicist Paul Dirac, when asked about how he made his epochal discoveries, replied: "I like to play about with equations, just looking for beautiful mathematical relations which maybe don't have any physical meaning at all. Sometimes they do."

And Richard Feynman said: "The game I play is a very interesting one. Its imagination, in a tight straitjacket." The straitjacket, he goes on to explain, is that if your goal is to discover new things about physical reality, you have to respect known facts, accumulated over centuries of research.

Perhaps the most impressive testimonial to scientific imagination came from James Clerk Maxwell, the leading theoretician of electromagnetism, in his tribute to Michael Faraday, its leading experimenter. The self-taught Faraday had to rely on his visual imagination, because his mathematical training was sketchy. This led him to new ways of thinking, as Maxwell described: Faraday, in his mind's eye, saw lines of force traversing all space where the mathematicians saw centers of force attracting at a distance: Faraday saw a medium where they saw nothing but distance; Faraday sought the seat of the phenomena in real actions going on in a medium.

Later, Maxwell converted Faraday's imaginative visions into wonderful new kinds of equations, which we still use today.

But imagination is only half the story. The process of imagining possibilities must be married to methods for evaluating their success.

In games, the final goal like winning or solving the puzzle is specified clearly. But in interesting games it's not possible to see a clear path to that goal straight away. To make progress you must form more limited, tractable, intermediate goals, and aim for those. In other words, you've got to decide what to wish for.

Wishful thinking, in this sense, is an essential part of problem-solving. This becomes even more true when we move outside the context of games, where often there are no set rules that supply the definition of ultimate success.

It's very plausible, then, that an important step toward achievement, whether for machines or human beings, is to cultivate smart, systematic wishful thinking. New Year's resolutions, business plans, and visionary "to-do" lists embody that strategy.

The issue of goals arises most keenly at the highest levels of learning and problem-solving. Trying to make a scientific breakthrough, write a novel or compose a symphony, or create some other great work of art can be hard, frustrating work. Success is not guaranteed, and the tangible, economic rewards are usually modest. What keeps people going?

Some motivations are obvious. The dopamine rush that accompanies successful problem-solving can be its own reward. And successful problem-solving can earn the esteem of others, another thing people find rewarding in itself. But that isn't the whole story.

For many of the greatest physicists, religion was a big motivator. Galileo, Newton, Faraday, and Maxwell were all deeply believing, if not entirely orthodox, Christians. Here's how John Maynard Keynes, the economist, described Isaac Newton, in his famous lecture "Newton, the Man":

> He looked on the whole universe and all that is in it as a riddle, as a secret which could be read by applying pure thought to certain evidence, certain mystic clues which God had lain about the world to allow a sort of philosopher's treasure hunt to the esoteric brotherhood. He believed that these clues were to be found partly in the evidence of the heavens and in the constitution of elements (and that is what gives the false suggestion of his being an experimental natural philosopher), but also partly in certain papers and traditions handed down by the brethren in an unbroken chain back to the original cryptic revelation in Babylonia. He regarded the universe as a cryptogram set by the Almighty.

And here is Maxwell again, delighting in his discoveries:

> The vast interplanetary and interstellar regions will no longer be regarded as waste places in the universe, which the Creator has not seen fit to fill with the symbols of the manifold order of His kingdom. We shall find them to be already full of this wonderful medium; so full, that no human power can remove it from the smallest portion of space, or produce the slightest flaw in its infinite continuity.

These scientists were determined, as Stephen Hawking put it, to "know the mind of God." That inspired them to work prodigiously hard.

Though Albert Einstein was not religious in any conventional sense, he, too, was driven by a passion to know. In his *Autobiographical Notes*, he recounts his fascination as a child when his father showed him a compass: "This experience made a deep and lasting impression upon me. Something deeply hidden had to be behind things." And elsewhere he wrote movingly of his struggle to reach the general theory of relativity: "The years of searching in the dark for a truth that one feels but cannot express, the intense desire and the alternations of confidence and misgiving until one breaks through to clarity and understanding."

Although I am no longer a believer, I am grateful for the training I received in Roman Catholicism, which taught me to see the world as having grandeur and hidden meaning. That vision helped inspire my wishful searching for grandeur and meaning in the physical world, which became habitual.

Finally, let me add that in deciding what to wish for, a feeling for beauty is an invaluable asset. Exposure to beautiful objects and sounds art and music as well as beautiful ideas can develop that sense.

It's a wonderful thing and not, I think, an accident that we humans naturally take delight in imagination and wishful thinking. They help us to solve problems and thrive. Teachers and managers should encourage them, and even the most practical, hard-headed engineers and scientists should cultivate them.

MIT, Cambridge, MA
February 2024

Frank Wilczek
2004 Nobel Laureate

Acknowledgment

In honor of Professors Bernd Krämer and Murat M. Tanik—Life Fellows of SDPS—for their lifetime contribution and achievement in the field of design and process science.

This book appears on the occasion of Prof. Bernd Krämer and Prof. Murat M. Tanik being named Life Fellows of the Society for Design and Process Sciences (SDPS) in January 2024, at a special event held at the AI in Design and Process Science (AIDPS) workshop during the 57th Hawaii International Conference in System Sciences (HICSS). To appreciate their work and honor them for their contribution and achievement in the field of design and process science, a wide range of scientists, engineers, educators, scholars, and practitioners, both from SDPS and from the international research community, dedicated chapters to this commemorative edition.

Recognition of Life Fellows at 2024AIDPS workshop in HICSS 57, Murat Tanik (left), Bernd Krämer (right), Sang Suh (center)

AIDPS workshop committee in HICSS 57, January 2024 in Honolulu, Hawaii

SDPS Leadership Summit and Vision Meeting on AI for Design and Process Science, January 2024

SDPS 20th Anniversary Celebration in Dallas, TX, November 2015

Contents

Contributors

Geetanjali Bihani Purdue University, West Lafayette, IN, USA

Joaquim Roberto Neves Campos ProcesSolution Consultoria Ltda, São Paulo, SP, Brazil

Yu Chen San Jose State University, San Jose, CA, USA

Francis Joseph Costello Sungkyunkwan University, Seoul, South Korea

Amal Elgammal Egypt University of Informatics, Cairo, Egypt

Cristiane Chaves Gattaz Innovarch Soluções em Educação e Inovação Ltda, São Paulo, SP, Brazil

Frank A. Gomez California State University Office of the Chancellor, Long Beach, CA, USA

Rey A. Gonzalez Purdue University, West Lafayette, IN, USA

Gabriel Granco Cal Poly Pomona, Pomona, CA, USA

Serkan Güldal Adiyaman University, Adiyaman, Turkey

Yunfei Hou California State University, San Bernardino, CA, USA

Manfred Huber University of Texas at Arlington, Arlington, TX, USA

Bernd Krämer Scientific Academy for Service Technology e.V. (ServTech), Potsdam, Germany

Man Lau Swinburne University of Technology, Hawthorn, VIC, Australia

Kung Chang Lee Sungkyunkwan University, Seoul, South Korea

Heather Macias California State University, Long Beach, CA, USA

Oscar Ivan Palma Pacheco OG Consultoria em Sistemas e Processos Ltda, Campinas, SP, Brazil

Lurong Pan Ainnocence Inc., Middletown, DE, USA

Michael P. Papazoglou Universities of New South Wales and Macquarie University, Sydney, NSW, Australia

Swetha Reddy Pathuri East Texas A&M University, Commerce, TX, USA

Julia Rayz Purdue University, West Lafayette, IN, USA

Frank M. Skidmore Analytical AI LLC, Birmingham, AL, USA

Fuad Gattaz Sobrinho Ambiência Sistemas de Informação Ltda, Campinas, SP, Brazil

Morteza Zangeneh Soroush Concordia University, Montreal, QC, Canada

Md Sakib Ullah Sourav Concordia University, Montreal, QC, Canada

Sang Suh East Texas A&M University, Commerce, TX, USA

Murat M. Tanik University of Alabama, Birmingham, AL, USA

Patrick Then Swinburne University of Technology, Kuching, Sarawak, Malaysia

Clement Ting Swinburne University of Technology, Kuching, Sarawak, Malaysia

Raghav Vadhera University of Texas at Arlington, Arlington, TX, USA

Quymã da S. Viana Banco Itaú, São Paulo, SP, Brazil

Yong Zeng Concordia University, Montreal, QC, Canada

AI for Social Good Education Through a Culturally Responsive Pedagogy

Yu Chen, Heather Macias, Gabriel Granco, Yunfei Hou, and Frank A. Gomez

Abstract The advances of artificial intelligence (AI) have impacted and opened opportunities for almost every single industry. Meanwhile, it also holds potential to address pressing societal issues such as traffic, climate change, and poverty. It is therefore crucial to educate the next generation of students from various disciplines to be capable of practical AI skills while having the awareness and confidence to innovatively contribute to their communities. We introduce the AI for Social Good (AI4SG) project that aims to teach AI through the lens of social good to students of multiple disciplines. We deployed the AI4SG curriculum among 514 undergraduate students in management information systems, geography, and computer science at three universities. Students reported increased level of interest and curiosity in learning AI, appreciated project-based learning, and developed learning space within and beyond their classroom.

Keywords Artificial intelligence · Education · Social good · Interdisciplinary education · AI for Social Good · Undergraduate education · STEM education culturally responsive pedagogy

---

Y. Chen (✉)
San Jose State University, San Jose, CA, USA
e-mail: yu.chen@sjsu.edu

H. Macias
California State University, Long Beach, CA, USA
e-mail: heather.macias@csulb.edu

G. Granco
Cal Poly Pomona, Pomona, CA, USA
e-mail: ggranco@cpp.edu

Y. Hou
California State University, San Bernardino, CA, USA
e-mail: yunfei.hou@csusb.edu

F. A. Gomez
California State University, Office of the Chancellor, Long Beach, CA, USA
e-mail: fgomez@calstate.edu

S. C. Suh (ed.), *Artificial Intelligence for Design and Process Science*,
https://doi.org/10.1007/978-3-031-67886-8_1

1 Introduction

Advances in new technologies, including artificial intelligence (AI), have fueled the Fourth Industrial Revolution affecting the way people live, work, and relate to one another. As part of its 2030 Agenda for Sustainable Development, the United Nations, in 2015, set up the 17 Sustainable Development Goals (SDGs) (e.g., reduce inequality, provide affordable and clean energy, improve health and education) which were a call for action by countries in a global partnership in AI innovation and education for social good [1]. These goals align with the mission of the California State Universities (CSUs), with 21 of 23 campuses being Hispanic-Serving Institutions (HSIs). Faculty and researchers from the CSU system have been exploring how AI can be used for social good by addressing societal challenges, thereby improving people's lives. This raises two questions for educators: (1) How can undergraduate students from diverse majors learn AI so they are equipped with the necessary skills for the future workforce and become tomorrow's model citizens and leaders? (2) How can student engagement and learning in AI be increased to reduce the equity gap in AI education?

The AI for Social Good (AI4SG) project aims to broaden AI education by developing and studying the efficacy of innovative learning practices and resources for AI education for social good. We have developed three AI learning modules for students to (1) identify social issues that align with the SDGs in their community (e.g., poverty, hunger, quality education), (2) learn AI through hands-on labs and business applications, and (3) create AI-powered solutions in teams to address social issues they have identified. Student teams are expected to situate AI learning in their communities and contribute to their communities. Students then use the modules to engage in an interdisciplinary approach, facilitating AI learning for social good in management information systems, geography, and computer science at three CSU HSIs (San Jose State University (SJSU), Cal Poly Pomona (CPP), and CSU San Bernardino (CSUSB)).

2 Related Work

2.1 Culturally Responsive, Relevant, and Sustaining Pedagogy (CRRSP)

Culturally Responsive, Relevant, and Sustaining Pedagogy (CRRSP) is a student-centered teaching framework, drawing upon decades' worth of research [2–6], that recognizes and affirms students' racial, linguistic, and cultural identities to develop their agency, encourage academic rigor and critical thinking skills, uplift marginalized voices, and empower students to become agents of change through a strong development of their sociopolitical or critical consciousness. CRRSP recognizes and responds to students' identities and needs by using the cultures, experiences, and narratives of culturally diverse students as resources for their own learning and the teaching of peers [7]. Teaching that recognizes the cultural characteristics, experiences, and perspectives of culturally diverse students affirms the cultural knowledge and skills they and their communities offer the classroom [3]. CRRSP realizes that student learning is impacted by factors that go beyond the classroom [3, 7]; integrating students' and communities of Color's knowledge and skills into classroom learning normalizes the knowledge and skills of communities of Color, enriches classroom learning, and promotes a curriculum that is accessible and relevant to all students [5], thereby increasing students' social, cultural, and academic success [8–11].

CRRSP does not replace rigor with inclusion or vice versa; rather, it intentionally empowers students intellectually, "socially, emotionally, and politically" [5] (p. 159). Because CRRSP integrates community and diverse academic knowledge and skills, students develop their critical consciousness and cultural awareness of society, others, and themselves [5, 7, 12]. A culturally affirming instructor integrates practices that simultaneously foster academic success and empower students to ask critical questions [2, 13]. Through the development of student agency, CRRSP builds students' critical literacies to connect their lives/cultures to examples of oppression in curricula, institutions, and disciplines [14].

In contrast to CRRSP's concern with connecting students' identities, cultures, and communities to the classroom, past research has made visible the lack of diversity in particular fields, including computer science (CS). CS has historically been inaccessible to racially marginalized groups, women, and students from working class communities [15]. Work has been done to take a culturally affirming approach to CS education by examining and diversifying what artifacts are produced, how courses are taught, and how to deepen student participation [16, 17]. From this work, culturally responsive computing (CRC) has emerged based on the principles of CRRSP to encourage students to engage, reflect, and build tools while simultaneously challenging the status quo in computing [18, 19].

CRC promotes equity in STEM by rooting the curriculum in a social critique lens [19, 20] to leverage the cultural and linguistic assets of the local community and students [21, 22]. Through CRC, students engage and challenge political, economic, and social issues, including oppressive conditions they have experienced. CRC has five main tenets that shape a culturally responsive computing environment: (1) every student is capable of digital innovation; (2) the learning context must support the transformational use of technology; (3) learning should be about one's self along various intersecting sociocultural lines that allow for technical innovation; (4) technology should be a vehicle for students to reflect and demonstrate understanding of their intersectional identities; and (5) standards for technological success must consider who creates, for whom, and to what end, rather than who endures socially and culturally irrelevant curriculum [19] (pp. 420–421). In sum, CRC's goals are similar to those of CRRSP: to create an educational (computing) environment that values student/family/community expertise, to provide opportunities for collaborations with local community organizations and community experts, and to focus not only on the content (i.e., tool design) but also on the design and implementation of a CRC curricula [22].

Past examples of CRC demonstrate the connection it has to CRRSP. Examples include teen girls using digital technology to educate their local community about relevant, but stigmatized, social issues (e.g., teen pregnancy) [23], using "social GIS" to explore social justice issues with data science and mapping tools [24], using computational skills to share Indigenous knowledge and language [20], and working with young women to develop a Zambian Women's Rights mobile app [25]. Past research has established that when students are encouraged to embed their identities, cultures, and communities into their STEM learning and computing, students' motivation is enhanced, which has the potential to also increase student agency and STEM participation [10, 26]. Teaching through a CRC lens creates opportunities to align the goals of instructors and community members through a collaboration that leverages "community assets" that are relevant to the students and their lived realities [22] (p. 5) while also promoting equity in CS [27].

3 AI4SG Curriculum Design

We designed AI learning modules called "AI for Social Good (AI4SG)" to educate undergraduates from STEM and non-STEM backgrounds. These instructional modules are a result of interdisciplinary work from the research team and are based on CRC and targeting sustainability as an application case [20]. CRC is particularly suitable for interdisciplinary, community-based, and inclusive AI education due to its five tenets: (1) all students are capable of digital innovation, modules will have varying levels of learning support and application; (2) the learning context supports transformational use of technology, modules will be designed to address relevant social issues in students' communities; (3) learning should be about one's self along various intersecting sociocultural lines that allow for technical innovation, modules are interdisciplinary and the exchange of cultural values will be incentivized; (4) technology should be a vehicle in which students reflect and demonstrate understanding of their intersectional identities, modules will be designed for students to express and bring their full self into the practice and community; and (5) barometers for technological success should consider who creates, for whom, and to what ends rather than who endures socially and culturally irrelevant curriculum, modules will emphasize the importance of social good, community, and ethics in AI, enabling students to contribute to their communities as they learn AI. In addition to CRC, the project also incorporated sustainability, particularly the United Nations' Sustainable Development Goals (SDGs), into the AI4SG modules. This integration aims to educate students about the role of AI in achieving these global goals and encourage them to consider sustainability in their AI projects as a case for social good.

We designed modules that (1) encourages students to choose topics that they care about—sustainability, (2) offers appropriate difficulty levels that students feel competent to work on, and (3) empowers students to create concrete solutions relevant and beneficial for their communities and future careers. Therefore, "AI for Social Good" is deployed as a student-team project with three modules [28–31]:

- Module 1: identifying sustainability challenges in students' communities (using the SDGs as guide)
- Module 2: learning AI concepts and applications through hands-on AI labs and study cases
- Module 3: learning AI innovation by proposing or creating, in teams, AI-powered solutions to address the social issues and discussing the benefits and risks

In Module 1: Social Problem, students were provided with material on the Sustainable Development Goals (SDGs) and local applications of the SDGs for initial ideation of possible topics of study. Additional material was provided on how to identify a social issue and connect it to the SDGs. Students formed teams and identified relevant social issues in their community through observation, taking photos, and interacting with the community. This task allowed students to connect the module content to their lived experiences, motivating them by choosing challenges that mattered to them. This module also helped students establish an intrinsic value to learn skills to address problems relevant to them and their communities.

In Module 2: AI Labs, students were provided with AI "toolkits" to learn the concepts and applications of AI. The purpose of providing these toolkits was to facilitate ideation on how they might use AI to address the social issue identified in Module 1. The project curated demonstrations (demos) of common AI applications and tutorials on how to use them from leading AI companies (e.g., IBM, Google). These AI applications covered machine learning, conversational agents, visual recognition, speech to text, text to speech, sentiment analysis, etc. This module encouraged students to learn AI concepts by using the provided AI demos and to summarize the definitions and functions of these AI applications. For advanced options, students participated in hands-on labs using an adapted version of existing AI platforms and tutorials from the industry to meet students' levels. The project team compared alternative platforms that best served project and student needs (i.e., Google, Microsoft). Subsequently, students were provided with short study cases in which companies and organizations use AI to create innovative solutions. Studying the technical and application aspects of AI helped them connect what they learned about AI to the problems in their communities they had selected. We expected that using cutting-edge technologies and application cases that matched students' capabilities allowed students to increase the attainment value in learning.

Finally, in Module 3: AI-Powered Innovation, students worked with their teams as simulated "startups" to create AI-powered solutions for pressing social issues in their communities. Having identified a social issue in Module 1 and learned about AI toolkits in Module 2, student teams integrated these modules and ideated how AI applications could be utilized to address their chosen topics. Students were guided through brainstorming based on a simplified design thinking framework, an analytical and creative problem-solving framework that engages a person to ideate, prototype, and evaluate solutions iteratively. Students were also instructed on a risk/benefit analysis to evaluate their plans of AI4SG in their communities [32]. For advanced options, student teams have created prototypes based on the hands-on AI labs they learned in Module 2. Students then presented their solutions, complete with a risk/benefit analysis, in front of gamified "investors"—external industry or community guests who served as judges for the student presentations. The AI4SG project guided students in developing AI solutions for community issues, emphasizing the value of their diverse backgrounds for innovation. Through a simulated "social entrepreneurship" experience, students presented their ideas to external judges, enhancing their sense of social citizenship and leadership. Furthermore, the project incorporated the SDGs, encouraging students to align their AI solutions with these goals. This fostered global citizenship and responsibility among students, positioning the AI4SG project as a tool for not just teaching AI but also promoting sustainable development and social good.

4 AI4SG Implementation

Our project aimed to implement AI4SG modules by engaging undergraduate students in practical projects across a range of disciplines and institutions, thereby promoting AI learning, community engagement, and inclusiveness. Adopting an interdisciplinary approach, we recognized the necessity of drawing upon multiple disciplines due to AI's broad applications across all industries and the complex nature of social problems. Consequently, the teaching modules developed in the project's initial phase were deployed across various disciplines to meet the diverse needs of undergraduate students at different academic levels. Lower division students were introduced to AI concepts, applications, and innovation, while upper division students gained hands-on experience by creating prototypes, preparing them for AI-related careers and potential startups.

We emphasized an interdisciplinary approach throughout the project. Before starting Module 1, students engaged with existing projects completed by their peers, as documented in studies [30, 31, 33], to understand the context for community-engaged projects. This step aimed to enhance students' appreciation for the value of their work. Before Module 2, we facilitated idea exchanges between students from different disciplines and campuses (SJSU, CSUSB, CPP), fostering an appreciation for disciplinary, cultural, and regional diversity. Following Module 3, students showcased their AI-powered social innovation projects in a workshop across the three campuses, further enhancing their understanding of the projects' utility value.

The project's commitment to diversity was evident in its execution across the three highly diverse CSU campuses. We engaged students from both upper and lower academic divisions, encouraging teamwork to explore AI solutions to social problems. For the upper division, students progressed beyond ideation to actually implement and deploy prototypes addressing social issues of their choice.

In Fall 2022 and Spring 2023, the project had reached 514 undergraduate students across 13 classes on the three campuses. These students represented a wide array of majors, including Management Information Systems, Finance, Business Analytics, Accounting Information Systems, Entrepreneurship, General Business, Marketing, International Business, Management, Psychology, Economics, Criminology, Advertising, Kinesiology, Mechanical Engineering, Computer Science, Computer Engineering, Geography, History, Anthropology, Geology, Urban and Regional Planning, Electrical Engineering, Landscape Architecture, Environmental Biology, Agribusiness, and Food Industry Management. This diverse participation underscored the project's comprehensive reach and impact on promoting interdisciplinary AI education and community engagement.

5 Findings

In Fall 2022, we conducted individual interviews with three students at the beginning and end of the semester to pilot the interview questions and to determine any initial themes that emerged to inform the focus groups next semester. During Spring 2023, the research team decided that focus groups would be the main data source for the qualitative data collection to ensure that the qualitative data was rich and robust, given the diversity of the student-participant pools. Thirteen students participated in the beginning-of-semester focus group and nineteen students in the end-of-semester focus group. To maintain independence and impartiality, the interview and focus group studies were conducted by a co-author from a different institution who had no direct involvement in the courses integrating AI4SG modules. This section presents three preliminary findings from our qualitative interview and focus group studies [34].

Developing an Interest and Curiosity in AI Technology Results indicate that students develop an interest in the potential application and development of AI technology over the course of the semester. Most students appear to take the courses because they are "required" for their major across all three institutions; during interviews at the start of the semester, very few students discuss being personally interested in the content of the courses.

However, by the end of the semester, findings indicate that students develop a clearer understanding of the uses of AI, the impact that AI has on people's lives, and the potential AI holds to improve people's lives (including for communities of Color), and, overall, many more students are interested in integrating AI into their future careers or are open to the possibility, should one arise. For example, one student who is unsure if something like AI would be used in their future career still states that "if my future company does have that [opportunity], I would love to be a part of those organizations that actually take time" to help bring computer science,

AI, and other technology to others, such as children and marginalized neighborhoods. The course and project sparked an interest in these students to share the benefits of AI technology with those who may not have access otherwise.

By the end of the course, students are able to discuss the limits of AI, including various ethical dilemmas that AI technology may present in the future as further developments are made. One student brings up the fact that "the people that are actually developing the technology will have their biases," while another student states that the potential for future developers working in AI have "a lot of power and with that comes a lot of responsibility." Many students agree that AI technology needs to be monitored because it can "definitely be used for good, but it can also be used for very bad things." Through the process of completing the project, including the group work (see finding #2) and the emphasis on community (see finding #3), students now understand there are both scientific implications and humanistic implications when developing AI technology.

Appreciation for Project-Based Learning Assessments Initial findings suggest that the learning modules used in the courses at the three institutions are the type of learning experiences students desire, as expressed in the interviews. For example, when asked what advice they would give course instructors about how to make course content more relevant to their lived experiences, at the beginning of the course, the majority of focus group students begin the semester wanting as many opportunities as possible to practice applying the course content in contextualized situations.

During focus groups at the end of the semester, students across all courses refer to the "AI for Social Good" project done in the present course as an example of what other STEM-related courses should use as a summative assessment.

"Project-based learning" (PBL) is a type of inquiry-based learning that provides students with opportunities to construct knowledge through real-world questions, problems, and practices [35] to create meaningful learning experiences [36] that include peer social interactions and the sharing of knowledge and understanding with others. As a PBL assessment, the students discuss aspects of the "AI for Social Good" project they enjoyed, including collaborating with their peers, applying their personal knowledge and expertise, and demonstrating their content knowledge through an authentic context. When talking about the advantages of collaboration, one student explains that "a huge advantage of working in a group is that you're able to get perspectives from so many different places," demonstrating their understanding of how effective group-based learning is compared to the traditional, passive learning found in lecture-based courses. Another student even calls the present course "an outlier" because "STEM courses tend to focus more on a technical understanding, or it's very just 'get it done,' instead of having that human factor to it," which, they feel, their course did take into consideration in relation to the course content, completing the PBL assessment with their peers, and designing the final product with other communities in mind.

Developing Community Inside and Outside the Classroom A final theme is how students discuss the importance of "community" both inside and outside the classroom. At the beginning of the course, when discussing a hypothetical scenario of a student of Color who is struggling to feel included in a STEM course, the topic of "community" is consistently brought up. Some students speak about struggles they experienced before finding their community on campus; other students mention their family and friends from home who support them emotionally and help them to persist through difficulties in school.

During focus groups at the end of the semester, students still hold the same views on the importance of community when unpacking another scenario with the hypothetical student of Color. The student's expressed disappointment with the hypothetical classmates in the scenario who are described as "unsupportive" or "mean." Several students contrast the scenario to their own positive group experiences during the "AI for Social Good" project; students across the courses characterize their learning environments as "welcoming," with one student feeling "very lucky and fortunate to have such a diverse class of people" to work with over the semester. Another student talks about how through this project their instructor created "a pretty strong bond within the class," revealing the class community that was created through the efforts of the instructors, the learning that linked course content to community, and the process of collaborating with peers. Likewise, several students share how their ideas for the group project are based on their own lived experiences (e.g., struggling with basic needs, searching for affordable textbooks) and were taken up by their group for the final project.

Worth noting is that students do not mention the role of communities geographically local to campus during focus groups at the start of the course; but, by the end of the course (Spring 2023 focus groups), students include the role of local communities in the context of their learning and future careers. For example, when asked what advice they would give instructors to make the courses more relevant to their lived experiences, students suggest instructors integrating more opportunities to integrate the local community, such as interviewing local community members and working with local community organizations to understand their needs and to "improve the social good" of the local community more directly.

Additionally, when asked to rank the importance of the course content to either their future careers, their daily lives, or improving the lives of communities of Color, by the end of the semester, less students prioritize themselves and instead, prioritize improving the lives of communities of Color. One student uses the class project as an example of improving the social good for others (over themselves), stating: "a great example of this [priority]was just in the class itself. A lot of the [group] projects were based on helping communities of Color, whether it be gaining access or knowledge about food, or bridging a gap between education, between different levels of income ... and I think it could be utilized in helping communities of Color." By leveraging their experiences within their own communities alongside their content knowledge and skills, initial findings indicate that through this project, students begin building connections between the self, others, and the greater good—something lacking in their previous STEM experiences. Any evidence of students developing an interest in investing in local and/or marginalized communities by the end of the semester will be further examined in future semesters.

6 Dissemination

To maximize the impact of the AI4SG project, we devised a strategic dissemination plan aimed at broadening the project's scope beyond our immediate academic and geographic confines. Central to this strategy was a project website, designed to showcase the diverse "AI for Social Good" projects undertaken by students across participating CSU campuses, available at https://www.aiforsocialgood.org/. This Web site not only highlights the innovative solutions our students have developed to address societal challenges through AI but also serves to inspire educators, stakeholders, and investors about the potential of AI for social improvement. It aims to connect the theoretical knowledge of AI with practical, community-focused applications, thereby engaging current students and motivating future participants.

Further amplifying our outreach, we organized a virtual symposium in collaboration with the CSU Chancellor's Office and STEM-NET, designed to foster cross-disciplinary and cross-institutional dialogues about AI's role in societal transformation. The First Annual CSU AI for Social Good Student Innovation Symposium brought together students, faculty, industry partners, and community stakeholders, facilitating a rich exchange of ideas and highlighting career opportunities in the field of AI. It attracted about 150 attendances in May 2023. Through these initiatives, our dissemination effort not only showcased the practical outcomes of the AI4SG project but also established a foundation for ongoing collaboration and innovation in the application of AI for Social Good.

7 Conclusion

In this study, we introduced the AI for Social Good (AI4SG) project, which aims to offer an innovative educational pedagogy to impart AI knowledge to undergraduate students from diverse academic disciplines, with a focus on societal betterment. Students were instructed to gain a multifaceted understanding of AI applications through case studies, practical hands-on lab sessions, and the prototyping of AI-driven solutions for local societal challenges. The AI4SG curriculum was implemented among three universities between Fall 2022 and Spring 2023 semesters, encompassing 514 students from three distinct disciplines. Students have reported increased level of curiosity and interests in learning AI and a stronger inclination toward AI-related careers. They also appreciated the project-based approach to address important social issues in their own community. Finally, students found it enriching to transcend the traditional classroom boundaries, taking their learning experience into their communities. With the promising preliminary results, we plan to continue to implement the project among more instructors from a variety of disciplines.

Acknowledgement We would like to thank the National Science Foundation for sponsoring this project under the grants #2142783, #2142439, #2142503, #2142490, and #2142594.

References

1. Keating, J., & Nourbakhsh, I. (2018). Teaching artificial intelligence and humanity. *Communications of the ACM, 61*(2), 29–32.
2. Brown, J. C., & Crippen, K. J. (2016). The Growing Awareness Inventory: Building capacity for culturally responsive science and mathematics with a structured observation protocol. *School Science and Mathematics, 116*(3), 127–138.
3. Gay, G. (2018). *Culturally responsive teaching: Theory, research, & practice* (3rd ed.). Teachers College Press.
4. Kelley, H. M., Siwatu, K. O., Tost, J. R., & Martinez, J. (2015). Culturally familiar tasks on reading performance and self-efficacy of culturally and linguistically diverse students. *Educational Psychology in Practice, 31*(3), 293–313.
5. Ladson-Billings, G. (1995). Toward a theory of culturally relevant pedagogy. *American Educational Research Journal, 32*(3), 465–491.
6. Paris, D. (2012). Culturally sustaining pedagogy: A needed change in stance, terminology, and practice. *Educational Researcher, 41*(3), 93–97.
7. Gay, G., & Kirkland, K. (2003). Developing cultural critical consciousness and self-reflection in preservice teacher education. *Theory Into Practice, 42*(3), 181–187.
8. Byrd, C. M. (2016). Does culturally relevant teaching work? An examination from student perspectives. *Sage Open, 6*(3), 1–7.
9. Howard, T. C. (2001). Telling their side of the story: African American students' perceptions of culturally relevant teaching. *The Urban Review, 33*(2), 131–149.
10. Hughes, R. M., Nzekwe, B., & Molyneaux, K. J. (2013). The single sex debate for girls in science: A comparison between two informal science programs on middle school students' STEM identity formation. *Research in Science Education, 43*(5), 1979–2007.
11. Wiggan, G., & Watson, M. J. (2016). Teaching the whole child: The importance of culturally responsiveness, community engagement, and character development in high achieving African American students. *The Urban Review, 48*, 766–798.
12. Sleeter, C. E. (2005). *Un-standardizing curriculum: Multicultural teaching in standards-based classrooms*. Teachers College Press.
13. Brown, J. C., & Crippen, K. J. (2016). Designing for culturally responsive science education through professional development. *International Journal of Science Education, 38*(3), 470–492.
14. Gutierrez, K. (2008). Developing a socio critical literacy in the third space. *Reading Research Quarterly, 43*(3), 148–164.
15. Zweben, S., & Bizot, B. (2018). 2017 CRA Taulbee survey. *Computing Research News, 30*(5), 1–47.
16. Fields, D.A., Landa, J., Nakajima, T.M., Margolis, J., Chapman, G., Kafai, Y.B., & Goode, J. (2016, October). Putting making in computer science classrooms: An electronic textiles high school curriculum for Exploring Computer Science. Palo Alto, CA: *Demonstration presented at the annual FabLearn conference*.
17. Fields, D. A., Lui, D., & Kafai, Y. B. (2017). Teaching computational thinking with electronic textiles: High school teachers' contextualizing strategies in Exploring Computer Science. In S.

C. Kong, J. Sheldon, & R. K. Y. Li (Eds.), *Conference proceedings of international conference on computational thinking education 2017* (pp. 67–72). The Education University of Hong Kong. isbn:978-988-77034-4-0.
18. Lachney, M. (2017). Culturally responsive computing as brokerage: Toward asset building with education-based social movements. *Learning, Media and Technology, 42*(4), 420–439.
19. Scott, K. A., Sheridan, K. M., & Clark, K. (2015). Culturally responsive computing: A theory revisited. *Learning, Media and Technology, 40*(4), 412–436.
20. Sandoval, C. D. M. (2013). Critical ancestral computing: A culturally relevant computer science education. *PsychNology Journal, 11*(1), 91–112.
21. Lachney, M., Babbitt, W., & Eglash, R. (2016). Software design in the "construction genre" of learning technology: Content aware versus content agnostic. *Computational Culture, 5.*
22. Lachney, M., Eglash, R., Bennett, A., Babbitt, W., Foy, L., Drazin, M., & Rich, K. M. (2021). pH empowered: Community participation in culturally responsive computing education. *Learning, Media and Technology*, 1–22.
23. Vilchis, M., Scott, K., & Besaw, C. (2015). COMPUGIRLS speak: How we use social media for social movements. In E. Middaugh & B. Kirshner (Eds.), *#youthaction: Becoming political in the digital age* (pp. 59–79). Information Age Publishing.
24. Tully, K. (2015). *Social GIS: Creating a mapping tool to engage middle and high school students with their neighborhoods and STEM.* Rensselaer Polytechnic Institute.
25. Buolamwini, J. (2013). *Proposal for pilot Rhodes year of service: Promoting women's rights through technology education.* http://zamrize.org/showcase/pdf/pilot.pdf
26. Reynolds, R. (2016). Defining, designing for, and measuring "social constructivist digital literacy" development in learners: A proposed framework. *Educational Technology Research, 64*(4), 735–762.
27. Scott, K. A., Aist, G., & Zhang, X. (2014). Designing a culturally responsive computing curriculum for girls. *International Journal of Gender, Science and Technology, 6*(2), 264–276.
28. Blumenfeld, P. C., Soloway, E., Marx, R. W., Krajcik, J. S., Guzdial, M., & Palincsar, A. (1991). Motivating project-based learning: Sustaining the doing, supporting the learning. *Educational Psychologist, 26*, 369–398.
29. Chen, Y., Albert, L. J., & Jensen, S. (2022). Innovation farm: Teaching artificial intelligence through gamified social entrepreneurship in an introductory MIS course. *Decision Sciences Journal of Innovative Education, 20*(1), 43–56.
30. Chen, Y., Albert, L. J., & Macias, H. (2023). *Prototyping AI-powered social innovation in an undergraduate MIS course. International conference on information systems 2023.*
31. Chen, Y., & Hill, T. R. (2023). AI for Social Good (AI4SG) education in an undergraduate introductory MIS course. *American conference on information systems 2023.*
32. Çetinkaya-Rundel, M. (2021). *Data science in a box.* Retrieved June 1, 2021, from https://datasciencebox.org/ethics.html
33. Creswell, J. W., Hanson, W. E., Clark Plano, V. L., & Morales, A. (2007). Qualitative research designs: Selection and implementation. *The Counseling Psychologist, 35*(2), 236–264.
34. Patton, M. Q. (1990). *Qualitative evaluation and research methods*. Sage.
35. Blumenfeld, P., Fishman, B. J., Krajcik, J., Marx, R. W., & Soloway, E. (2000). Creating usable innovations in systemic reform: Scaling up technology-embedded project-based science in urban schools. *Educational Psychologist, 35*(3), 149–164.
36. Wurdinger, S., Haar, J., Hugg, R., & Bezon, J. (2007). A qualitative study using project-based learning in a mainstream middle school. *Improving Schools, 10*(2), 150–161.

A Communication Dynamics Representation of Electron Energy of S-Orbitals in Hydrogen-Like Atoms

Lurong Pan, Frank M. Skidmore, Serkan Güldal, and Murat M. Tanik

Abstract This paper delves into the inherent role of energy within the proposed theoretical framework, communication dynamics, which draws inspiration from Shannon's communication theory. Beginning with the foundational understanding of atoms as quintessential carriers of energy, especially evident in electron orbital structures, we explore the centrality of energy in varying computational models, from classical mechanics to quantum mechanics. A pivotal observation reveals the confluence of information and energy, suggesting that in many systems, particularly in quantum realms, information transfer necessitates energy interactions. Further, we probe the energy implications within particle-wave duality, indicating dual energy manifestations for entities. By emphasizing energy's universality, we argue for its role as a bridge in the multi-scale model integration of communication dynamics with diverse scientific fields. We posit that for the holistic success of this new framework, a coherent understanding and representation of energy across multiple scales and domains is imperative.

Keywords Communication theory · Communication dynamics · Quantum mechanics

---

L. Pan
Ainnocence Inc, Middletown, DE, USA

Integrated Systems Center, University of Alabama at Birmingham, Birmingham, AL, USA

F. M. Skidmore
Analytical AI, LLC, Birmingham, AL, USA

S. Güldal (✉)
Integrated Systems Center, University of Alabama at Birmingham, Birmingham, AL, USA

Department of Physics, Art and Science Faculty, Adiyaman University, Adiyaman, Turkey
e-mail: sguldal@adiyaman.edu.tr

M. M. Tanik
Integrated Systems Center, University of Alabama at Birmingham, Birmingham, AL, USA

Department of Electrical and Computer Engineering, UAB, Birmingham, AL, USA
e-mail: mtanik@uab.edu

S. C. Suh (ed.), *Artificial Intelligence for Design and Process Science*,
https://doi.org/10.1007/978-3-031-67886-8_2

1 Introduction

The Concept of Communication Dynamics (CD)

The groundbreaking communication dynamics theory is built on four foundational assumptions:

Assumption 1 The universe (nature) displays anisotropy.

Assumption 2 The universe adheres to the second law of thermodynamics (arrow of time), implying that time is an evolving metric of the universe's entropy. The continual increase in the total entropy of the universe denotes that time is irreversible.

Assumption 3 A shift from a low entropy state to a higher one is perceived as acceleration. This apparent acceleration is consistent with the general theory of relativity, meaning that as the universe accelerates, the temporal speed (measured in clock ticks) varies across microsystems. Such variances might be perceived as different colors by observers (Wilczek, 2015).

Assumption 4 The universe's essence is encapsulated as a one-dimensional communication system in acceleration. All observations, including those hinting at multi-dimensionality, stem from this singular, accelerating dimension termed space-time.

To craft a model founded on these assumptions, certain concepts warrant clarification:

Definition 1: Computing A universal state of existence, equally applicable to both natural and artificial systems across every accuracy scale. In the realm of communication dynamics, we substitute traditional physics terms such as interactions, conduction, and entanglement with "computing." Here, a consistent rule set governs the exchange of information, with computations taking place in what we term as space-time.

Definition 2: Space-Time Point In the intricate tapestry of communication dynamics, a space-time point, represented as x + it, belongs to the complex domain. Time is symbolized by "it," while space by "x."

Definition 3: T-Vectors and U-Matrices Introducing the timed vector (T-vector), a novel mathematical object in communication dynamics is designed to seamlessly incorporate space-time. Expanding the typical vector definition, the T-vector is characterized by magnitude, direction, and uniquely, frequency. Fourier series aptly capture the frequency attributes of T-vectors. A distinct matrix made of T-vectors is denominated as the U-matrix.

Definition 4: Eigenvalue In the lexicon of communication dynamics, the eigenvalue associated with T-vectors and U-matrices symbolizes energy, providing an insightful metric to understand the energy attributes of systems.

2 Approach

Mathematical models of atomic and molecular systems, grounded in both classical and quantum physics, utilize three-dimensional spatial portrayals of atoms. Such models emerge from the classical mechanics assumption that space and time are distinct dimensions. However, this premise, questioned by Einstein's theory of general relativity, limits these models in terms of accuracy and computational efficiency. We propose that the constructs of 3D space and time are predominantly human-derived perceptions, suggesting that mathematics can depict the universe beyond these confines. To enhance computational capabilities and represent physical reality across scales, it's essential to rethink the 3D space-time paradigm.

We developed the communication dynamics model that challenges the conventional space-time belief, offering a unified mathematical formulation that encapsulates physical significance. In this model, space-time is represented as a one-dimensional frequency space evolving hyperbolically over a clock time (or T-vector). Our model permits representation across varying system scales, introducing an adjustable precision mechanism. With this model, precision can range from the minutest quantum unit, represented by Planck's constant (h), to expansive entities like atoms, molecules, and even complex biomolecules such as proteins and DNA. This model facilitates seamless cross-scale integration using a uniform formula, presenting an avenue to refine foundational physics theories by shifting from a 3D space-time representation to a frequency-vector model.

Communication dynamics systematically analyze and compare chemical structures at any chosen scale. It holds the potential to address data-heavy and computationally demanding challenges in chemical systems. In prior work [1], we introduce unique communication channel representations for every element in the periodic table, conceptualizing electron orbitals as distinct communication channels. This innovative approach allowed for the depiction of intrinsic orbital properties, including energy and radius. The approach is translatable to modeling complex chemical systems. In this paper, we begin an exploration of the modeling of complex chemical systems.

Our approach to chemical systems starts with the concept of building a communication channel representation of electron shell structure. We approach this concept by taking inspiration from Shannon's capacity theory, which defines the maximum amount of information, or data capacity, that can be sent over any channel of medium. As a first principle, we assume that space-time is fundamentally dynamic and, at a smallest level, can be most efficiently described as a periodic evolving function (Eq. 4). Evolution is conceptualized as occurring in quantum "jump steps," represented in a complex number plane. Subsequently, we develop this approach to accommodate four quantum numbers (Table 1). In this section, we first review Shannon and relate his approach to our error content graph, and we then detail a process by which we develop a quantum number-based approach, using communication dynamics, to represent electron shells.

Table 1 Quantum numbers and Fourier matrix parameters

Quantum numbers	Symbol	Orbital meaning	Range of values	Fourier series polygon parameters
Principal quantum number	n	Shell	$1 \leq n$	Vertices ($n = n + 1$)
Azimuthal quantum number (angular momentum) $\ell = 0, 1, 2$ (s, p, d)	ℓ	Subshell (*s* orbital is listed as 0, *p* orbital as 1, etc.)	$0 \leq \ell \leq \mathrm{n} - 1$	Summation interval ($1 = \ell + 1$)
magnetic quantum number, (projection of angular momentum) $m\ell = -2, -1, 0, 1, 2$	$m\ell$	Energy shift (orientation of the subshell's shape)	$-\ell \leq m\ell \leq \ell$	Summation interval ($[-1, 1]$)
Atomic number A	A	Number of protons in a nucleus	$1 < A < 118$	Coefficient A

3 Compounded Error Content Graphs in Communication Dynamics

Our mathematical models are developed based on the concept that communication theory can represent various scales of biological units including electrons, atoms, molecules, cells, and organisms. Compounded error communication channels (error contained, compounded channels) represent the interactions and assemblies between signal generation and moments in space-time where signal is modeled to be received. Figure 1 shows a sample communication and a related error (or information) content graph.

The symbols on the left side correspond to a signal, and the symbols on the right side show the mapping of the sent and received signals. On the left in Fig. 1, we show Shannon's representation of an error content graph. In this representation, the information content of the lowercase and uppercase symbols is the same. If lowercase letter corresponds to the same letter (uppercase) on the other side, no error is encountered in the communication. In the formulation of Shannon, therefore (left), $a \rightarrow \mathrm{B}$, $b \rightarrow \mathrm{C}$, $c \rightarrow \mathrm{D}$, $d \rightarrow \mathrm{E}$, and $e \rightarrow \mathrm{A}$ represent errors that occur.

In the polygon formulation (Fig. 1, right), each of these symbols may be considered to be a point on a circle and the error pairs as line segments joining these points. Inherently, in the polygon, we understand $a \rightarrow a$, $b \rightarrow b$, etc. can represent an error-free transmission over space-time, whereas $a \rightarrow b \rightarrow c \rightarrow d \rightarrow e \rightarrow a$ efficiently represents the dynamic error content of the graph [2], or equivalently, we can call this the information entropy [1]. This polygon can be considered an error content graph that represents the transmission error in the communication channel.

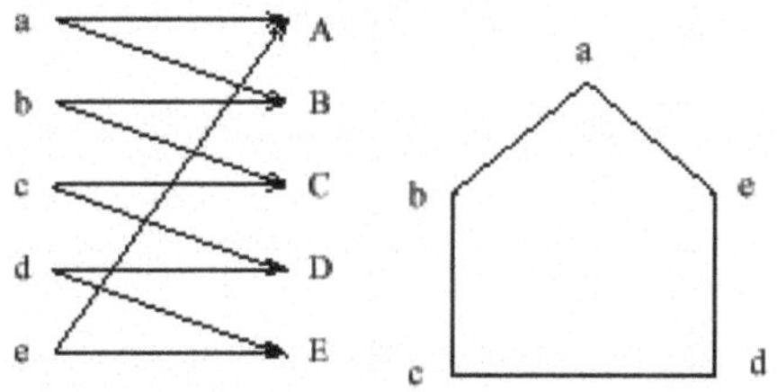

Fig. 1 A sample communication channel and its error content graph

A Fourier series representation of this error content graph can be expressed as [3]:

$$u_{n,a}(p,t) = \sum_{\ell=-p}^{p} \frac{e^{j(a+nl)t}}{(a+nl)^2} \tag{1}$$

where a is the jump step or jump speed and n is the number of vertices. In other words, n determines number of vertices of the polygon, l determines the interval $l \in [-p, p]$ in which the Fourier series will be calculated, and p is the resolution parameter.

Following [4], let $\chi_{n,\,[a]}([p], t)$ denote an irregular-shaped error content graph that has n vertices, where the jump speed a is not a constant, but is a vector that has n elements. Moreover, $[p]$ does not have to be constant for each side of the irregular-shaped error content graph. One can assume that the resolution parameter p is used to represent some parameter in the system being modeled. For example, let $a = [c, d, c, e, \ldots, h, q, d]$ where each distinct element of a corresponds to a different jump speed. The length of jump vector a is n, the number of vertices, revealing the fact that the irregular-shaped error content graph $\chi_{n,\,[a]}([p], t)$ is composed of pieces out of the regular-shaped error content graphs. Since the error content graphs can be represented as Fourier series, then a communication channel can be represented with a Fourier series [5]:

$$U(n,p,q) = \sum_{i=-p}^{p} \sum_{t_r=0}^{2\pi} \frac{e^{j(q+nl)t_r}}{(q+nl)^2} \tag{2a}$$

The matrix expression of this formula is:

$$U(n,p,q)$$

$$= \begin{bmatrix} \frac{e^{i[q+n(-p)]t_1}}{[q+n(-p)]^2} & \frac{e^{i[q+n(-p)]t_2}}{[q+n(-p)]^2} & \cdots & \frac{e^{i[q+n(-p)]t_{N-1}}}{[q+n(-p)]^2} & \frac{e^{i[q+n(-p)]t_N}}{[q+n(-p)]^2} \\ \frac{e^{i[q+n(-p+1)]t_1}}{[q+n(-p+1)]^2} & \frac{e^{i[q+n(-p+1)]t_2}}{[q+n(-p+1)]^2} & \cdots & \frac{e^{i[q+n(-p+1)]t_{N-1}}}{[q+n(-p+1)]^2} & \frac{e^{i[q+n(-p+1)]t_N}}{[q+n(-p+1)]^2} \\ \vdots & \vdots & & \vdots & \vdots \\ \frac{e^{i[q+n(-1)]t_1}}{[q+n(-1)]^2} & \frac{e^{i[q+n(-1)]t_2}}{[q+n(-1)]^2} & \cdots & \frac{e^{i[q+n(-1)]t_{N-1}}}{[q+n(-1)]^2} & \frac{e^{i[q+n(-1)]t_N}}{[q+n(-1)]^2} \\ \frac{e^{i[q+n(0)]t_1}}{[q+n(0)]^2} & \frac{e^{i[q+n(0)]t_2}}{[q+n(0)]^2} & \cdots & \frac{e^{i[q+n(0)]t_{N-1}}}{[q+n(0)]^2} & \frac{e^{i[q+n(0)]t_N}}{[q+n(0)]^2} \\ \frac{e^{i[q+n(1)]t_1}}{[q+n(1)]^2} & \frac{e^{i[q+n(1)]t_2}}{[q+n(1)]^2} & \cdots & \frac{e^{i[q+n(1)]t_{N-1}}}{[q+n(1)]^2} & \frac{e^{i[q+n(1)]t_N}}{[q+n(1)]^2} \\ \vdots & \vdots & & \vdots & \vdots \\ \frac{e^{i[q+n(p-1)]t_1}}{[q+n(p-1)]^2} & \frac{e^{i[q+n(p-1)]t_2}}{[q+n(p-1)]^2} & \cdots & \frac{e^{i[q+n(p-1)]t_{N-1}}}{[q+n(p-1)]^2} & \frac{e^{i[q+n(p-1)]t_n}}{[q+n(p-1)]^2} \\ \frac{e^{i[q+n(p)]t_1}}{[q+n(p)]^2} & \frac{e^{i[q+n(p)]t_2}}{[q+n(p)]^2} & \cdots & \frac{e^{i[q+n(p)]t_{N-1}}}{[q+n(p)]^2} & \frac{e^{i[q+n(p)]t_N}}{[q+n(p)]^2} \end{bmatrix} \tag{2b}$$

This matrix, which we term the U-matrix, is a unique nonstationary space state matrix, in which each term in the matrix is nonstationary.

For example, the Fourier series representing the "polygon" in 1 will specifically be:

$$u_{5,1}(p,t) = \sum_{\ell=-p}^{p} \frac{e^{j(1+5l)t}}{(1+5l)^2} \tag{3}$$

Using MATLAB and the Fourier series representation for this communication channel, we plotted the directed graph as represented in Fig. 2. Note that Fig. 2 is produced from the error content graph equation, and it is an analytical representation of noise in the communication channel. However, Fig. 2 is simply a directed graph produced from Shannon's channel representation scheme. The biological significance of the quantum Fourier representation depicted in Fig. 2 is that each directed "edge" is a mathematical computation. That is the reason we can claim that electronic, atomic, molecular, and larger assembly representations can be expressed as a series of computations in complex domain. This computational representation also connects the communication channel formalism to quantum electrodynamics (QED) [6].

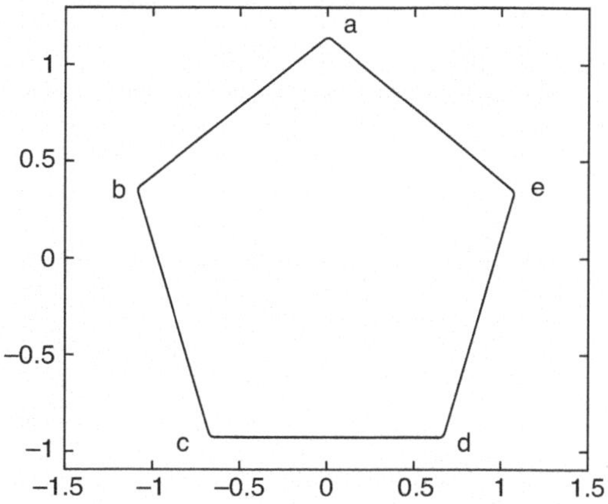

Fig. 2 Fourier series representation of the error content graph that describes the noise in the communication channel in Fig. 3

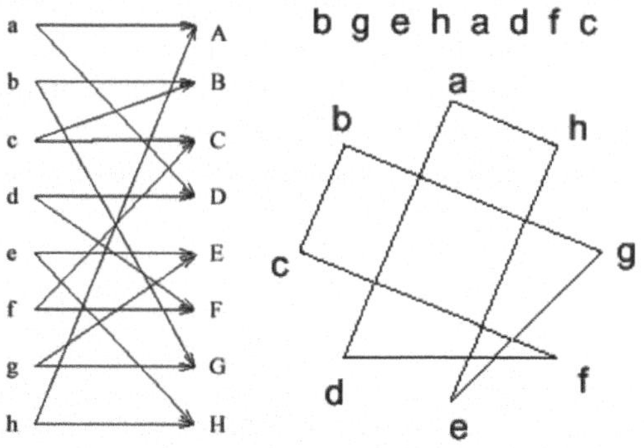

Fig. 3 An irregular communication channel and its error content graph

A more realistic example would be the representation of irregular "polygons" as in Fig. 3.

As represented in Fig. 3, we can see that a communication channel formulated in this fashion is able to describe systems with low or high degrees of symmetry. The noise component of signal transduction process can be quantified as information entropy, which is consistent with the concept of entropy described in thermodynamics and statistical mechanics. This concept also bridges the application of communication theory to a broader avenue in modern physics.

4 Electron Orbitals as Communication Channels

We can build a communication channel representation atoms and their electron shells using the above communication dynamics formulation. To be able to accommodate four quantum numbers (Table 1) as well as improve rigor, we introduced minor modifications to our notation. We can start by considering periodic functions.

A periodic function $f(t)$ with $w_0 = 1$ can be represented by complex (exponential) form of the Fourier series where:

$$f(t) = \sum_{k=-\infty}^{\infty} c_k e^{ikt} \tag{4}$$

with $|c_k e^{ikt}| = |c_k|$. The Fourier series of a uniform polygon is given as:

$$f_n(t) = \sum_{k \equiv 1(n)} \frac{e^{ikt}}{k^2} \tag{5}$$

where $k = q + n\ell$ with $\ell = -p, \ldots, p$ and $\ell \in [-p, p]$.

The following parameters are defined to represent the polygon with the Fourier series: $q \in Z^+$ corresponds to the jump step value of uniform polygon; $n \in Z^+$ corresponds to the number of vertices of the uniform polygon; $l \in Z^+$ determines the summation interval $[-p, p]$, in which the Fourier series will be calculated; and $N \in Z^+$ is the sampling factor for the numerical algorithms and it determines the number of samples $t \in [t_0, 2\pi + t]$.

Including all of the parameters of the algorithm, the new equation is obtained:

$$u(\ell, t) = \frac{e^{i(q+n\ell)t_r}}{(q+n\ell)^2} \tag{6}$$

where $t_r = t_0, t_1, \ldots, t_{N-1} = (2\pi + t_0)$ and $\ell = -p, -p+1, \ldots, -1, 0, 1, \ldots, p-1, p$. Since the resulting Fourier series calculation is the sum of each Fourier term at time t_0, we can rewrite the equation for $u(\ell, t)$ as:

$$u(\ell, t) = \sum_{\ell=-p}^{p} \frac{e^{i(q+n\ell)t}}{(q+n\ell)^2} \tag{7}$$

By observing the quantum numbers in Table 1 and the parameters of our equation, we produced our next equation (Eq. 8).

After replacing n, p, and ℓ parameters [7] in Eq. (8) with principal quantum number n, azimuthal quantum number ℓ, and magnetic quantum number m_l, respectively, our equation for the Fourier series becomes:

$$u'_\ell(t) = \sum_{m_\ell=-\ell}^{\ell} \frac{e^{i(q+lm_\ell)t}}{(q/n + lm_\ell)^2} \tag{8}$$

An obvious interpretation of this equation would suggest that it represents a subshell depending on the value of ℓ. Note that each matrix component corresponds to a m_ℓ value. If we continue with our interpretation, each of these components would represent an electron orbital. Let us name these components as $u_{m_\ell}(t)$:

$$u_{m_\ell}(t) := \frac{e^{i(q+lm_\ell)t}}{(q/n + lm_\ell)^2} \tag{9}$$

By extending the same analogy, we can represent the nth shell by taking a summation over ℓ, from 0 to $n - 1$. Then, this U-matrix could be shown as:

$$u''_n(t) = \sum_{\ell=0}^{n-1} \sum_{m_\ell = -\ell}^{\ell} \frac{e^{i(q+lm_\ell)t}}{(q/n + lm_\ell)^2} \tag{10a}$$

In order to incorporate the effect of nuclei on electrons, Eq. (8) is further modified by introducing atomic number (A) (number of protons in the nuclei) and **q = 1 for nonradioactive isotopes**, and y as the period number:

$$u'_\ell(t) = \sum_{m_\ell = -\ell}^{\ell} \frac{2 * n * n * y * e^{i(A+l*m_\ell)t}}{\left(\frac{A}{n} + l * m_\ell\right)^2} \tag{10b}$$

y is the row number of the periodic table, A is the atomic number, and n is the principal quantum number.

Eigenvalues play a pivotal role in linear algebra, particularly in the context of matrices and linear transformations. Typically defined in relation to a matrix and its associated eigenvectors, these values gain unique significance in the realm of communication dynamics. Within this theory, the eigenvalue of the U-matrix $u'_\ell(t)$ intrinsically symbolizes the energy of the communication channel, aligning seamlessly with traditional physics interpretations.

5 Integrating the Communication Dynamics Approach to a Quantum Mechanics Representation of Electron Energy

A spectrum describes the condition in which a value varies continuously [8]. The electromagnetic spectrum is a well-known example, encompassing a continuous range of energy from radio frequencies (low energy) to ultrahigh frequencies such as x-rays and gamma rays [2]. As shown in Fig. 4, visible light occupies a very small portion of the electromagnetic spectrum. Although it is not possible to show the limits of electromagnetic waves, the best guess is that the longest wavelength is the size of the universe, and the shortest electromagnetic wavelength size is equal to the Planck length $\approx 1.616199(97) \times 10^{-35}$ m.

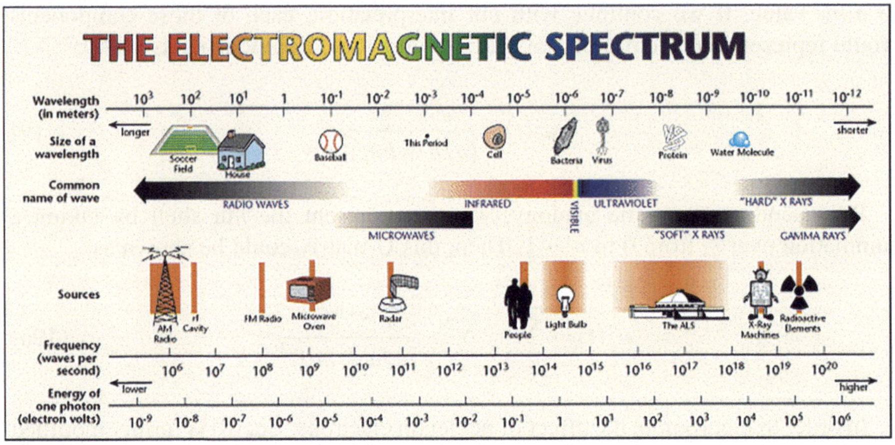

Fig. 4 The electromagnetic spectrum image that is obtained from [9]

Table 2 Electronic structure of the first two shells for $n = 1$ and $n = 2$

n	l	m_l	m_s	Shell	Subshell
1	0	0	½	K	1 s
	0	0	−½		
2	0	0	½	L	2 s
	0	0	−½		
2	1	1	½	L	2p
	1	1	−½		
	1	0	½		
	1	0	−½		
	1	−1	½		
	1	−1	−½		

5.1 Hydrogen Energy Spectrum

To understand the energy spectrum of hydrogen atom, the structure of the atom needs to be known. Hydrogen atoms are mainly composed of a nucleus and electron (s) orbiting around the nucleus. The electron rotates in different levels with respect to its energy. The lowest orbit is $n = 1$, $m_s = \frac{1}{2}$. n is the principal quantum number and m_s is the spin magnetic quantum number [1]. The first shell is named *K* level, and there is only one subshell, 1 s (Table 2).

Moving between shells and subshells is possible by observing or emitting energy. While an electron moves to the lower energy level, it emits radiation. Wavelengths of these radiations are given by Rydberg's formula as:

[1]Electron's spin is ½, so electron's spin magnetic quantum number can only be ½ and −½ .

Table 3 Hydrogen's first three energy spectrum series (Adopted from [10])

Lyman series ($n' = 1$)		Balmer series ($n' = 2$)		Paschen series ($n' = 3$)	
n	λ, vacuum (nm)	n	λ (nm)	n	λ, air (nm)
2	121.57	3	656.3	4	1875
3	102.57	4	486.1	5	1282
4	97.254	5	434.0	6	1094
5	94.974	6	410.2	7	1005
6	93.780	7	397.0	8	954.6
∞	91.175	∞	364.6	9	922.9
				∞	820.4

Table 4 Hydrogen's second three energy spectrum series (Adopted from [10])

Brackett series ($n' = 4$)		Pfund series ($n' = 5$)		Humphreys series ($n' = 6$)	
n	λ, air (nm)	n	λ, vacuum (nm)	n	λ, vacuum (μm)
5	4051	6	746	7	12.37
6	**2625**	**7**	**465**	**8**	**7.503**
7	2166	8	374	9	5.908
8	**1944**	**9**	**329**	**10**	**5.129**
9	1817	10	303	11	4.673
∞	**1458**	∞	**227**	∞	**3.282**

$$\frac{1}{\lambda} = R_H\left(\frac{1}{n'^2} - \frac{1}{n^2}\right) \tag{11}$$

where n is the upper energy level, n' is the lower energy level, and R is the Rydberg constant, $1.09678 \times 107\ \text{m}^{-1}$ (Tables 3 and 4). Rydberg's discovery has an important impact in quantum mechanics.

Lyman series ($n' = 1$)
Balmer series ($n' = 2$)
Paschen series (Bohr series; $n' = 3$)
Brackett series ($n' = 4$)
Pfund series ($n' = 5$)
Humphreys series ($n' = 6$)
Further ($n' > 6$)

5.2 *Hydrogen Atom Energy Level*

Starting from Bohr's model of hydrogen atom, the radius of the stationary orbits and electron energy levels (eV) can be calculated with the following equations:

$$r_n = n^2 a_0 \tag{12}$$

$$E = \frac{-13.6Z^2}{n^2} \tag{13}$$

where $a_0 = 0.0529$ nm is Bohr's radius and Z is the number of protons in an atom (in this case is 1).

Bohr's model is only successful in describing hydrogen-like atoms but fails in all other elements. It also fails to successfully describe many quantum mechanics features of atoms and electrons. The current quantum mechanics description of atomic orbital generally adopts the Schrödinger equation using wave functions. The Schrödinger equation (Eq. (14)) is an eigenvalue equation. For example, the Hamiltonian operator (H) operates on a function (Ψ, a wave function) and the result equals to a real number (E, energy value) times the same function. The scalar number is called the eigenvalue; the function is an eigenfunction of that operator. For hydrogen atom, the atomic orbital can be described by using spherical polar coordinates in the form of a radial function $R_{n,\ l}$ with a radial variable r and a spherical harmonic function Y_{l,m_l} with angular variables θ and ϕ [10]:

$$\widehat{H}\Psi = E\Psi \tag{14}$$

$$\varphi_{\mathrm{n,l,m}_l} = R_{\mathrm{n,l}} Y_{\mathrm{l,m}_l} \tag{15}$$

The wave functions of all hydrogen orbitals ($Z = 1$) can be found here:

The expectation value of the orbit radius ($<r>$) is used to describe the average of radial probability, which resembles the probabilistic expected value of the result (measurement) from an experiment as:

$$<r> = \int \varphi_{\mathrm{n,l,m}_l} * \widehat{r}\varphi_{\mathrm{n,l,m}_l} dV \tag{16}$$

where dV is the spherical polar coordinate that contains the following function:

$$dV = r^2 \sin \theta \mathrm{d}r\mathrm{d}\theta\mathrm{d}\phi \tag{17}$$

For example, for 1s orbital, the solution $<r> = \frac{3a_0}{2Z}$. This also explains why heavier atom has smaller core orbital (1 s) that when Z increases, the $<r>$ of 1s orbital becomes more compact.

Further, the probability density of an electron shell at distance r can be described using $P(r)$, which has a relation with radial wave function R as:

$$P(r) = 4\pi r^2 R^2 \tag{18}$$

The maximum of *P*(*r*) is obtained by setting $dP/dr = 0$ and solving *r*. For 1s orbital, the maximum of *P*(*r*) is when $r = \frac{a_0}{Z}$. For hydrogen ($Z = 1$), the expectation value of 1s orbital radius <*r*> is 1.5 times of the maximum probability radius *r* that is the Bohr radius. For 2 s, $r = \frac{2a_0}{Z}$ and for 3 s $r = \frac{3(3+\sqrt{3})a_0}{2Z}, \frac{3(3-\sqrt{3})a_0}{2Z}$ (two nodes).

On the other hand, the H atom spectrum can be described by using the Rydberg equation. This implies a series of discrete energy levels as:

$$E_n = -hcR_H \frac{1}{n^2} \tag{19}$$

The eigen equation for the radial function $R_{n,\,l}$ can be expressed as follows and the eigenvalue of which is the energy:

$$-\frac{\hbar^2}{2me}\left(\frac{\partial^2 R}{\partial r^2} + \frac{2\partial R}{r\partial}\right) + \left(\frac{\hbar^2}{2\mu r^2} l(l+1) - \frac{Ze^2}{4\pi r\epsilon_0}\right) R = ER \tag{20}$$

where $\mu = \frac{m_{\text{electron}} m_{\text{Nuclues}}}{m_{\text{electron}} + m_{\text{Nuclues}}}$ Therefore, when $l = 0$:

$$\mathrm{E} = -\frac{Z^2 \mu e^4}{32\epsilon_0{}^2 \pi^2 \hbar^2} \frac{1}{n^2} = -13.6 \frac{Z^2}{n^2} \tag{21}$$

which is the same as Eq. (20) when $Z = 1$, indicating that both theories are in agreement at H atom.

When $n_2 \to \infty$, the electron is free from nucleus and this process is called ionization. The ionization energy for electrons in the valence shell $Ei = -E(26)$; when *n* is a constant, the ionization energy increases as *Z* increases. Because the amount of energy required for ionization (ionization energy) is the same for a given quantum number *n*, the atom orbital exhibited energy levels of 2 n^2 degeneracy (e.g., second shell 2 s + 2p has eight degenerate states).

6 Energy Degeneracy and Vertices

On the other hand, the eigen equation for the radial function $R_{n,\,l}$ can be expressed as in Eq. (22) and the eigenvalue of which is the energy:

$$-\frac{\hbar^2}{2me}\left(\frac{\partial^2 R}{\partial r^2}+\frac{2\partial R}{r\partial}\right)+\left(\frac{\hbar^2}{2\mu r^2}l(l+1)-\frac{Ze^2}{4\pi r\epsilon_0}\right)R=ER \tag{22}$$

where $\mu=\frac{m_{\text{electron}}m_{\text{Nuclues}}}{m_{\text{electron}}+m_{\text{Nuclues}}}$, which is approximately equal to m_{electron}. Therefore, when $l=0$, for s orbitals, solving Eq. (22) acquires:

$$E=-\frac{Z^2\mu e^4}{32{\epsilon_0}^2\pi^2\hbar^2}\frac{1}{n^2}=-13.6\frac{Z^2}{n^2} \tag{23}$$

where Z is the effective nuclear charge, which is the same as Eq. (19) when $Z=1$, indicating that both theories are in agreement at H atom.

7 Comparison Between Quantum Mechanics and Communication Dynamics (Calculation of Electron Energies)

Based on this nonrelativistic wave function solution from the Schrödinger equation, Eq. (15) only works for single electron atoms, in other words the hydrogen-like atoms, including H, He^+, Li^{2+}, Be^{3+}, and B^{4+}. The corresponding energy levels with the increase of n using Eq. (15) are shown in Fig. 5.

The results shows that the correlation between QM calculated energy levels and CD eigenvalues are correlated in the same manner for all five elements.

8 Conclusions

By calculating and inserting the corresponding eigenvalues to the adjacent U-matrix, we propose and construct a new communication dynamics representation of orbital energy levels with the mathematical model we developed. Our approach effectively describes orbital energy levels. In the future, we propose to use our model to describe internal atomic orbital structures.

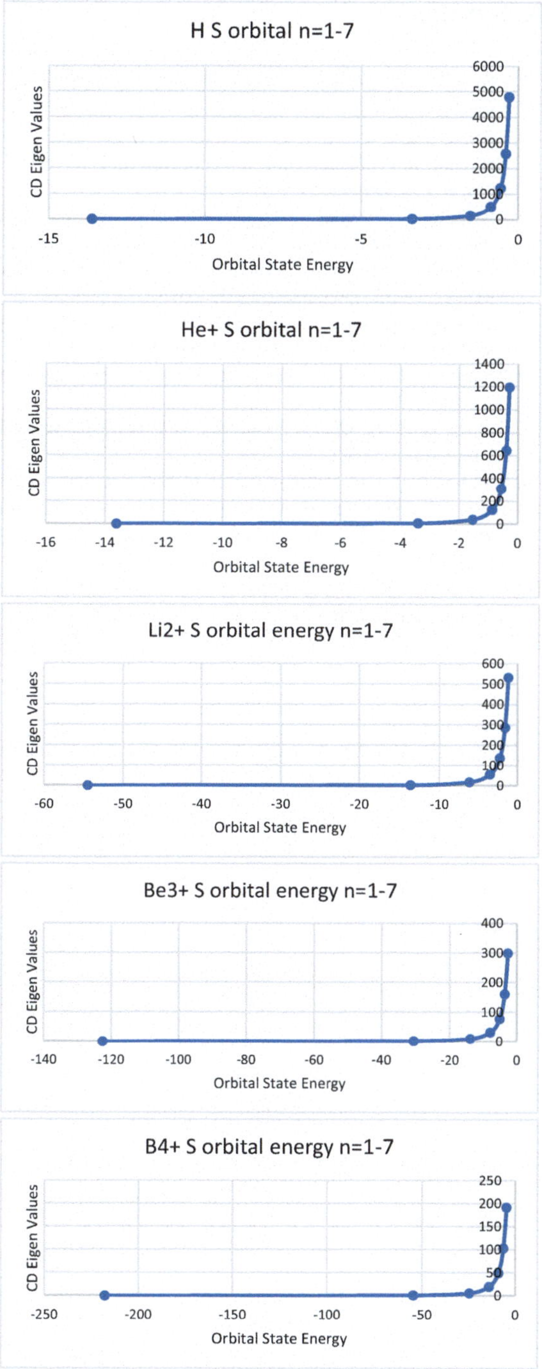

Fig. 5 Energy levels of s orbitals for hydrogen-like atoms with the increase of the principal quantum number ($n = 1, 7$) in comparison between QM and CD eigenvalues

References

1. The theory of communication dynamics application to modeling the valence shell orbitals of periodic table elements, transactions of the SDPS: *Journal of Integrated Design and Process Science* 2021.
2. Eckmann, J. P., Kamphorst, S. O., & Ruelle, D. (1987). Recurrence plots of dynamical systems. *Europhysics Letters*, 973–977.
3. Wikipedia [Online]. Available: https://en.wikipedia.org/wiki/Electromagnetic_spectrum. [Accessed 1 July 2015].
4. *Wikipedia* [Online]. Available: http://www2.lbl.gov/MicroWorlds/ALSTool/EMSpec/EMSpec2.html. [Accessed 1 july 2015].
5. *Hydrogen Spectral Series* [Online]. Available: https://en.wikipedia.org/wiki/Hydrogen_spectral_series. [Accessed 2 July 2015].
6. Weisstein, E. W. *Incircle*. MathWorld [Online]. Available: http://mathworld.wolfram.com/Incircle.html
7. Bell, J. A. S. B. (2009). A survey of known results and research areas for n-queens. *Discrete Mathematics, 309*(1, 6), 1–31.
8. Webber, C. L., Jr., & Zbilut, J. P. (1994). Dynamical assessment of physiological systems and states using recurrence plot strategies. *American Physiological Society*, 965–973.
9. Strang, G. (2009). *Introduction to linear algebra* (4th ed.). Wellesley-Cambridge Press and SIAM.
10. Reference, M. O. *Convex polygon*. [Online]. Available: http://www.mathopenref.com/polygonconvex.html

Creativity and AI

Morteza Zangeneh Soroush, Md Sakib Ullah Sourav, and Yong Zeng

Abstract The advancement of artificial intelligence (AI) has enabled researchers to apply this effective tool to several complex cognitive processes, one of which is creativity. Different applications such as creativity assessment, human-AI co-creation, and team creativity enhancement are examples of AI applications to creativity. Although several studies have reported AI applications being effective in the field of creativity, there are major shortcomings and open questions from different aspects which should be addressed. In this chapter, we introduce these applications, then review related recent studies, and finally open a discussion to point out the gaps and available research areas for future studies. We believe that the present chapter can shed light on AI-based creativity studies and boost researchers' understanding of that.

Keywords Creativity · Artificial intelligence · Creative ideation · AI · Creativity assessment · Human-AI co-creation

1 Introduction

Creativity, which is a key aspect of human intelligence, is defined as the ability to develop useful, appropriate, and novel ideas [1]. Creativity is vital for human survival and is needed in various problem-solving and decision-making scenarios. It helps in finding innovative solutions and improving efficiency [2]. This indicates that creativity, as an inseparable part of our lives, is of great importance [3, 4].

Creativity has been explored in various fields such as design, engineering, business, and others. The papers by Zeng et al. [5] and Nguyen and Zeng [6] present mathematical and theoretical models for understanding the factors that lead to a creative design, using the axiomatic theory of design modeling (ATDM) and environment-based design (EBD). Gero et al. [7] explore the modeling of creativity

M. Z. Soroush · M. S. U. Sourav · Y. Zeng (✉)
Concordia University, Montreal, QC, Canada
e-mail: yong.zeng@concordia.ca

S. C. Suh (ed.), *Artificial Intelligence for Design and Process Science*,
https://doi.org/10.1007/978-3-031-67886-8_3

and knowledge-based creative design, underscoring the significance of computer-aided design in nurturing creativity. Badran [8] introduces an engineering creativity enterprise diagram aimed at amplifying creativity and innovation in engineering education. Boden [9] delves into computer-generated models of creativity, illuminating the potential of technology in comprehending and simulating creative processes. It underscores the importance of harnessing technological advancements and integrating creativity tools to foster innovation and cultivate creative thinking.

Creativity undoubtedly stands as one of humanity's most complex and advanced cognitive tasks [10–12], engaging both mental and physical activities [6, 13]. It operates as a recursive, complex, and nonlinear cognitive process, encompassing tasks like problem understanding, idea generation, and idea evolution [14–16]. Despite numerous theoretical investigations, there are unexplored facets of creativity, including assessment methods and human-machine collaboration, which necessitate exploration [17, 18]. These uncharted research domains present opportunities for advancement through the application of AI [19–22].

The progress in artificial intelligence (AI) has empowered researchers to investigate intricate processes like human cognitive tasks, including creativity. AI tools have been developed into highly sophisticated instruments capable of surpassing their programmed functionalities [23, 24]. This suggests that these complex algorithms exhibit a form of "creativity." Nonetheless, artificial creativity may diverge from human creativity across various dimensions. This suggests that exploring AI in creativity is of great importance.

Although AI has seen extensive use and discussion across various disciplines, its application in the realm of creativity remains relatively understudied, leaving several questions unanswered and prompting ongoing research. Some of these questions include the following:

1. How can AI be leveraged to augment human creativity?
2. How can AI effectively evaluate a creative product or solution?
3. In what ways can AI and humans collaborate in creativity tasks?
4. Is there a potential for AI to surpass human creativity?

These inquiries have been and continue to be focal points within the field of creativity. They serve as the driving force behind our exploration of AI's applications in creativity. Several studies compared human and artificial creativity concerning several aspects [9, 19, 21–23, 25–27]. Our main aim in this chapter is to address the abovementioned questions to the fullest extent possible based on the existing literature.

In this chapter, we explore AI applications in creativity going over several aspects such as (1) AI as a creative tool, (2) AI-human co-creation, (3) creativity assessment by AI tools, and (4) AI creativity versus human creativity. We also provide some information regarding creativity tests and assessments.

2 Two Creativity Tests: AUT and TTCT

The Alternate Uses Task (AUT) and the Torrance Test of Creative Thinking (TTCT) are represented in the following sections. These creativity tests have been widely employed in the literature as they are well-documented, structured, and straightforward. These tests have also been used in the field of AI and creativity as benchmarks.

2.1 Alternate Uses Task

The Alternate Uses Task (AUT), pioneered by J.P. Guilford in 1967 [28], is a prominent psychological assessment tool utilized to gauge divergent thinking, a crucial aspect of creativity. In the AUT, participants are tasked with brainstorming new and unconventional applications for everyday items. Each item is typically presented twice: first in its standard (common) condition and second in its unusual condition. During the common condition, participants are instructed to contemplate typical, everyday uses for the items. Conversely, in uncommon conditions, they are prompted to devise unique, inventive applications for the items [29–31]. The test includes various items for exploration, such as bricks, foil, hangers, helmets, keys, magnets, pencils, and pipes.

2.2 Torrance Test of Creative Thinking

Developed by E. Paul Torrance in the late 1960s, the Torrance Test of Creative Thinking (TTCT) [32] stands as a foundational tool for appraising creative thinking abilities as it offers a structured assessment of creativity, contrasting with the more open-ended approach of the AUT [33].

The TTCT comprises two versions: verbal and figural. The verbal component, TTCT-Verbal, is available in Forms A and B [34], including various subtests. These include tasks such as Asking Questions and Making Guesses, Improvement of a Product, Unusual Uses, and Supposing, all designed to elicit creative responses from participants based on specified criteria as outlined by Torrance. Similarly, the figural component, TTCT-Figural, also exists in two versions, featuring tasks involving drawing creation, completion of unfinished drawings, and development of new drawings from parallel lines. For example, participants may be asked to creatively finish a partially drawn image, with evaluations based on predetermined criteria [14, 35].

3 AI Applied to Creativity

In recent times, AI has significantly boosted creativity through the utilization of advanced tools like technical AI chatbots such as ChatGPT, Google Bard, Microsoft Bing, Jasper, Bard, Mid Journey, and Dalle-2, all of which are built upon vast language models and generative intelligence [36]. These tools have played a vital role in enhancing divergent thinking. AI programs aim to emulate human strategies and problem-solving approaches, particularly in tasks involving creativity [27]. What sets AI systems apart from other computerized systems is their ability to adapt fluidly, sometimes surpassing their initial programming [37]. This adaptability is key to their effectiveness in fostering creativity. AI-based models excel in generating creative solutions or designs, evaluating creativity tests or products, and aiding humans in enhancing their creativity [26].

In this chapter, we delve into the basics of AI in fostering creativity, focusing on three main aspects: artificial creativity versus human creativity, the collaborative potential of AI and humans in creativity, and the role of AI in assessing creativity.

3.1 Artificial Creativity Versus Human Creativity

AI has demonstrated immense potential in domains that demand reasoning and creative decision-making, prompting inquiries into how it compares with human creativity [22, 38]. Numerous studies have undertaken this comparison, employing established creativity tests such as AUT and TTCT [21, 24, 26, 39, 40]. Through these investigations, we gain valuable insights into the interplay between human and AI creativity.

In a study [22], 256 participants engaged in AUT experiments through an online platform, with their results later compared to those generated by AI chatbots. The researchers evaluated the performance of AI chatbots, including ChatGPT3.5, ChatGPT4, and Copy.ai, alongside human participants in a standard divergent thinking task. On average, the AI chatbots surpassed human participants in both mean scores (the average of all responses to an object) and max scores (the best response to an object). This superiority was evident in the semantic distance of responses and subjective ratings of creativity provided by impartial human raters. The findings indicate that AI has reached, if not exceeded, the level of the average human's idea generation ability. However, the study concludes that while AI chatbots generally outperform humans, the most skilled humans can still rival them.

In the study [21], the creative prowess of GPT-4 was scrutinized using the Torrance Tests of Creative Thinking. Compared to human samples, ChatGPT's performance was evaluated in terms of fluency, flexibility, and originality. Findings revealed that ChatGPT scored in the top 1% for originality and fluency, displaying commendable scores for flexibility as well. In terms of generating novel and unexpected outputs, and based on prevailing conceptions and assessment criteria of creativity, this study concludes that AI exhibits creativity and, in many instances, outperforms humans.

In another study [39], a Turing test was conducted to assess DALL·E's ability to achieve combinational creativity in comparison to human designers. To compare the performance of DALL·E with human novice designers, two datasets were prepared for evaluation: one for machines and one for humans. Both DALL·E and novice designers were given the same textual prompts containing combinational design ideas as input, and they generated images corresponding to these prompts as output. After selections were made, an equal amount of data was saved for both the machine and human datasets. Subsequently, three tests were conducted: a Turing test, a computational test, and an expert test. The results indicated that DALL·E could achieve combinational creativity at a level comparable to that of novice designers, shedding light on the distinctions between computer and human creativity.

In a review [40], various creative machines applied to the AUT were examined. The reviewed studies suggest that systems based on large language models (LLMs) perform at or slightly above human levels in terms of originality and usefulness scores. Additionally, similarities were observed between human and LLM model data in the AUT, such as output order effects and a negative correlation between originality and value or utility. However, it was concluded that despite generating novel and useful responses, systems like GPT-3 and similar ones do not exhibit creativity because they lack agency and operate solely on algorithms. The performance of GPT-based chatbots in the AUT seems to improve with the increasing power of the chatbots from GPT-3 to GPT-4.

The study [24] investigates the correlation between creativity and the origin of the creator by analyzing paintings produced by both AI and humans across various artistic genres. Through a mathematical approach employing entropy analysis, utilizing Shannon entropy and a complexity measure based on multi-scale entropy, the findings reveal differences between AI and human art not only in the schematic representation but also in color changes. The AI struggles more with representing painting styles lacking well-defined objects and with handling color changes involving pixels of similar intensity values. The study draws two main conclusions: (1) Paintings generated by AI exhibit significantly higher standard deviation values for both features compared to human artworks. (2) Both features are smaller for AI-generated drawings compared to human artworks.

In a separate study [38], both human participants and GPT-4 were tasked with responding to the AUT, Consequences Task, and Divergent Associations Task. Human and artificial participants were recruited using GPT-4. Responses were evaluated for fluency, originality, and elaboration. The study revealed that AI consistently displayed greater creativity across all measures of divergent thinking compared to human counterparts. Specifically, when considering response fluency, AI exhibited higher levels of originality and elaboration. Overall, GPT-4 demonstrated higher levels of originality and elaboration than humans across all divergent thinking tasks, even after controlling for response fluency.

3.2 AI-Human Co-creativity

Computational co-creative systems represent a burgeoning field where human users collaborate with AI agents to produce creative works [36]. These systems, particularly in design, allow users to move beyond their initial ideas and overcome design fixation by working together with an AI agent on open-ended creative tasks throughout the design process. While some research in computational creativity focuses on generative creativity, co-creative systems emphasize how systems implementing generative creativity can collaborate with humans on creative tasks. For instance, sketching is a common technique used in creativity tasks where designers generate and refine design ideas. In the realm of design creativity, AI has proven valuable in assisting designers with ideation and overcoming fixation issues.

Co-creative systems hold significant promise for enhancing human creativity across various domains by fostering and encouraging designers' creative thinking. Understanding the influence of co-creative systems on the ideation process is crucial for designing effective generative AI models within these systems and assessing their impact on human creativity. Co-creative systems have found application in diverse creative fields such as art, music, dance, drawing, and game design. What sets co-creativity apart from computational creativity is its collaborative nature, where multiple parties contribute to the creative process in a blended manner. However, evaluating co-creative systems remains an ongoing research challenge, as there is currently no standardized metric for measuring the effectiveness of co-creative approaches.

The study [41] introduces a co-creative system called the Collaborative Ideation Partner (CIP), designed to bolster design creativity by encouraging the exploration of design solutions during the initial idea generation phase. CIP facilitates this process by offering inspirational sketches that align with both visual and conceptual aspects of sketches created by a designer. To evaluate the effectiveness of ideation within this co-creative system, the researchers devised a method that encompasses both outcome and process approaches. The study emphasizes the importance of image quality within the dataset for AI-based creativity. Notably, it suggests that inspirations derived from conceptual similarity to the target design have a more significant impact on ideation than those based solely on visual resemblance to sketches drawn by a designer.

In a separate study [36], the authors investigated the impact of an AI model that gauges both visual and conceptual similarity to select sketch responses as inspiration for a user's ongoing sketch. They examined participants' behaviors and responses in a human-AI co-creative sketching system, reporting the outcomes of a user study that analyzed user reactions to the Creative Sketching Partner's (CSP) sketches.

The authors developed an AI model to facilitate the mapping process between visual and conceptual spaces, aiding users in making connections between these categories to generate fresh ideas for their design tasks. By utilizing deep learning models trained on a large dataset of sketches, users could adjust the level of visual and conceptual similarity in the AI-generated responses when seeking inspiration from the CSP.

The tool translates the user's sketch into another category that shares structural and semantic characteristics, with users able to control the degree of similarity in both visual and conceptual aspects to inspire their current designs.

Fifty design students participated in the study, and their interactions and self-reports were analyzed. Participant behavior clustered into three types of design creativity: combinatorial, exploratory, and transformational. The results indicate that the tool effectively facilitates ideation and helps overcome design fixation. Moreover, the analysis suggests that inspiration linked to conceptual similarity is more associated with transformational creativity, while inspiration based on visual similarity is more prevalent during the detailed design stages and is closely tied to combinatorial creativity.

3.3 Creativity Assessment Through AI

Assessing creativity has long been a practice in various fields of study, often relying on expert evaluation. Researchers commonly administer tests of creative thinking, spanning from verbal tasks like word association to visual tasks like sketches [42]. However, they face the challenge of quantifying creative outputs from such tests efficiently [43]. One common approach is to rely on human raters to provide subjective judgments for each response, akin to the classic Consensual Assessment Technique (CAT). While subjective scoring can be reliable and valid, it is also time-consuming and resource-intensive, slowing down research progress and posing a barrier for researchers and practitioners lacking the necessary human resources to support subjective scoring methods like the CAT [44, 45].

Despite the effectiveness of subjective scoring, its resource-intensive nature can hinder the pace of research, making it challenging for those without adequate human resources to employ such methods [46]. Recently, the field of creativity has achieved a notable milestone with the emergence of advancements in AI. AI holds the potential to transform creativity assessment methods, offering cost-effectiveness, automation capabilities, and enhanced reliability compared to human raters [21, 45].

3.3.1 Creativity Measures

Participants' responses in creativity tests are typically assessed across several dimensions, including fluency, originality, and flexibility [47, 48]. Some creativity tests may also incorporate additional indices such as usefulness and elaboration [47, 48]. Fluency refers to the total number of ideas generated for each object. Fluency-valid, on the other hand, considers only unique and non-repeated ideas, providing a valid count of ideas. Flexibility measures the diversity of idea categories produced for each object. Originality evaluates the rarity or novelty of the ideas relative to those generated by all participants. Elaboration assesses the level of detail in the responses, while usefulness gauges the functional utility of the idea [49].

3.3.2 Creativity Assessment Studies

The evolution of computational approaches to creativity assessment, from Guilford's (1950) prediction to today's AI-based methods, can be delineated into four distinct phases.

In the first phase, the focus was on text-mining statistics derived from responses, including word length, word counts, and punctuation usage. The second phase saw the application of latent semantic analysis to divergent thinking (DT) tasks. Unlike the linguistic characteristics emphasized in the first phase, the latent semantic analysis considered both the DT prompt and the responses, quantifying originality through semantic distance. The third phase witnessed a transition from latent semantic analysis to Global Vectors for Word Representation. This shift capitalized on superior corpus size and neural network capabilities, offering a better approximation of human thought processes. Research indicated that this approach surpassed latent semantic analyses in predicting human ratings. In the fourth phase, there was a shift from unsupervised to supervised learning approaches. This phase leveraged large language modeling techniques to significantly enhance scoring accuracy [44].

In a study [46], a creativity assessment system called AuDrA—an Automated Drawing Assessment platform—was employed to extract visual creativity scores from simple drawing productions. Using a collection of line drawings and human creativity ratings, they trained AuDrA and tested its generalizability to untrained drawing sets, raters, and tasks. This work employed four distinct datasets of rated drawings—totaling over 13,000 drawing-rating pairs. They focused on training the model to perform the abstract drawing task to optimize its predictive capacity for that specific task. They opted to use ResNet [50] as the computer vision backbone for AuDrA [46].

The model successfully learned to predict the creativity scores of human drawings. It was not trained on with remarkably high accuracy.

The model showed evidence of learning visual features of drawings, beyond simply predicting their level of elaboration. Critically, AuDrA generalized to predict the creativity of sketches from entirely independent datasets of human ratings that were not used in training the model. They found AuDrA scores to be highly correlated with human creativity ratings for new drawings on the same drawing task. Importantly, correlations between AuDrA scores and human raters surpassed those between drawings' elaboration (i.e., ink on the page) and human creativity raters, suggesting that AuDrA is sensitive to features of drawings beyond a simple degree of complexity.

AuDrA showed poorer performance on a drawing task it was not trained on, pointing to a boundary condition of its predictive power. It is the first extensively trained and vetted demonstration that machine learning methods can be reliably used to predict human creativity on drawing tasks, routinely used in creativity research [46].

In the study [43], machine learning, in the form of a convolutional neural network (CNN), was applied to automate the scoring of the Test of Creative Thinking-Drawing Production (TCT-DP). The TCT-DP is a figural test of creativity designed to assess creativity from a more gestalt-oriented perspective compared to traditional, quantitatively oriented divergent thinking tests. The TCT-DP utilizes incomplete and irregular figural fragments (such as a semicircle, a right angle, or a dot) within a large square frame to elicit creative responses. The study utilized a training dataset comprising 414 samples, with all images scored by at least two trained raters.

Various models were employed to explore the capabilities of the proposed method, utilizing different numbers of classes ranging from two (representing low and high creativity) to seven (corresponding to the classes defined in the TCT-DP test manual). The study considered factors such as model accuracy (percentage of correctly classified images), sensitivity to the size of the training dataset, sensitivity to model parameters (e.g., number of epochs, learning rate), and utility (ability to provide useful information). Overall, the models achieved high accuracies (above 85% in all cases) in assessing creativity.

3.4 Design Creativity and AI

In the previous sections, we covered the AI applications related to creativity. Here, we would like to highlight the differences between creativity and design creativity and report on some of the studies employing AI in design creativity research.

To the best of our knowledge, there exist some studies such as [36, 51–53] targeting the AI applications in design creativity and how AI can help design/design creativity. In contrast, the authors studied the effects of design thinking on the cognition of AI learning, attitudes toward AI, idea creativity, and the product creativity of AI applications [54]. This study found that design thinking significantly enhances conceptual cognition of AI learning, particularly in relational conjunctions and classes of AI concepts, though it had no significant effect on cross-linking and examples. Design thinking also positively affects learning attitudes toward AI, fostering more positive views on AI input and processing due to its real-life applicability. Additionally, design thinking improves the creativity of AI-generated works, notably in their novelty, value, functionality, and elaboration, though not in material, style, and structure.

There also exist comprehensive reviews [23, 55, 56] investigating the effects of AI, specifically generative adversarial networks as toolbox for design practitioners [55], on human-machine collaborations. In [56], AI-powered applications in design (in the last 15 years) are reported which indicates the wide usage of AI in design [57]. However, according to our investigation, in the field of design creativity, fewer AI-related studies can be found. It should be noted that like other applications of AI or machine learning, design creativity research powered by AI has been increasing by leaps and bounds. In other reviews [58], shorter communications, and editorial letters [58–60], AI has been reported as a pivotal part of future design creativity research indicating the importance of exploring opportunities to employ AI in design creativity processes.

4 Discussion

Creativity spans various disciplines and intersects with numerous fields. With the advancement of AI and computational machines, AI has found applications in various creativity studies. While much of the research has focused on creativity assessment, human-AI co-creativity, and the comparison between artificial and human creativity, there is a notable gap in exploring other aspects, such as simulating creativity using AI based on neurophysiological findings.

Existing literature predominantly emphasizes general or artistic forms of creativity. However, there is a pressing need for further investigation into the challenges and limitations of machine learning and deep generative models, particularly in domains like design creativity, constraint handling, and simultaneous modeling of form and functional performance.

While many studies have primarily targeted tasks like AUT and TTCT, there is a lack of exploration in other creativity tasks. Although most studies suggest that AI outperforms average human creativity levels in AUT and TTCT, it is crucial to consider additional factors like validity, appropriateness, and usefulness to comprehensively compare human and AI creativity.

In this domain, various AI methods and models have been employed, yet there is room for exploration and comparison with other AI methods. Choosing the appropriate AI method tailored to specific creativity applications is essential, considering each method's unique capabilities and potential limitations. Future researchers should prioritize understanding AI methods, with workshops on prompt engineering being particularly beneficial.

Moreover, the social and psychological implications of AI application in creativity warrant attention. Future studies should investigate how AI impacts students' problem-identification capacity, convergent thinking, and long-term creativity when integrated into educational settings.

We would like to shed light on the aspect that has been less discussed in the literature. While several studies have applied AI or explored it in the realm of creativity, there are just a few studies that targeted the considerations of AI applications in design creativity. Investigating design creativity presents significant challenges due to its multifaceted nature, involving nonlinear cognitive processes and various subtasks such as divergent and convergent thinking, perception, and memory retrieval.

Considering the points mentioned above, AI can be employed to investigate or model the intricate processes of design creativity. However, there is a necessity to understand the differences between creativity, design, and design creativity which provide the foundation for future AI-based research in this field. To explore these intricate considerations, we shall begin with the definitions to understand the connections between creativity and design to better understand design creativity. As mentioned before, creativity is defined as the ability to develop useful, novel, and surprising ideas [10–12, 61]. Design aims at changing existing situations into desired ones [62]. The design process is nonlinear and complex [63] and lies at the heart of creativity [64–67]. On the one hand, by definition, creativity is a measure of the process of creating, for which design, either intentional or unconscious, is an indispensable constituent. On the other hand, it is important to note that not all designs are inherently creative; many designs follow established patterns and resemble existing ones, differing only in their specific context. Design creativity typically denotes a scenario where the resulting product embodies creativity. Creative design is inherently unpredictable; at times, it may seem implausible—yet it happens. It is noteworthy that different designers may propose varied solutions to the same design problem, and even the same designer might generate diverse design solutions for the same problem over time [10]. Creativity may spontaneously emerge even if one does not intend to conduct a creative design, whereas creative design just may not come out no matter how hard one tries. Moreover, it is conceivable that a designer may lack creativity, while the product itself demonstrates creative attributes, and conversely, a designer may exhibit creativity, while the resulting product does not [16].

Concerning what was covered in this chapter, future studies are recommended to focus on AI-powered design creativity and the explainability of AI methods applied to creativity and design creativity. Although there exist several papers on "AI and creativity," deep explorations are required to associate complex and abstract concepts of design creativity with AI-related ones. In addition, for the differences between creativity and design creativity, researchers should focus on AI-based design creativity studies as there is a relatively limited number of studies in this field.

5 Conclusion

In conclusion, the exploration of AI in creativity is still in its early stages, and there is a need to adopt advanced and updated AI methods to further enrich this area of research. Although the literature indicates some clear applications of AI in creativity, other types of AI-powered research, such as man-machine creativity, AI in teams, and machine-machine creativity, will soon emerge due to the advancement of AI methods. Generative neural networks, for example, have the potential to be employed in creativity and design creativity applications. In this chapter, we aimed to cover the most pivotal topics in the realm of AI applications in creativity and design creativity. We covered artificial creativity versus human creativity, creativity assessment using AI, human-AI co-creation, and AI in design creativity. The intricate considerations must be taken into account when applying AI to design creativity, as there are several nuanced differences between design, creativity, and design creativity. These differences should be explored further in future studies to design AI methods that specifically meet the criteria for design creativity. This chapter aims to provide insight into these controversial topics and motivate readers to explore new directions of research in this area.

References

1. Sternberg, R. J., & Lubart, T. I. (1996). Investing in creativity. *The American Psychologist, 51*, 677–688. https://doi.org/10.1037/0003-066X.51.7.677
2. Cropley, D. H. (2015). Chapter 2 - The importance of creativity in engineering. In D. H. Cropley (Ed.), *Creativity in engineering* (pp. 13–34). Academic. https://doi.org/10.1016/B978-0-12-800225-4.00002-1
3. Corazza, G. E. (2016). Potential originality and effectiveness: The dynamic definition of creativity. *Creativity Research Journal, 28*(3), 258–267. https://doi.org/10.1080/10400419.2016.1195627
4. Moran, S. (2010). The roles of creativity in society. In J. C. Kaufman & R. J. E. Sternberg (Eds.), *The Cambridge handbook of creativity* (pp. 74–90). Cambridge University Press. https://doi.org/10.1017/CBO9780511763205.006
5. Zeng, Y., et al. (2004). Mathematical foundation for modeling conceptual design sketches1. *Journal of Computing and Information Science in Engineering, 4*(2), 150–159. https://doi.org/10.1115/1.1683825
6. Nguyen, T. A., & Zeng, Y. (2012). A theoretical model of design creativity: Nonlinear design dynamics and mental stress-creativity relation. *Journal of Integrated Design and Process Science, 16*(3), 65–88.
7. Gero, J. S., & Lou Maher, M. (2013). *Modeling creativity and knowledge-based creative design*. Psychology Press.
8. Badran, I. (2007). Enhancing creativity and innovation in engineering education. *European Journal of Engineering Education, 32*(5), 573–585. https://doi.org/10.1080/03043790701433061
9. Boden, M. A. (2009). Computer models of creativity. *AI Magazine, 30*(3), 23–34. https://doi.org/10.1609/aimag.v30i3.2254
10. Boden, M. A. (2004). *The creative mind: Myths and mechanisms* (2nd ed.). Psychology Press. https://doi.org/10.4324/9780203508527
11. Simonton, D. K. (2012). Taking the U.S. Patent Office criteria seriously: A quantitative three-criterion creativity definition and its implications. *Creativity Research Journal, 24*(2–3), 97–106. https://doi.org/10.1080/10400419.2012.676974
12. Sternberg, R. J., & Lubart, T. I. (1999). The concept of creativity: Prospects and paradigms. In *Handbook of creativity* (pp. 3–15). Cambridge University Press.
13. Mazza, A., et al. (2022). Beyond alpha-band: The neural correlate of creative thinking. *Neuropsychologia, 179*(November), 2023. https://doi.org/10.1016/j.neuropsychologia.2022.108446
14. Jia, W., & Zeng, Y. (2021). EEG signals respond differently to idea generation, idea evolution and evaluation in a loosely controlled creativity experiment. *Scientific Reports, 11*(1), 2119. https://doi.org/10.1038/s41598-021-81655-0
15. Jia, W., von Wegner, F., Zhao, M., & Zeng, Y. (2021). Network oscillations imply the highest cognitive workload and lowest cognitive control during idea generation in open-ended creation tasks. *Scientific Reports, 11*(1), 24277. https://doi.org/10.1038/s41598-021-03577-1
16. Yang, J., Quan, H., & Zeng, Y. (2022). Knowledge: The good, the bad, and the ways for designer creativity. *Journal of Engineering Design, 33*(12), 945–968. https://doi.org/10.1080/09544828.2022.2161300

17. Rominger, C., et al. (2019). Creativity is associated with a characteristic U-shaped function of alpha power changes accompanied by an early increase in functional coupling. *Cognitive, Affective, and Behavioral Neuroscience, 19*(4), 1012–1021. https://doi.org/10.3758/s13415-019-00699-y
18. Rominger, C., et al. (2022). Functional brain activation patterns of creative metacognitive monitoring. *Neuropsychologia, 177*, 108416. https://doi.org/10.1016/j.neuropsychologia.2022.108416
19. Boden, M. A. (1998). Creativity and artificial intelligence. *Artificial Intelligence, 103*(1–2), 347–356. https://doi.org/10.1016/s0004-3702(98)00055-1
20. De Garrido, L. (2022). Conceptual design of a creative artificial intelligence system based on the neurocognitive bases of human creativity in the brain. *Creativity Research Journal, 34*(3), 273–294. https://doi.org/10.1080/10400419.2021.2005309
21. Guzik, E. E., Byrge, C., & Gilde, C. (2023). The originality of machines: AI takes the Torrance Test. *Journal of Creativity, 33*(3), 100065. https://doi.org/10.1016/j.yjoc.2023.100065
22. Koivisto, M., & Grassini, S. (2023). Best humans still outperform artificial intelligence in a creative divergent thinking task. *Scientific Reports, 13*(1), 1–10. https://doi.org/10.1038/s41598-023-40858-3
23. Anantrasirichai, N., & Bull, D. (2022). *Artificial intelligence in the creative industries: a review* (Vol. 55, no. 1). Springer. https://doi.org/10.1007/s10462-021-10039-7
24. Papia, E.-M. M., Kondi, A., & Constantoudis, V. (2023). Entropy and complexity analysis of AI-generated and human-made paintings. *Chaos, Solitons and Fractals, 170*(January), 113385. https://doi.org/10.1016/j.chaos.2023.113385
25. Chen, L., Wang, P., Shi, F., Han, J., & Childs, P. R. N. N. (2018). A computational approach for combinational creativity in design. *DS 92 Proceedings of the DESIGN* 2018 15th *international design* conference (vol. 4, pp. 1815–1824). doi: https://doi.org/10.21278/IDC.2018.0375.
26. Cropley, D. (2023). Is artificial intelligence more creative than humans? *Learning Letters, 2*(March), 13. https://doi.org/10.59453/ll.v2.13
27. Habib, S., Vogel, T., Anli, X., & Thorne, E. (2024). How does generative artificial intelligence impact student creativity? *Journal of Creativity, 34*(1), 100072. https://doi.org/10.1016/j.yjoc.2023.100072
28. J. P. Guilford, The nature of human intelligence. 1967.
29. Benedek, M., Schickel, R. J., Jauk, E., Fink, A., & Neubauer, A. C. (2014). Alpha power increases in right parietal cortex reflects focused internal attention. *Neuropsychologia, 56*(1), 393–400. https://doi.org/10.1016/j.neuropsychologia.2014.02.010
30. Martindale, C., & Hasenfus, N. (1978). EEG differences as a function of creativity, stage of the creative process, and effort to be original. *Biological Psychology, 6*(3), 157–167. https://doi.org/10.1016/0301-0511(78)90018-2
31. Stevens, C. E., & Zabelina, D. L. (2020). Classifying creativity: Applying machine learning techniques to divergent thinking EEG data. *Neuroimage, 219*(August 2019), 116990. https://doi.org/10.1016/j.neuroimage.2020.116990
32. Torrance, E. P. (1966). *Torrance tests of creative thinking*. Personnel Press.
33. Kim, K. H. (2006). Can we trust creativity tests? A review of the torrance tests of creative thinking (TTCT). *Creativity Research Journal, 18*(1), 3–14. https://doi.org/10.1207/s15326934crj1801_2
34. Almeida, L. S., Prieto, L. P., Ferrando, M., Oliveira, E., & Ferrándiz, C. (2008). Torrance test of creative thinking: The question of its construct validity. *Thinking Skills and Creativity, 3*(1), 53–58. https://doi.org/10.1016/j.tsc.2008.03.003
35. Rominger, C., Papousek, I., Perchtold, C. M., Weber, B., Weiss, E. M., & Fink, A. (2018). The creative brain in the figural domain: Distinct patterns of EEG alpha power during idea generation and idea elaboration. *Neuropsychologia, 118*(September 2017), 13–19. https://doi.org/10.1016/j.neuropsychologia.2018.02.013

36. Karimi, P., et al. (2020). Creative sketching partner: An analysis of human-AI co-creativity. *International conference on intelligent user interfaces, Proceedings of IUI, 10*, 221–230. https://doi.org/10.1145/3377325.3377522
37. Haase, J., & Hanel, P. H. P. P. (2023). Artificial muses: Generative artificial intelligence chatbots have risen to human-level creativity. *Journal of Creativity, 33*(3), 100066. https://doi.org/10.1016/J.YJOC.2023.100066
38. Hubert, K. F., Awa, K. N., & Zabelina, D. L. (2024). The current state of artificial intelligence generative language models is more creative than humans on divergent thinking tasks. *Scientific Reports, 14*(1), 3440. https://doi.org/10.1038/s41598-024-53303-w
39. Chen, L., Sun, L., & Han, J. (2023). A comparison study of human and machine-generated creativity. *Journal of Computing and Information Science in Engineering, 23*(5), 1–10. https://doi.org/10.1115/1.4062232
40. Gilhooly, K. (2024). AI vs humans in the AUT: Simulations to LLMs. *Journal of Creativity, 34*(1), 100071. https://doi.org/10.1016/j.yjoc.2023.100071
41. Kim, J., Lou Maher, M., & Siddiqui, S. (2021). Studying the impact of AI-based inspiration on human ideation in a co-creative design system. *CEUR Workshop Proceedings, 2903*, 0–3.
42. Sung, Y. T., Cheng, H. H., Tseng, H. C., Chang, K. E., & Lin, S. Y. (2022). Construction and validation of a computerized creativity assessment tool with automated scoring based on deep-learning techniques. *Psychology of Aesthetics, Creativity, and the Arts*. https://doi.org/10.1037/ACA0000450
43. Cropley, D. H., & Marrone, R. L. (2022). Automated scoring of figural creativity using a convolutional neural network. *Psychology of Aesthetics, Creativity, and the Arts*. https://doi.org/10.1037/ACA0000510
44. Acar, S. (2023). Creativity assessment, research, and practice in the age of artificial intelligence. *Creativity Research Journal, 00*(00), 1–7. https://doi.org/10.1080/10400419.2023.2271749
45. Rowe, J., & Partridge, D. (1993). Creativity: a survey of AI approaches. *Artificial Intelligence Review, 7*(1), 43–70. https://doi.org/10.1007/BF00849197
46. Patterson, J. D., Barbot, B., Lloyd-Cox, J., & Beaty, R. E. (2023). AuDrA: An automated drawing assessment platform for evaluating creativity. *Behavior Research Methods, 1*(0123456789), 1–18. https://doi.org/10.3758/S13428-023-02258-3/FIGURES/10
47. Cropley, A. J. (2000). Defining and measuring creativity: Are creativity tests worth using? *Roeper Review, 23*(2), 72–79. https://doi.org/10.1080/02783190009554069
48. Runco, M. A., & Acar, S. (2012). Divergent thinking as an indicator of creative potential. *Creativity Research Journal, 24*(1), 66–75. https://doi.org/10.1080/10400419.2012.652929
49. Prent, N., & Smit, D. J. A. (2020). The dynamics of resting-state alpha oscillations predict individual differences in creativity. *Neuropsychologia, 142*, 107456. https://doi.org/10.1016/j.neuropsychologia.2020.107456
50. He, K., Zhang, X., Ren, S., Sun, J. (2016). Deep residual learning for image recognition. In *2016 IEEE conference on computer vision and pattern recognition (CVPR)* (pp. 770–778). doi: https://doi.org/10.1109/CVPR.2016.90.
51. Bartlett, K. A., & Camba, J. D. (2024). Generative artificial intelligence in product design education: Navigating concerns of originality and ethics. *The International Journal of Interactive Multimedia and Artificial Intelligence, 8*(5), 55–64. https://doi.org/10.9781/ijimai.2024.02.006
52. Hanafy, N. O. (2023). Artificial intelligence's effects on design process creativity: 'A study on used A.I. Text-to-Image in architecture'. *The Journal of Building Engineering, 80*(September). https://doi.org/10.1016/j.jobe.2023.107999
53. Liao, J., Hansen, P., & Chai, C. (2020). A framework of artificial intelligence augmented design support. *Human-Computer Interact, 35*(5–6), 511–544. https://doi.org/10.1080/07370024.2020.1733576
54. Chang, Y. S., & Tsai, M. C. (2021). Effects of design thinking on artificial intelligence learning and creativity. *Educational Studies*. https://doi.org/10.1080/03055698.2021.1999213

55. Hughes, R. T., Zhu, L., & Bednarz, T. (2021). Generative adversarial networks–enabled human–artificial intelligence collaborative applications for creative and design industries: A systematic review of current approaches and trends. *Frontiers in Artificial Intelligence, 4*(April), 1–17. https://doi.org/10.3389/frai.2021.604234
56. Yüksel, N., Börklü, H. R., Sezer, H. K., & Canyurt, O. E. (2023). Review of artificial intelligence applications in engineering design perspective. *Engineering Applications of Artificial Intelligence, 118*(October 2022), 105697. https://doi.org/10.1016/j.engappai.2022.105697
57. Figoli, F. A., Mattioli, F., & Rampino, L. (2022). *Artificial intelligence in the design process: The impact on creativity and team collaboration*. FrancoAngeli s.r.l.
58. Cascini, G., et al. (2022). Perspectives on design creativity and innovation research: 10 years later. *International Journal of Design Creativity and Innovation, 10*(1), 1–30. https://doi.org/10.1080/21650349.2022.2021480
59. Gero, J. S. (2020). Nascent directions for design creativity research. *International Journal of Design Creativity and Innovation, 8*(3), 144–146. https://doi.org/10.1080/21650349.2020.1767885
60. Goldschmidt, G. (2019). Design creativity research: Recent developments and future challenges. *International Journal of Design Creativity and Innovation, 7*(4), 194–195. https://doi.org/10.1080/21650349.2019.1646387
61. Runco, M. A., & Jaeger, G. J. (2012). The standard definition of creativity. *Creativity Research Journal, 24*(1), 92–96. https://doi.org/10.1080/10400419.2012.650092
62. Simon, H. A. (1996). *The sciences of the artificial* (3rd ed.). MIT Press.
63. Zeng, Y. (2001). An axiomatic approach to the modeling of conceptual product design using set theory. *The Department of Mechanical and Manufacturing Engineering*, 218.
64. Gero, J. S. (1996). Creativity, emergence and evolution in design. *Knowledge-Based Systems, 9*(7), 435–448. https://doi.org/10.1016/S0950-7051(96)01054-4
65. Guilford, J. P. (1959). Traits of creativity. *Creativity and Its Cultivation*, 142–161.
66. Jung, R. E., & Vartanian, O. (2018). *The Cambridge handbook of the neuroscience of creativity*. Cambridge University Press. https://doi.org/10.1017/9781316556238
67. Xie, X. (2023). The cognitive process of creative design: A perspective of divergent thinking. *Thinking Skills and Creativity, 48*(February 2022), 101266. https://doi.org/10.1016/j.tsc.2023.101266

Demystifying Computer Science: A Sentence Transformers and Neural Networks-Powered Chatbot

Sang C. Suh and Swetha Reddy Pathuri

Abstract A significant challenge faced by many students and parents is the lack of clear information about the diverse range of available courses and career paths in the ever-evolving landscape of higher education. This informational gap often results in students making uninformed choices, leading to academic struggles and disappointment for both students and their parents. Particularly in the field of computer science, where numerous bright majors and rewarding careers exist, many students lack awareness of the available opportunities and how to navigate the learning process. Recognizing the pivotal role of emerging technologies, this paper introduces an AI-driven chatbot called CSACbot (Computer Science as Career bot) developed using neural networks, sentence transformers, and PyTorch. This chatbot serves as an innovative solution to provide comprehensive information about the field of computer science, guiding students and parents in making informed decisions about courses, majors, and potential careers. By efficiently and accurately addressing user queries, this AI-driven chatbot aims to bridge the information gap, empowering students to embark on successful academic journeys in computer science.

Keywords Educational chatbot · Generative AI · Sentence transformers · Computer science education

1 Introduction

In the rapidly evolving landscape of AI applications in academia, various studies have explored the integration of AI tools to enhance different aspects of education. The growing workload and expansion of academic programs in universities create stress for academic staff. To address this, an AI-based chatbot using the K-Nearest Neighbor (K-NN) method was introduced to assist with tasks typically handled by academic officers [1]. The evaluation based on user responses indicates that chatbots

S. C. Suh (✉) · S. R. Pathuri
East Texas A&M University, Commerce, TX, USA
e-mail: Sang.Suh@tamuc.edu; SPathuri@leomail.tamuc.edu

S. C. Suh (ed.), *Artificial Intelligence for Design and Process Science*,
https://doi.org/10.1007/978-3-031-67886-8_4

significantly improve efficiency in providing academic information. In the COVID pandemic situation, many youngsters feel restless and dissatisfied due to syllabus incompletion. To address this issue, a student friendly AI-powered chatbot called EDUBOT and the Learning Management System (LMS) were developed to provide students with the resources they need on any topic they are interested in and resolve their problems [2]. Generative artificial intelligence (GAI) tools can in general help efficiently manage and create innovative business methods. Companies like Microsoft, Google, and Facebook are investing in the development of these tools. Research done with 100 students and 100 professors involved suggests that the ease of use positively influences GAI adoption emphasizing the increasing importance of incorporating generative AI in various aspects of life including academics [3]. Challenges of recommending suitable educational resources in the field of E-Learning necessitated a new recommendation approach that utilizes AI techniques which aims to provide real-time responses to learner queries and offers a relevant set of suggestions tailored to their specific needs in the context of E-Learning [4].

A key aspect of an effective chatbot's functionality lies in its ability to understand and accurately interpret user intent from its messages, a task commonly known as intent classification. Intent classification involves classifying user utterances into predefined categories, each representing a distinct goal [5]. Successful intent classification provides the basis for generating relevant, contextualized responses, thereby enhancing the user experience. Traditionally, intent classification was achieved using rule-based systems or feature engineering approaches, which often struggled to capture the complexities of natural language and are also time-consuming.

The emergence of pre-trained models, such as all_MiniLM_L6_v2, which is one of the models of sentence transformer along with neural networks, has revolutionized NLP tasks, including intent classification. These models pre-trained on large quantities of text data have an inherent understanding of linguistic structures and contextual indices. Their application to intent classification offers the potential to improve accuracy, adapt to diverse domains, and reduce reliance on hand-crafted features.

In the dynamic landscape of higher education, students and parents often face challenges in navigating the multitude of available courses and career paths. The lack of clear information leads to uninformed choices contributing to academic struggles and disappointment. This research paper addresses this issue by introducing an innovative solution—an AI-driven chatbot specifically designed to provide comprehensive insights into the field of computer science. The primary purpose of this chatbot is to empower students and parents with accurate and efficient information about available courses, majors, and potential careers in computer science. By leveraging advanced technologies such as neural networks, sentence transformers, and PyTorch, the chatbot aims to bridge the informational gap and guide users towards well-informed decisions, ultimately enhancing the success and satisfaction of students in their academic journeys.

Through the integration of neural networks, sentence transformers, and PyTorch, the AI-driven chatbot boasts a robust foundation for effectively addressing user queries. These technologies enable the chatbot to understand and respond intelligently to a diverse range of inquiries ensuring accuracy and efficiency in delivering information. By combining the power of artificial intelligence with the state-of-the-art natural language processing techniques, this chatbot serves as a valuable resource offering users a seamless and informative experience as they explore the dynamic and promising landscape of computer science education and careers.

2 Related Work

Chatbots that are powered by AI are a big help to education [6]. These interactive agents give prompt answers and are great resources for both educators and students. AI chatbots are beneficial to education since they can help with a variety of learning tasks, provide prompt feedback, and tailor personalized instructions. Research and development, teaching, administration, assessment, and advisory are among the areas where chatbot technology is being used in a rapid fashion in education [7]. It is noteworthy that the majority of chatbot applications are in teaching and learning domain (66%), with the remainder going to research and development (19%), administration (5%), evaluation (6%), and advisory (4%) [6]. These results highlight how chatbots have the ability to completely change how education is delivered and made accessible.

The studies of chatbots reported in [8–10] helped to establish a solid foundation for the understanding of key concepts, design principles, historical context, structure, and developmental intricacies and development techniques for the chatbots. A nuanced understanding of the classification and organization of Open Educational Resources (OERs) tailored for computer science education was given in [11]. This work has been pivotal in identifying relevant OERs and navigating the challenges and opportunities in OER reuse. Work provided in [9] provided valuable perspectives on developments in computational methods and applications in science and engineering. This understanding is particularly beneficial for addressing information gaps faced by students and parents.

Ample amount of information about courses and careers in computer science was provided in the context of historical and current perspectives of computer science education [12], whereas the insights into the comprehensive landscape of state-of-the-art chatbots in education were given in [13]. These works provided guidance on the understanding of how chatbots can effectively engage learners, personalize learning activities, and support educators. Furthermore, valuable insights were given for the potential and challenges of leveraging AI, particularly ChatGPT, for science education [14]. This knowledge has been instrumental in considering the integration of AI tools in teaching and learning. The understanding of the academia-industry gap offered valuable insights that have proven invaluable in assisting students to make informed decisions in the complex landscape of computer science education and careers [15]. Guidance for the general framework and architecture was given for developing chatbots with deep learning techniques, such as natural language processing and neural networks [16].

Various chatbot types were detailed in [17] to provide a foundation for designing effective educational chatbots and addressing specific educational queries. Further, in [18], an understanding of neural network architecture and training processes were facilitated, guiding the development of chatbots' language processing capabilities. The systematic review presented in [13] has been insightful in focusing on chatbot-learner interaction design techniques in education, whereas the utilization of neural networks (RNNs and CNNs) in a student chatbot was demonstrated providing practical insights into working with neural networks [19]. In [20], further impact of AI-based chatbots, including ChatGPT, and their potential to enhance the educational experience was discussed by offering personalized answers and guidance. Resources from https://action.bot/blog/using-chatbots-in-education/ and https://sendpulse.com/blog/education-chatbots have provided real-world insights into how AI chatbots are revolutionizing interactions between schools/universities and students. This knowledge has been instrumental in considering practical tips for creating effective chatbots in education covering such aspects as student communication and personalization.

3 Methodology

3.1 Data Collection

A specialized dataset was crafted, aimed at enhancing question-answering models focused on computer science education and career-related inquiries. The dataset compilation process involved gathering questions and answers through two primary methods as shown in Fig. 1. Firstly, surveys were conducted among university students, resulting in the collection of 8500 questions. Additionally, through an AI model, OpenAI's ChatGPT, 10,000 questions and answers were generated. Subsequently, a meticulous filtering process was employed to eliminate irrelevant or redundant questions, resulting in a refined repository of pertinent queries.

Following the filtration phase, a comprehensive curation process ensued, whereby 2163 questions and answers were carefully selected based on their relevance to computer science education and career exploration. This curated subset was formatted into a structured JSON format to facilitate seamless integration into the model training pipeline. The resulting dataset comprising high-quality and domain-specific questions and answers is embedded into the model to train it.

To facilitate model training, a sentence embedding module is utilized enabling the conversion of textual input into vectorized representations. The PyTorch-based neural network consists of an input layer matching the sentence embedding's vector size, a hidden layer, and an output layer representing the unique tags assigned to each question. The model is trained using the Adam optimizer with a cross-entropy loss function.

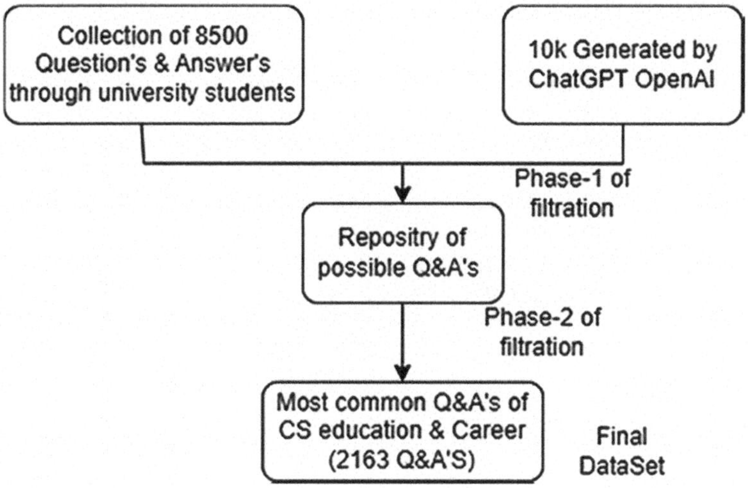

Fig. 1 Data collection process

The training process is executed over 100 epochs, during which the model learns to map input questions to their corresponding tags effectively. The training pipeline is optimized to run on either CPU or GPU. The model's performance is continuously monitored, and training is halted if no improvement is observed over a set patience threshold. Upon successful completion of training, the model's state, architecture details, and associated metadata (input and output sizes, tags, etc.) are stored in a "model.pth" file.

3.2 *Integration of Transformative Encoding and Neural Network*

The chatbot collects input from users and utilizes the sentence transformer, specifically the "all-MiniLM-L6-v2" model to encode the input sentences into a 384-dimensional vector. This model undergoes several key steps to process the input and generate meaningful representations:

(a) Word embedding: The first step involves converting input words into numerical vectors. This process is known as word embedding and helps the model represent words in a format suitable for mathematical operations.
(b) Positional encoding: To capture the sequential relationships in a sentence, positional encoding is introduced. Since traditional embeddings don't convey word order information, positional encoding adds positional information to the word vectors. This ensures that the model understands the sequential structure of the input.

Table 1 Example of 384-dimensional vector

	How	Are	You
Word embedding	[0.2, 0.3, 0.5, ...]	[0.1, 0.4, 0.6, ...]	[0.3, 0.2, 0.7, ...]
Positional encoding	[0.2, 0.3, 0.5, ...] + [0.1, 0.2, −0.3, ...] = [0.3, 0.5, 0.2, ...]	[0.1, 0.4, 0.6, ...] + [−0.1, 0.3, 0.2, ...] = [0.0, 0.7, 0.8, ...]	[0.3, 0.2, 0.7, ...] + [0.2, −0.1, 0.4, ...] = [0.5, 0.1, 1.1, ...]
Self-attention	[0.3, 0.5, 0.2, ...]	[0.2, 0.8, 0.1, ...]	[0.5, 0.2, 0.3, ...]
FFNN	[0.4, −0.1, 0.6, ...]	[0.6, −0.2, 0.4, ...]	[−0.3, 0.7, 0.1, ...]
Add and norm	[0.3, 0.5, 0.2, ...] + [0.4, −0.1, 0.6, ...] = [0.7, 0.4, 0.8, ...]	[0.0, 0.7, 0.8, ...] + [0.2, 0.8, 0.1, ...] + [0.6, −0.2, 0.4, ...] = [0.8, 1.3, 1.3, ...]	[0.5, 0.1, 1.1, ...] + [0.5, 0.2, 0.3, ...] + [−0.3, 0.7, 0.1, ...] = [0.7, 1.0, 1.5, ...]

(c) Self-attention: Self-attention is a mechanism where each word in the input sentence decides how much attention to give to other words. This attention mechanism allows the model to focus on different parts of the input when encoding, enabling it to capture dependencies and relationships between words more effectively.
(d) Feedforward neural network: Following self-attention, the output is processed through a feedforward neural network. This network consists of six linear layers, each followed by a Rectified Linear Unit (ReLU) activation function. The purpose of the feedforward network is to capture complex relationships within the data by transforming the representations learned from self-attention.
(e) Add and norm: After passing through the feedforward network, the output is combined with the original information using an "add" operation. This residual connection helps in mitigating potential vanishing gradient problems during training. The combined output is then normalized to ensure that the information is in a suitable state for further processing. This step, known as normalization, stabilizes and standardizes the output.

The sentence transformer utilizes the processed information to encode the input sentences into a 384-dimensional vector. This vector serves as a meaningful representation of the input capturing both semantic and sequential information.

For example, let's consider the sentence "How are you?". The process can be elaborated by following the abovementioned five steps and is shown in Table 1 and depicted in the sentence transformer part of Fig. 2.

The 384-dimensional vector output from the sentence transformer is fed into a simple feedforward neural network. This network processes the vector through multiple layers, and it generates a vector representing the predicted output at the final layer (output layer). The predicted output vector is then passed through a SoftMax activation function which converts the raw output into a probability distribution assigning probabilities to different classes. This is crucial for identifying the most likely class or response. The class with the highest probability in the

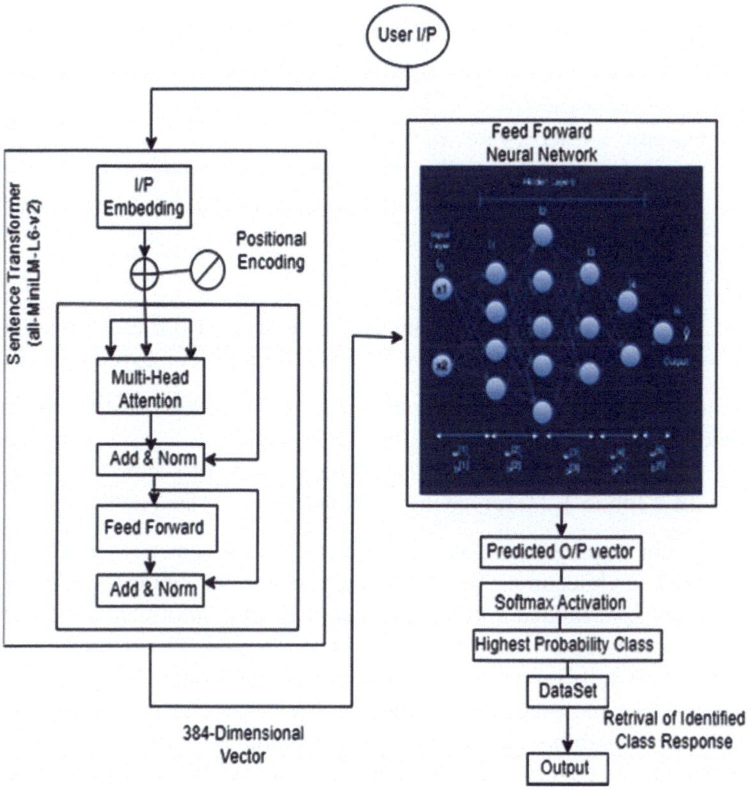

Fig. 2 Architecture of encoder and neural network model

distribution is identified as the predicted class. This class corresponds to a specific response in the dataset. Finally, the response associated with the identified class is retrieved from the dataset. This response is then generated as the output in the user interface providing a seamless and contextually appropriate interaction experience for users interacting with the chatbot system.

4 Experiment

The data for CSACbot primarily originated from ChatGPT by OpenAI. The dataset stored in the "2kintents_ques_gen.json" file encapsulates various intents, each comprising tags, patterns, and responses. With a total of 2163 tags corresponding to distinct classes, each class is associated with a set of seven similar questions and a response. The dataset structure takes the following format:

```
{
  "intents": [
   {
     "tag": "greeting",
     "patterns": ["Hi", "Hello", "Hey"],
     "responses": ["Hello! How can I assist you today?"]
   }
  ]
}
```


Python 3.11.2 was used with Microsoft's Visual Studio Code as the programming language and in code IDE, respectively. The key libraries employed include:

- PyTorch 2.1.0 for building, training neural network models, loading, and making predictions
- TQDM 4.65.0 to display progress during the creation of vectorized training data
- scikit-learn's Joblib 1.2.0 for saving and loading vectorized data

The CSACbot employs a two-step process integrating sentence embedding and a neural network architecture. The sentence transformer library using the "all-MiniLM-L6-v2" pre-trained model captures semantic information by encoding input sentences into high-dimensional vectors of size 384. The NeuralNet architecture consists of six fully connected layers with ReLU activation designed to process embedded features and predict responses. The SoftMax function is applied to the output layer for probability distributions over potential responses.

A curated dataset covering diverse computer science queries and corresponding responses was utilized for training and evaluation. The model parameters were optimized using the cross-entropy loss function and the Adam optimizer. Training involved 100 epochs with a batch size of 8. Model evaluation was conducted on a separate test set to assess generalization capabilities. The training process involved two steps: sentence embedding using the sentence embedding class and neural network training using the NeuralNet class. The dataset was vectorized and backpropagation was employed to optimize parameters with the Adam optimizer and cross-entropy loss.

The chatbot model was implemented in the "Chat.py" script facilitating real-time interaction. Users provide input queries for the model to generate predicted responses based on confidence thresholds as shown in Fig. 3. CSACbot is initiated by user questions related to computer science education and careers. The bot will respond with the answers with relevant information. Sample interaction with CSACbot is shown in Fig. 3.

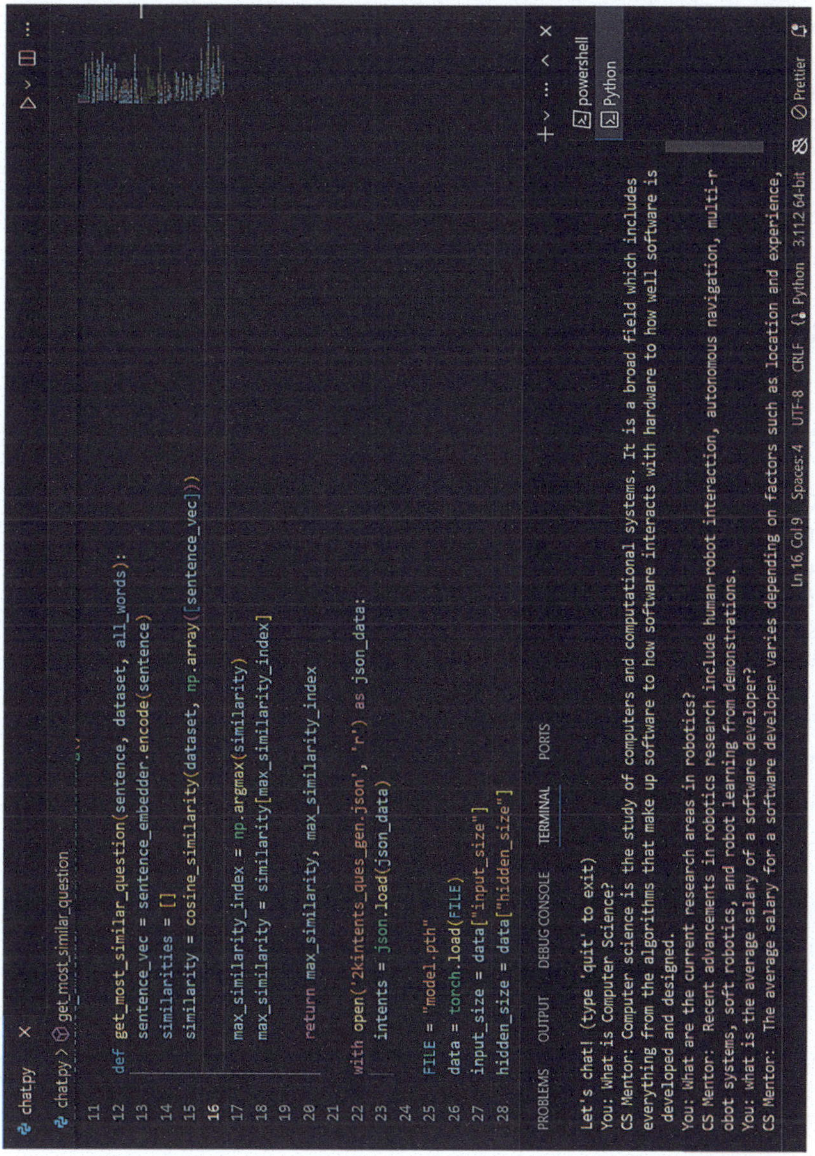

Fig. 3 A snapshot of CSACbot interaction

5 Results and Discussions

The CSACbot demonstrated commendable accuracy in addressing a wide range of queries related to computer science offering valuable insights for students and parents alike. Through meticulous training and integration of advanced techniques, the bot effectively provided relevant information contributing to enhanced user experiences. However, certain limitations were observed particularly in handling queries outside the scope of its training data. Despite these occasional shortcomings, the CSACbot showcased promising performance in delivering informative responses. Table 2 shows a comparative analysis of various chatbots to illustrate a better view of how CSACbot compares with other chatbots.

6 Future Work

Moving forward, further efforts can be focused on further enhancing the capabilities of the CSACbot to ensure continuous improvement and adaptability in terms of range of questions it can handle. The integration of advanced learning mechanisms akin to ChatGPT will enable the bot to engage in more nuanced interactions and provide tailored responses. Additionally, the exploration of multimodal interaction modes such as graphical- and image-based interfaces will enrich user experiences and cater to diverse learning preferences. Furthermore, the incorporation of a voice synthesis feature can be envisioned to augment user-friendliness and facilitate seamless interactions and accessibility. These future directions underscore the commitment to ongoing innovation and refinement to position the CSACbot as a versatile and indispensable resource in the realm of computer science education and career guidance.

Table 2 Comparison of related chatbots

Type	Features	
Sentiment analysis	Methodology	Combination of bag of words and word2vec
	Dataset	Used existing IDMB dataset
	Accuracy	90%
	Impact/ significance	Addresses the challenge of correctly interpreting the sentiment of tweets, which is important for understanding public opinion in various industries
	Novelty	Combination of bag of words and word2vec improves system effectiveness; contribution is toward better sentiment classification of tweets, which can be beneficial for analyzing public opinion on movies
Essay scorer	Methodology	ChatGPT-3 text-davinci-003 model
	Dataset	Existing dataset from TOEFL11 consisting of 12,000 essays
	Accuracy	Gives only certain level of accuracy
	Impact/ significance	AI language models could revolutionize writing evaluation and feedback methods
	Novelty	Linguistic features can improve the accuracy and potential integration of AI in learning system
IT career bot	Methodology	NLP techniques
	Dataset	NA
	Accuracy	NA
	Impact/ significance	Address career-related queries
	Novelty	Tailors career advices based on market trends
Customer service bot	Methodology	Experimental method through survey
	Dataset	Survey-based dataset
	Accuracy	NA
	Impact/ Significance	Understanding user compliance with chatbot requests
	Novelty	Exploring the impact of anthropomorphism and consistency on compliance
Medical chatbot	Methodology	Neural networks
	Dataset	Existing dataset
	Accuracy	80%
	Impact/ significance	Automating expert work in healthcare
	Novelty	Applying neural networks to medical chatbots
EduBot	Methodology	CNN, RNN
	Dataset	Relational database containing user and chatbot questions
	Accuracy	Compares two chatbots—Visualdialog.cloudcv and CloudCV—and concludes as CloudCV gives better results
	Impact/ significance	Provides convenient way of learning while confining to their homes
	Novelty	It is potential to cover more domains in the future
Python-bot	Methodology	Used SnatchBot platform to design and implement Python-bot

(continued)

Table 2 (continued)

Type	Features	
	Dataset	Uses predefined messages in SnatchBot to give response to user
	Accuracy	Not mentioned explicitly but provided accurate suggestions when tested with university students
	Impact/ significance	Supports novice programmers in understanding Python-programming language
	Novelty	Innovative educational tool that simplifies learning and supports students outside of the traditional classroom setting
Education chatbot	Methodology	NLP and ML Algorithms.
	Dataset	Collected data from open-source Web site
	Accuracy	NA
	Impact/ significance	To provide a user-friendly interface for students, staff, and parents to get information quickly
	Novelty	Reducing the need for in-person visits to college offices for information
Major chatbot	Methodology	Rasa framework
	Dataset	Collected data from students
	Accuracy	NA
	Impact/ significance	By providing personalized recommendations, it can guide students toward more informed decisions
	Novelty	Combining chatbot technology, NLP, and personality assessment for major assessment
CSACbot	Methodology	Sentence transformer, neural networks, PyTorch
	Dataset	Prepared a dataset of 2163 QnAs through filtration process among 18,500 QnAs
	Accuracy	98%
	Impact/ significance	Providing guidance to students and parents about computer science career
	Novelty	Combination of encoder and neural networks gives efficient results as user friendly

References

1. Hardi, R., Che Pee, A. N., Muhammad Haziq Lim Bin, A., Pitogo, V. A., Pribadi, A. S., & Rusdi, J. F. (2022). Academic smart chatbot to support emerging artificial intelligence conversation. *2022 International conference of science and information technology in smart administration (ICSINTESA)* (pp. 194–199). doi:https://doi.org/10.1109/ICSINTESA56431.2022.10041632.
2. L. G, B. S, R. D. M, D. J., & S. N. (2022). AI-powered digital classroom, 2022 international conference on communication. *Computing and Internet of Things (IC3IoT)* (pp. 1–6). doi: https://doi.org/10.1109/IC3IOT53935.2022.9767944.
3. Fegade, A., Raut, R., Deshpande, A., Mittal, A., Kaul, N., & Khanna, V. (2023). Unleashing the power of generative artificial intelligence: Exploring its boundless potential and overcoming challenges in academic environments. *2023 6th international conference on contemporary computing & informatics (IC3I)* (pp. 1243–1249). doi:https://doi.org/10.1109/IC3I59117.2023.10397917.

4. Souali, K., Rahmaoui, O., Ouzzif, M., & El Haddioui, I. (2019). Recommending moodle resources using chatbots. *2019 15th international conference on signal-image technology & internet-based systems (SITIS)* (pp. 677–680). doi:https://doi.org/10.1109/SITIS.2019.00110.
5. Souha, A., Ouaddi, C., Benaddi, L., & Jakimi, A, (2023). Pre-trained models for intent classification in chatbot: Comparative study and critical analysis. *2023 6th international conference on advanced communication technologies and networking (CommNet)* (pp. 1–6). doi:https://doi.org/10.1109/CommNet60167.2023.10365312.
6. Okonkwo, C. W., & Ade-Ibijola, A. (2021). Python-bot: A chatbot for teaching python programming. *Engineering Letters, 29.*
7. Zawacki-Richter, O., Marín, V. I., Bond, M., & Gouverneur, F. (2019). Systematic review of research on artificial intelligence applications in higher education - where are the educators? *International Journal of Educational Technology in Higher Education, 16*(39). https://doi.org/10.1186/s41239-019-0171-0
8. Nißen, M., Selimi, D., Janssen, A., Cardona, D., Breitner, M., Kowatsch, T., & Wangenheim, F. (2022). See you soon again, chatbot? A design taxonomy to characterize user-chatbot relationships with different time horizons. *Computers in Human Behavior, 127*, 107043. https://doi.org/10.1016/j.chb.2021.107043
9. Adamopoulou, E, & Moussiades, L, (2020). An overview of chatbot technology. *IFIP (International federation for information processing) International conference on AI applications and innovations (AIAI20)* (pp. 373–383). doi:https://doi.org/10.1007/978-3-030-49186-4_31.
10. Cahn, J. (2017). *Chat bot: Architecture, design, & development.* Senior Thesis (EAS499) University of Pennsylvania, School of Engineering and Applied Science, Department of Computer and Information Science.
11. Simão de Deus, W., & Barbosa, E. F. (2022). A systematic mapping of the classification of open educational resources for computer science education in digital sources. *IEEE Transactions on Education, 65*(3), 450–458. https://doi.org/10.1109/TE.2021.3128019
12. Thibodeau, P. (2017). A tech bubble killed computer science once, can it do so again? *IEEE-USA InSight.* https://insight.ieeeusa.org/articles/a-tech-bubble-killed-computer-science-once-can-it-do-so-again/
13. Kuhail, M. A., Alturki, N., Alramlawi, S., & Alhejori, K. (2023). Interacting with educational chatbots: A systematic review. *Education and Information Technologies, 28*(1), 973–1018. https://doi.org/10.1007/s10639-022-11177-3
14. Cooper, G. (2023). Examining science education in ChatGPT: An exploratory study of generative artificial intelligence. *Journal of Science Education and Technology, 32*, 444–452.
15. Stepanova, A., Weaver, A., Lahey, J., Alexander, G., & Hammond, T. (2021). Hiring CS graduates: What we learned from employers. *ACM Transactions on Computing Education, 22*, Article 5, 5:2–5:20. doi:https://doi.org/10.1145/3474623.
16. Chopde, A., & Agrawal, M. (2023). *Chatbot using deep learning*. Vishwakarma Institute of Technology, Pune.
17. Gao, J., Galley, M., & Li, L. (2018). Neural Approaches to Conversational AI. *Proceedings of ACM SIGIR conference (SIGIR 2018)*, Article 4. doi:https://doi.org/10.1145/3209978.3210183.
18. Chempavathy, B., Varshitha, D. R., Prabhu, S. N., Vinita, & Yaratapalli, L. (2022). AI based chatbots using deep neural networks in education. *Proceedings of the second international conference on artificial intelligence and smart energy (ICAIS-2022)*, IEEE. doi:https://doi.org/10.1109/ICAIS53314.2022.9742771.
19. Sophia, J. J., & Jacob, T. P. (2021). EDUBOT - A chatbot for education in Covid-19 pandemic and VQAbot comparison. *Proceedings of the second international conference on electronics and sustainable communication systems (ICESC-2021)*, IEEE. doi:https://doi.org/10.1109/ICESC51422.2021.9532611.
20. Morales Chan, M., Amado-Salvatierra, H. R., Hernandez-Rizzardini, R., De La Roca, M., (2023). The potential role of AI-based chatbots in engineering education. Experiences from a teaching perspective. *2023 IEEE frontiers in education conference (FIE)*, 10343296.

A Revolutionary Artificial Intelligence Framework for a Business Value-Centric Living Laboratory

Cristiane Chaves Gattaz, Fuad Gattaz Sobrinho, Joaquim Roberto Neves Campos, Oscar Ivan Palma Pacheco, and Quymã da S. Viana

Abstract The convergence of big data and artificial intelligence (AI) technologies has revolutionized the landscape of business processes, necessitating a profound understanding of Legacy Data semantics and its synchronization with expected values, highlighting the application of environmental, social, and governance (ESG) principles and sustainable development goals (SDGs) in the global economy. This chapter introduces an AI framework for a business value-centric living laboratory (BVLL), leveraging semantic modeling for big data analytics. Through AI-driven transformation and integration of Legacy Data, organizations can extract meaningful insights and drive informed decision-making in alignment with human transformation objectives. The framework emphasizes the contextual nature of data analysis, recognizing the importance of AI technologies such as machine learning and natural language processing in unlocking business potential sustainability. By exploring the synergy of AI and semantic modeling, businesses can navigate complex global landscapes, enhance operational and governance efficiency, and drive economic prosperity while contributing to environmental and social sustainability. This chapter presents the PRIMETHOD methodology and P3Tech architecture model, showcasing how AI integration revolutionizes process management, value realization, and operational excellence in line with ESG and SDG principles. The results highlight the transformative power of AI in unlocking business value and

---

C. C. Gattaz (✉)
Innovarch Soluções em Educação e Inovação Ltda, São Paulo, SP, Brazil

F. G. Sobrinho
Ambiência Sistemas de Informação Ltda, Campinas, SP, Brazil
e-mail: fuad@ambiencia.com

J. R. N. Campos
ProcesSolution Consultoria Ltda, São Paulo, SP, Brazil

O. I. P. Pacheco
OG Consultoria em Sistemas e Processos Ltda, Campinas, SP, Brazil

Q. d. S. Viana
Banco Itaú, São Paulo, SP, Brazil
e-mail: quyma.viana@itau-unibanco.com.br

S. C. Suh (ed.), *Artificial Intelligence for Design and Process Science*,
https://doi.org/10.1007/978-3-031-67886-8_5

driving sustainable growth. Future prospects focus on the continued exploration of AI technologies and their impact on business processes in the evolving landscape of human-technology interactions and digital era with a focus on ESG and SDG frameworks for self-transformative communities.

Keywords Artificial intelligence · Big data · Legacy data · Business value · Semantic engineering · Process management · Decision-making · Human-technology interaction · Sustainable growth · Self-transformative community

1 Introduction

The concept of big data encompasses a diverse array of applications, including the management of large datasets, social media analytics, advanced data management capabilities, real-time data processing, and data mining, among others [1].

In the context of business processes engineering with a focus on environmental, social, and governance (ESG) principles and sustainable development goals (SDGs) [2, 3], understanding the semantics of Legacy Data and its alignment with expected values and outcomes is crucial for navigating the complexities of the globally interoperated economy. Also, there is a growing need to leverage artificial intelligence (AI) to comprehend the semantics of Legacy Data and synchronize it with expected values [4].

This chapter introduces an AI framework for a business value-centric living laboratory (BVLL), utilizing a context-dependent methodology and information communication technology (ICT) to drive semantic modeling for big data analytics in alignment with ESG and SDG frameworks [5–13].

Within this framework, Legacy Data undergoes AI-driven transformation and integration, ensuring its relevance and quality for analysis [14]. The AI algorithms employed focus on understanding the nuances of data semantics, enabling more insightful and accurate analytics [15]. The living laboratory concept fosters an environment where AI technologies can be experimented with and refined in real-world scenarios, maximizing their value to the business and contributing to sustainable development goals [16–20].

Organizations, industries, and society at large are actively seeking methods, techniques, and tools to leverage Big Data for meaningful insights and value creation in alignment with ESG and SDG principles [21]. AI technologies such as machine learning, natural language processing, and knowledge representation play a pivotal role in this endeavor, enabling organizations to extract insights from massive datasets, uncover hidden patterns, and make data-driven decisions based on the value chain [7, 8, 22].

Furthermore, the framework recognizes the contextual nature of data analysis, understanding that approaches may vary based on specific business circumstances and societal impacts [23]. By leveraging AI technologies within this context, businesses can effectively navigate the complexities of the global economy, extract actionable insights from their data to drive informed decision-making, and promote sustainable growth [24].

To address the challenges and opportunities presented by big data and AI technologies through an ESG and SDG lens, upfront assessments with a transdisciplinary approach are essential [25–30]. This problem-solving space requires a holistic understanding of diverse perspectives and methodologies, as highlighted by various researchers [25, 26, 29–33].

2 Exploring the Synergy of Artificial Intelligence and Semantic Modeling for Maximizing Business Value in Complex Global Landscapes

In today's fast-paced business environment, organizations face various challenges such as low quality, productivity issues, high costs, and inefficiencies [34]. Recognizing the need for improvement, executives are turning to data analytics to gain deeper insights into business behavior [16, 35].

However, despite the buzz around data analytics, obtaining accurate information about organizational performance requires complex thinking and transdisciplinary approaches that consider the impact on environmental, social, and governance factors and sustainable development goals [16, 35]. This involves developing advanced analytical models to understand and solve complex business problems.

AI further emphasizes the importance of advanced data analysis. With AI technologies requiring massive datasets and high processing capabilities [36], organizations must develop sophisticated models to ensure AI systems can interpret data effectively and achieve desired outcomes.

Despite the potential benefits, many organizations struggle to adopt advanced analytical techniques [5]. They often overlook fundamental principles of process and complexity, hindering their ability to effectively model and act upon business value differences emphasizing the importance of integrating environmental, social, and governance considerations and sustainable development goals into their analytical approaches [11, 12, 37–39].

In summary, integrating AI with advanced analytical approaches is essential for organizations to navigate today's complex business landscape effectively. It requires a comprehensive understanding of data dynamics and the adoption of innovative problem-solving methodologies that consider the implications for environmental, social, and governance factors and sustainable development goals to drive meaningful business and human transformation outcomes.

2.1 *Empowering Human Transformation: The Role of Artificial Intelligence in a Technology-Driven World*

The need for human evolution and adaptation is more pressing than ever in today's fast-paced world of technological innovation and societal upheaval. From individuals to institutions and from local communities to global organizations, the demand to forge alliances with pioneers in innovation and transformation has become paramount [31–33, 40]. This imperative extends beyond basic survival needs; it encompasses the profound quest for new purposes, perspectives, and processes capable of navigating the complexities of our rapidly changing environment.

Citizens, students, professionals, researchers, and organizations are grappling with circumstances that demand rapid adaptation and growth in the face of disruptive changes. These changes, whether driven by technological advancements, societal shifts, or environmental challenges, require a reevaluation of established norms and practices and the cultivation of new skills, ideas, and ventures. Moreover, they underscore the importance of integrating ethical considerations into the fabric of technological progress [5, 6, 22, 31–33, 37, 41].

In this context, the integration of artificial intelligence (AI) frameworks and tools emerges as a critical catalyst for human transformation. There is a compelling call to harness the potential of AI to drive meaningful change in society [40, 42]. From optimizing decision-making processes and managing risks to fostering innovation and collaboration, AI offers a myriad of capabilities that can empower individuals and organizations to thrive in an era of uncertainty and disruption.

However, unleashing the full power of AI requires more than just technical proficiency; it demands a commitment to ethical principles and responsible governance. By leveraging AI within a framework of ethical stewardship, technology-savvy stakeholders can forge connections, bridge divides, and cultivate a culture of continuous learning and adaptation [43].

In this narrative, the journey toward human transformation is not simply about acquiring new technologies or resources; it is about fostering a collective consciousness that values sustainability, equity, and resilience. It is about empowering individuals and communities to envision a future that transcends the limitations of the present and to embark on a journey of growth and evolution that is both technologically sophisticated and ethically grounded [44].

2.2 *Navigating Challenges in Human-Technology Interactions: Privacy, Information Overload, User Experience, and Ethical Considerations*

In the current era of human-human, human-technology, and technology-technology interactions, business stakeholders have been facing four main challenges in the process of exploring the synergy of AI and semantic modeling [27, 42, 44]:

Privacy and Data Security: With the increasing reliance on technology for communication and interaction, ensuring the privacy and security of personal data has become a significant challenge. Data breaches, cyberattacks, and unauthorized access to sensitive information pose risks to individuals and organizations alike. Balancing the benefits of interconnected systems with the need for data protection remains a complex issue in the digital age. Ensuring the protection of sensitive information and maintaining data security is crucial when exploring the synergy of artificial intelligence and semantic modeling in human-technology interactions. The integration of AI and semantic modeling may involve the processing of large amounts of data, raising concerns about data privacy, unauthorized access, and potential breaches. Addressing these challenges is essential to build trust and confidence in AI-driven systems.

Information Overload and Digital Fatigue: The abundance of information available through various technological channels can lead to information overload and digital fatigue among individuals. Constant connectivity and notifications from multiple devices can overwhelm users, affecting their ability to focus, make decisions, and maintain meaningful human connections. Finding ways to manage and filter the vast amount of information available in a digital world is crucial for maintaining well-being and productivity.

Ethical and Social Implications of AI and Automation: The rapid advancement AI and automation technologies raises ethical and social challenges in human-technology interactions. Concerns about job displacement, algorithmic bias, and the impact of AI on decision-making processes are increasingly relevant. Ensuring transparency, accountability, and fairness in the development and deployment of AI systems is essential to address these challenges and build trust between humans and technology. The use of AI and semantic modeling in human-technology interactions may introduce ethical challenges related to bias, fairness, and transparency. AI algorithms can inadvertently perpetuate biases present in the data used for training, leading to discriminatory outcomes. Understanding and mitigating bias in AI systems, ensuring transparency in decision-making processes, and upholding ethical standards are critical considerations when exploring this synergy.

User Experience and Adoption: Enhancing user experience and facilitating the adoption of AI-driven technologies are key challenges in exploring the synergy of AI and semantic modeling in human-technology interactions. Designing intuitive interfaces, providing meaningful insights from AI-powered systems, and addressing user concerns about privacy and trust are essential for successful integration. Overcoming barriers to adoption and ensuring that users feel comfortable and empowered when interacting with AI technologies are important factors to consider in navigating these challenges.

Navigating these challenges requires a transdisciplinary approach that considers the perspectives of technology developers, policymakers, and end users to foster responsible and beneficial interactions in an increasingly interconnected world.

2.3 Education and Training Using AI-Driven Technologies: Preparing Tomorrow's Minds for Serving Humanity

Educators face a daunting task in today's rapidly evolving landscape of AI. They must navigate through complex algorithms, neural networks, and machine learning models to prepare students for a future where AI permeates every aspect of society. Challenges arise in developing curricula that not only teach the technical aspects of AI but also foster critical thinking, ethical decision-making, and creativity in students [9, 31]. Moreover, educators must stay abreast of the latest advancements in AI technology, constantly updating their knowledge and teaching methods to ensure relevance and effectiveness. Balancing theoretical concepts with hands-on experience becomes crucial, as students need practical skills to apply AI algorithms to real-world problems [32]. Additionally, inclusivity and accessibility in AI education present significant challenges, as the field has historically been dominated by certain demographics. Efforts to diversify the AI workforce must start in the classroom, with initiatives to engage underrepresented groups and provide equal access to AI education resources. Despite these challenges, the potential benefits of AI education are immense, empowering students to harness the power of AI responsibly and shape a future where technology serves humanity [43].

2.3.1 Charting the Course: Challenges and Opportunities in the Age of AI and Innovation Educational Transformation

Even before the advent of transformative technologies like ChatGPT in education, a pressing need for radical innovation in the post-pandemic educational landscape was already evident [45]. The traditional models no longer sufficed, demanding urgent implementation of new ideas and methodologies.

In Brazil, echoing global discourse, discussions on reforming education—from curriculum and workload to teacher training and assessment criteria—became prevalent, stirring chaos in staff rooms. However, it's crucial to recognize that this is not a new phenomenon; the quest for educational reform spans back to the nineteenth century [43]. Figures like Paulo Blikstein have long been champions of radical innovation, advocating for approaches that transcend traditional paradigms.

According to Campos and Blikstein [46], "We have been thinking about new school formulations since the moment in time. that the school has become institutionalized, and the examples cross cultures and geographies – ranging from tsarist Russia, with the school founded by Tolstoy in Yasnaya Polyana, to John Dewey's laboratory school, from the modern school of Ferrer and Guardia to the Montessori revolution. In addition to the experiences of these schools, there are educators who have also become a reference in radical innovation, inspiring schools around the world. In Brazil, literacy methods have been based on the perspective of reading the world and its emancipatory power, transforming society vision of the role of the school and the teacher."

Their perspectives, coupled with AI frameworks and tools that can revolutionize business value-centric living laboratories, can guide the creation of educational processes and environments that are value-oriented, self-recurring, and inclusive.

Accelerating the development of innovative educational models requires training of all stakeholders in value-oriented processes, akin to value-based business process management [9, 10]. However, implementation challenges abound:

1. **Resistance to Change:** Teachers, students, and administrators may resist new methodologies due to comfort with existing practices or skepticism.
2. **Financial Resources:** Implementing new technologies and pedagogical approaches often requires significant investments.
3. **Teacher Training:** Effective integration of innovations necessitates adequate training and support for teachers.
4. **Technological Infrastructure:** Insufficient infrastructure like Internet access and devices can hinder innovation.
5. **Socioeconomic Inequalities:** Technological innovations may exacerbate disparities among students if not all have equal access.
6. **Assessment and Accountability:** Evaluating the impact of innovations requires robust accountability systems, which are still evolving.

These challenges are formidable but surmountable with a strategic, collaborative approach involving all stakeholders in the educational process [43].

3 Business Value-Centric Living Laboratory Model: Unlocking Business Potential Through AI-Driven Organizational Learning

The concept of a business value-centric living laboratory (BVLL) serves as an environment where AI takes the lead in integrating business values, fostering autonomous organizational learning through real-time data analysis from both internal and external sources [13, 18].

Experiments within the BVLL aim to leverage AI capabilities to grasp, model, simulate, emulate, and enact the complexities of evolving business dynamics. This involves addressing intricate dependencies within the business network to bridge existing gaps [38, 47, 48].

Furthermore, the BVLL delves into understanding patterns of change amidst diverse and unexpected scenarios [19, 49–51].

The BVLL model, illustrated in Fig. 1, encompasses several synchronized key dimensions organized into five pillars.

As illustrated above, the following five pillars are:

1. Business values differences: Addressing the diverse needs of the client base

    References: Providing guidance for navigating the needed directions

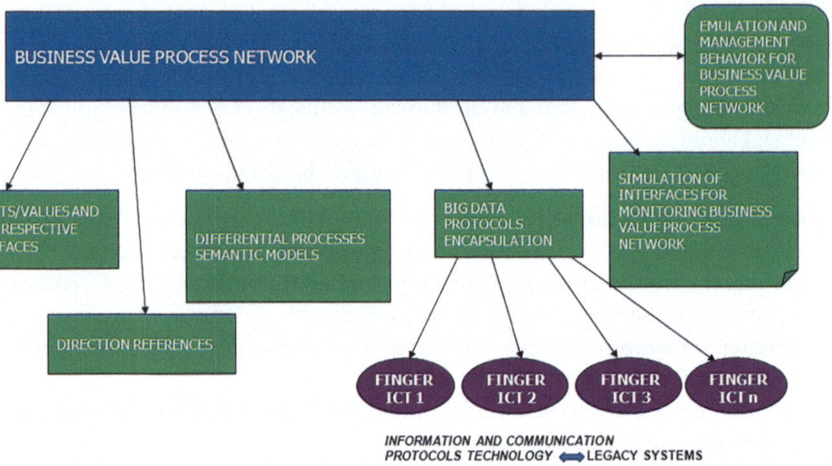

Fig. 1 Business value-centric living laboratory architecture. Source: Elaborated by the authors

2. Differential process equations: Explicitly defining the semantics of differences between current and desired multivariable states of business value
3. Content, interface, platform, and transmission protocols: Enabling the gathering of human, environmental, technological, and data resources and facilitating interaction with AI to correlate contextual variables
4. Monitoring and management context: Proactively managing change to mitigate undesirable side effects

The main components shown in Fig. 1 are aligned and structured within two architectures discussed in the upcoming sections of this chapter: PRIMETHOD, a method for managing Process Reality Intelligence, and P3TECH, a three-dimensional system bus for a value-based process management network [9, 10, 13].

4 PRIMETHOD Architecture: Navigating Business Value Realities with Process Intelligence Management

Value-centered process models developed using value business process management notation [10–12, 31] are capable of capturing different states of business value differences [7, 8]. Here are seven well-known recommendations, backed by scientific research [9, 52], that serve as a methodology for managing Process Reality Intelligence:

1. Value identification: Organizations should prioritize identifying their values before undergoing any process transformation to effectively address variety and volume filters.

2. Planning based on value engineering: Planning should revolve around the needs of value engineering, understanding that demand and supply are driven by needs.
3. Alignment with value chains: Organizational needed values should naturally align with the value chains of its business, ensuring traceability among initial, intermediary, and final values while meeting veracity requirements.
4. Contextual metric system: Establishing a contextual metric system allows for the evaluation of needed values across their multi-variable state space, addressing the variety of data states.
5. Modeling differential process equations: Modeling differential process equations helps accommodate tolerant differences between intermediary values and final values, considering the precision allowed by the adopted metric system.
6. Guiding differential processes: The directions of differential processes, indicating convergence toward needed final values, are determined by restrictions/references on the multi-variable state space of intermediary values to be added.
7. Synchronization for transformation: Synchronization among references, intermediary values to be added, and the technological, environmental, and human infrastructure are facilitated by the added final/intermediary values, triggering transitions for transformation and velocity.

These recommendations aim to induce the value needs, value veracity, value velocity, value variety, and value volume required for data analytics on business value.

A living laboratory, as deemed necessary by MIT Living Lab (2015), is essential for measuring and validating the necessary alignment and convergence of big data to satisfy the organizational needed values for the business within its value chain [5, 6].

The Architecture of the Process Reality Intelligence Management Method—PRIMETHOD—is shown in Fig. 2.

The PRIMETHOD approach designs numerous alternatives to address the behavioral processes of differential changes of business value shown in Fig. 3 when [9, 13, 52, 53]:

1. Identifying and designing differences of business value of contextual processes
2. Analyzing the evaluation by simulating ripple effects within process change management
3. Synthesizing the evaluation by emulation of the evolutionary or abrupt change process management
4. Explicating the complexity of organizational learning on the connection of business values
5. Innovating by design within a living laboratory of ill-structured business values when managing changes, inclusions, parallelisms, exponentiations, interoperations, zero time decisions, and so many other reality intelligences

This methodology utilizes a three-dimensional architecture, detailed in the following section, to bring the BVLL framework to life.

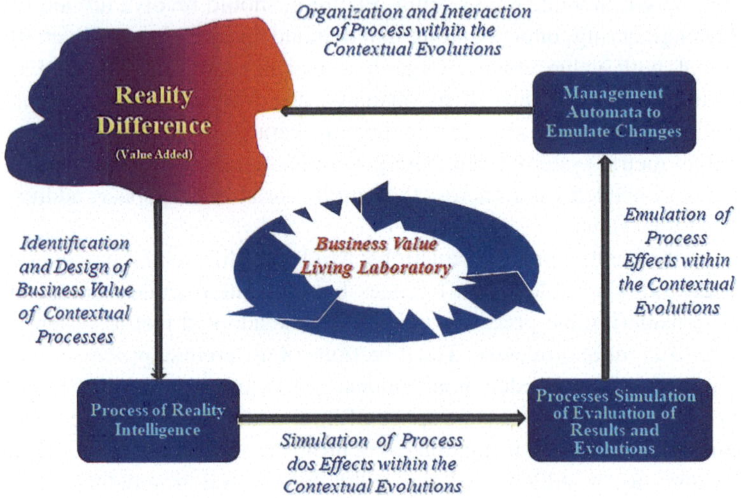

Fig. 2 PRIMETHOD architecture. Source: Elaborated by the authors

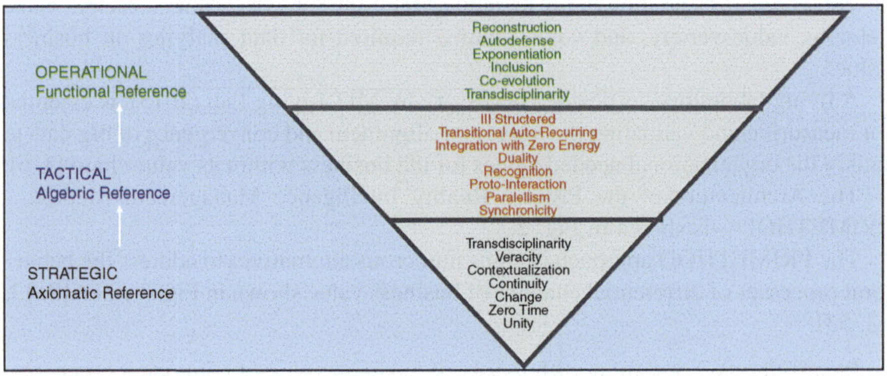

Fig. 3 Three-dimensional PRIMETHOD methodology. Source: Elaborated by the authors

5 Innovative Insights into the P3Tech Architecture: Revolutionizing Process Management and Value Realization

The P3Tech architecture, created by Gattaz Sobrinho in 2000, is a sophisticated three-dimensional system bus that leverages artificial intelligence principles to oversee a value-based process management network. It features key components like PArchitect for architectural aspects, PFingers for seamless interoperability, and PSynthesizer for synthesizing process models, as illustrated in Fig. 4.

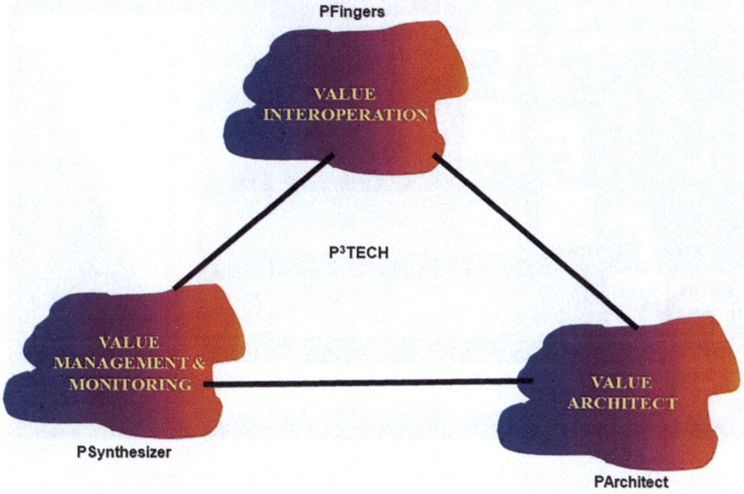

Fig. 4 P3Tech architecture. Source: Elaborated by the authors

The core elements of this architecture involve:

1. Defining specifications, interfaces, transformations, measurements, and interoperability of business values
2. Modeling the relationships between initial, intermediary, and final values in a business network
3. Ensuring synchronization to trigger the necessary transitions through protocols accessing human, technological, environmental, and data resources, according to the axioms or references required by the real world
4. Identifying potential repercussions of altering business values
5. Spotting inefficiencies in differential processes to boost value enhancement
6. Aligning business values and legacy systems (human, technology, environment, data) with the required business values

The challenges of synchronicity and conflicting interfaces in interoperating legacy systems across organizations necessitate P3Tech to be a versatile multiplatform development environment equipped with editing tools, interface construction tools, and runtime classes that amalgamate into a comprehensive ecosystem. This technology should cater to a broad spectrum of business solutions, from stand-alone departmental applications to complex distributed systems aimed at addressing enterprise challenges over long distances [54]. Additionally, it should serve as a robust tool for resolving interoperability issues and critical missions across various platforms and operating systems.

The P3Tech architecture encompasses five configurations of PArchitect, PFingers, and PSynthesizer, Initial, Management, Process, Measurement, and

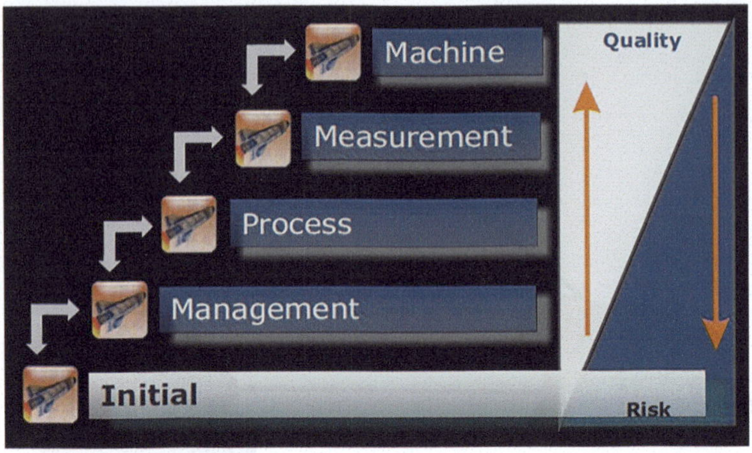

Fig. 5 P3Tech architecture configurations. Source: Elaborated by the authors

Machine, each with specific requirements detailed by Gattaz Sobrinho, Gattaz, and Pacheco in 2011 and described in the following sections of this chapter.

The architecture, visually represented in Fig. 5, showcases the seamless integration of these components to drive efficient process management and value realization in business operations.

5.1 P3Tech Initial: AI-Driven Technological Advancements in Development Environments

5.1.1 Advancing Technological Frontiers with Cutting-Edge Upgrades

In the realm of cutting-edge technical upgrades, the fusion of AI with development environments is reshaping the landscape of innovation. From autonomously partitioning applications to creating multilingual dictionaries seamlessly, AI is driving a wave of transformation in business operations. Empowering users with intuitive interfaces and optimizing efficiency through distributed application development, AI capabilities are propelling us into a new era of technological advancement. By embracing AI algorithms in versatile trans-platform environments and integrating essential operating system protocols, this section presents the holistic integration of AI contexts to enhance system intelligence and performance.

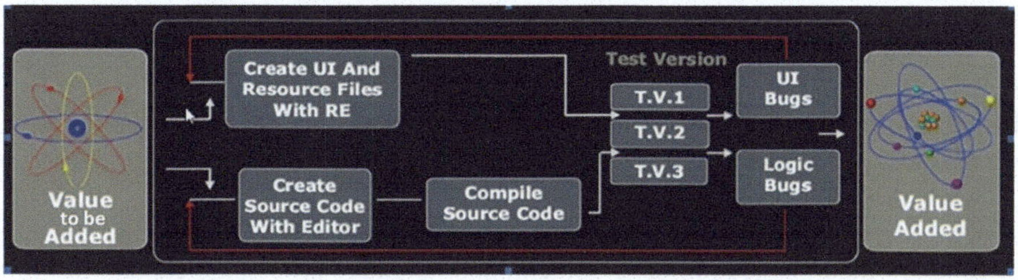

Fig. 6 P3Tech Initial Configuration. Source: Elaborated by the authors

The P3Tech Initial configuration illustrated in Fig. 6 explores the limitless possibilities at the intersection of AI and technology, from which the future is unfolding before our eyes:

- Harnessing AI in the development environment to partition applications and autonomously create multilingual dictionaries without manual intervention in the application code
- Intuitive interface development environment empowering business users to visually manage geometry and seamlessly distribute elements, irrespective of the underlying application code
- Leveraging AI capabilities in the development environment for distributed applications, focusing on individual elements of the business process for enhanced efficiency
- Embracing AI algorithms in a versatile trans-platform development environment for streamlined operations
- Multiplatform environment integrating essential operating system protocol libraries for optimal memory management, mutexes, conditions, trace statements, and efficient process control
- Holistic integration of AI contexts to elevate the system's overall intelligence and performance

As we conclude our exploration into the fusion of AI with development environments, it becomes evident that we are on the cusp of a technological revolution. The seamless integration of AI capabilities, from autonomously partitioning applications to enhancing efficiency through distributed development, signifies a paradigm shift in how businesses operate and innovate. The holistic integration of AI contexts has not only elevated system intelligence but has also paved the way for unprecedented advancements in performance and functionality. As we navigate the ever-evolving intersection of AI and technology, the limitless possibilities that lie ahead serve as a testament to the transformative power of AI in shaping the future of innovation. Embrace the journey as we witness the unfolding of a new era where AI drives us toward unparalleled heights of technological excellence.

5.1.2 AI-Powered Value Innovations: Revolutionizing System Efficiency and Cost-Effectiveness

In the fast-paced world of technology, the integration of AI is reshaping how businesses operate and innovate. This section delves into the game-changing impact of AI-driven value propositions, such as semantic code preservation to eliminate system interface maintenance costs, AI-powered distribution services for streamlined distributed application development, and language processing capabilities for efficient multilingual content management.

As shown in Fig. 7, the following three main aspects describe the P3Tech Initial configuration economic value propositions and explore how these innovative AI-driven solutions are revolutionizing system efficiency and cost-effectiveness and redefining the future of technology:

- Elimination of system interface maintenance costs and time through AI-driven semantic code preservation.
- Achieve a minimum 30% reduction in active effort required for developing distributed applications by leveraging AI-powered distribution built-in services.
- No resources development and maintenance costs and time associated with presenting content in multiple languages through AI-enabled language processing capabilities.

As we move forward, the impact of AI on system optimization and cost-effectiveness will continue to redefine the technological landscape, paving the way for a future where intelligent solutions drive sustainable growth and success.

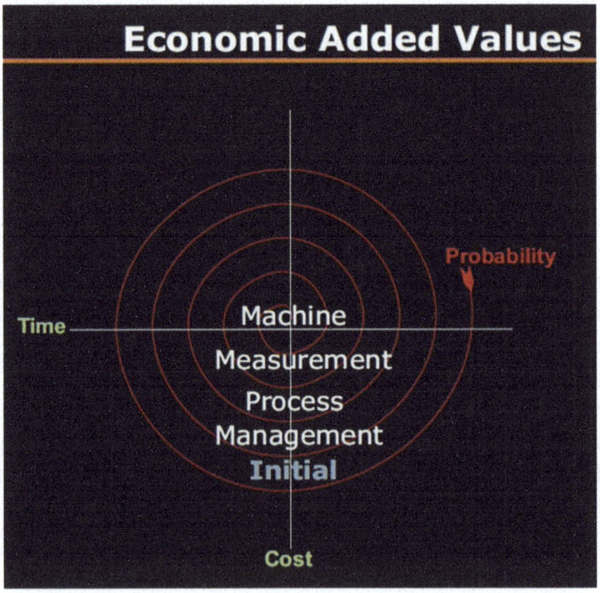

Fig. 7 P3Tech Initial value innovations. Source: Elaborated by the authors

5.2 P3Tech Management: Revolutionizing Technical and Economic Dimensions with AI Integration

P3Tech Management configuration stands out as a visionary framework that harnesses the power of AI to revolutionize technical and economic dimensions. By seamlessly integrating AI concepts, P3Tech Management offers a sophisticated approach to enhance operational efficiency, drive innovation, and optimize resource utilization. From advanced technical enhancements like multiplatform resource utilization and automated software generation to compelling economic benefits such as reduced maintenance costs and increased productivity, this framework reshapes traditional paradigms. Through a careful balance of technical sophistication and economic viability, P3Tech Management sets a new standard for organizations seeking to thrive in the age of AI-driven solutions through the following technical and economic aspects, illustrated in Fig. 8:

Technical benefits:

- Utilization of multiplatform resources for efficient representation, storage, location, and recovery of application resources
- Customizable look and feel tailored by the user
- Seamless zero-energy integration for sustainability
- Identification and detailed understanding of customer, product, and system requirements
- Simulation of requirements using different scenarios
- Automated generation of distributed and multiplatform software based on modeled requirements

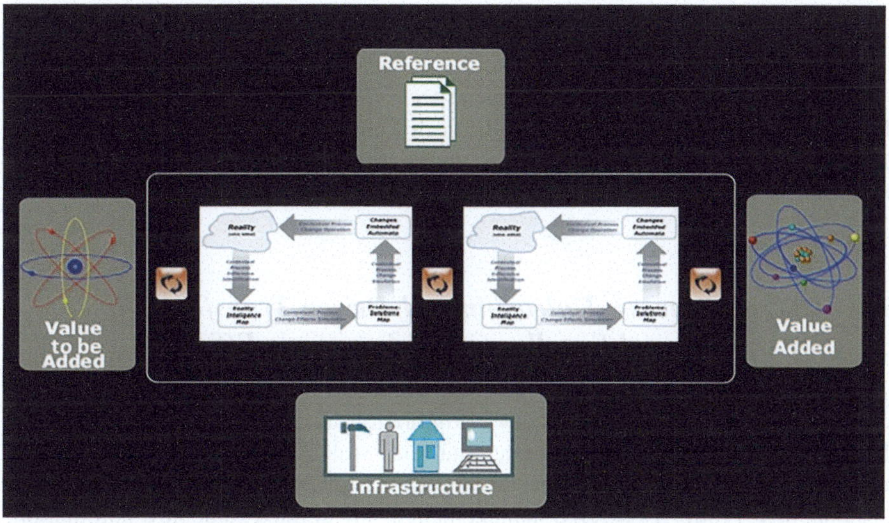

Fig. 8 P3Tech Management configuration. Source: Elaborated by the authors

- Evaluation and simulation of secondary effects that may occur due to requirement changes, facilitated by partition operators and software processes
- Platform for sharing requirements and best practices among stakeholders
- Tools to address dualities and implement self-defenses for all requirements
- Capability to identify, analyze, and simulate the operational aspects of organizational development processes for effective project planning and monitoring
- Tools to identify, analyze, and mitigate wastes and residues associated with requirements
- Automated integration of requirements to streamline processes
- Ensuring integrity and traceability of models and simulation scenarios in developed systems and processes, enabling transparent decision-making with the support of AI

Economic benefits:

- Reduction or elimination of system maintenance costs and time requirements.
- Significant productivity increase of at least 30% by reallocating human resources from maintenance and coding tasks.
- User interfaces can operate independently of platform-defined look and feel without requiring explicit user approval.
- Mitigation of system configuration and installation risks by 30%.
- Elimination of traditional coding phase, saving 20–30% of development effort in CMM Level 2 organizations and 40–60% in CMM Level 1 organizations.
- Assurance of alignment between requirements specification and the final system, facilitating auditing and control processes.
- Automatic registration of all process and software changes at no additional cost.
- Reduction of organizational inefficiencies caused by lack of synchronization in internal and external interactions through Web-based solutions.
- Integration of AI processes to support organizational compliance and enhance decision-making procedures.

The outlined technical and economic aspects, as illustrated in Fig. 8, demonstrate the profound impact and potential of P3Tech Management in reshaping traditional paradigms and paving the way for sustainable success in today's rapidly evolving landscape.

5.3 P3Tech Process: Unleashing AI-Driven Transformation for Operational Excellence and Economic Efficiency

Within the realm of P3Tech Process configuration lie a plethora of advancements that revolutionize operational, managerial, and structural processes, harmonizing with business objectives to propel organizations toward enhanced efficiency and sustainability. From AI-powered management to streamlined value flow automation, the integration of AI technologies promises exponential growth, insightful

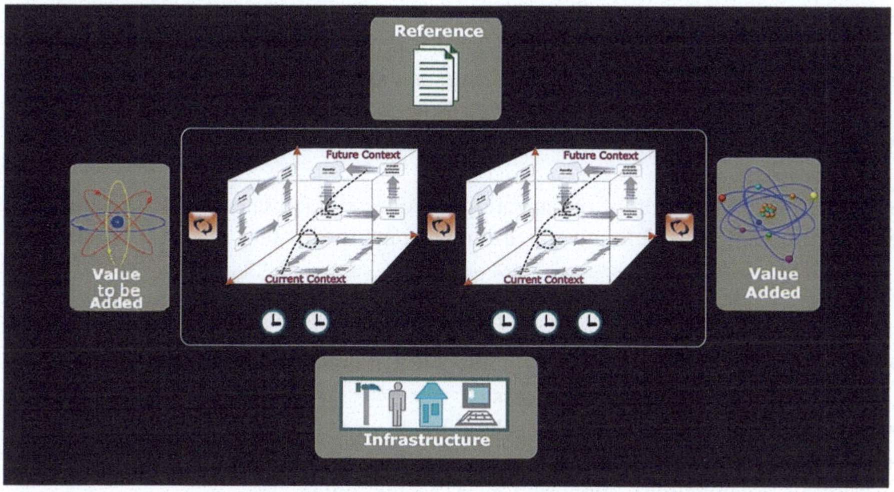

Fig. 9 P3Tech Process configuration. Source: Elaborated by the authors

transformations, and cost-saving strategies in the modern business landscape. In this dynamic environment, the fusion of AI capabilities with organizational frameworks paves the way for unprecedented value creation and economic efficiencies, redefining the very fabric of technological progress and business success by means of the following P3Tech Process technical and economic characteristics, illustrated in Fig. 9:

- Evolution of three-dimensional processes encompassing operation, management, and structure, evolving independently and in synchronism with business added values, driven by artificial intelligence concepts
- AI-powered management of modeled and simulated processes, enabling tracking, command, and control
- Integration with zero-energy consumption, enhancing sustainability and efficiency
- Generation of one-for-one software tailored to modeled, distributed, and multiplatform processes, ensuring seamless alignment with business needs
- Automated value flow generation aligned with business processes, streamlining operations through AI automation
- Environment for quantitative and qualitative verification and validation of processes and systems, leveraging AI capabilities
- Establishment of a unified communication protocol among various business competences, facilitated by AI technologies
- Exponential generation of new business possibilities through AI-driven insights and innovations
- Sharing environment for competencies and best practices, fostering collaborative AI-driven solutions

- Environment for explicit identification of dualities and implementation of self-defenses for all elements of organizational processes, guided by AI intelligence
- Platform for identifying, characterizing, and synthesizing wastes and residues in organizational processes, optimizing resource utilization with AI assistance
- Documentation generation for all organizational processes automated through AI technologies
- Automatic integration of organizational processes facilitated by AI systems
- Environment for defining three-dimensionality in the context of artificial intelligence

Besides, the following are the P3Tech Process economic added values:

- Elimination of the systems integration phase, reducing development total time by 30%, with AI streamlining processes
- Cost-free systems integration, enabled by AI-driven automation
- Elimination of codification phase, saving 20% of development efforts in CMM Level 3 organizations, supported by AI technologies
- Reduction of management systems development costs and time through AI optimization
- Decrease of configuration and installation risks in organizational business processes by 45%, with AI risk mitigation strategies
- A 45% decrease in configuration and installation risks of Legacy Systems, supported by AI integration
- A 50% decrease in costs of quality improvement projects like ISO and maturity processes, leveraging AI solutions
- A 20% increase in quality and productivity of teamwork, empowered by AI-driven efficiencies
- Zero-cost materials production for organizational training, reducing expenses with AI assistance
- Elimination of organization turnover risks, ensuring stability and continuity with AI systems
- A 50% decrease in total cost and time of projects requiring integration of multiple protocols and technologies, facilitated by AI-based solutions
- Environment for process-based artificial intelligence integration, enhancing economic efficiencies and outcomes

As organizations embrace the transformative power of AI, the convergence of P3Tech Process technical and economic added values emerges as a cornerstone of modern business evolution. Through AI-driven innovations, businesses can achieve unprecedented levels of operational excellence, cost efficiency, and strategic foresight. The symbiotic relationship between technology and economic outcomes underscores a new era of possibilities, where P3Tech Process serves as a catalyst for growth, resilience, and continuous improvement. By harnessing the potential of AI technologies, organizations can not only optimize processes and mitigate risks but also unlock a realm of untapped potentials, shaping a future where innovation and efficiency go hand in hand to drive sustainable success in a rapidly changing world.

5.4 The AI-Driven Revolution of P3Tech Measurement: Empowering Operational and Economic Excellence

In the context of P3Tech Measurement configuration, the infusion of AI concepts catalyzes a transformative shift in technical and economic values. By integrating AI-driven innovations, organizations delve into a world where processes are refined, interactions are optimized, and decision-making is enhanced through sophisticated AI algorithms. This marriage of technical advancements and economic efficiencies reshapes operational landscapes, promising heightened accuracy, efficiency, and cost-effectiveness. Through the lens of AI, P3Tech Measurement configuration emerges as a beacon of modernization, offering a paradigm shift in how businesses navigate complexities, streamline operations, and drive sustainable success in a dynamic and evolving business environment. The following technical added values describe the potential of P3Tech Measurement configuration and are illustrated in Fig. 10:

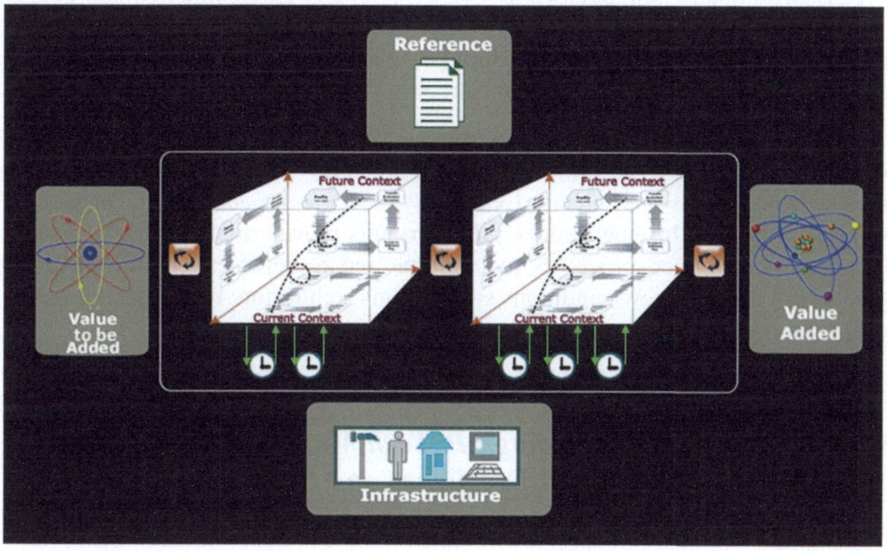

Fig. 10 P3Tech Measurement configuration. Source: Elaborated by the authors

- Incorporates AI-driven proto-interactions: refining process prototypes and fostering interactions among distributed prototypes
- Emulates the organizational business process map using AI algorithms
- Emulates communication protocols with AI integration
- Implements AI-based quantitative and qualitative management of organizational processes
- Records every action as a new process integrated into the organizational process
- Measure network behavior to assess the consistency of AI decisions across various scenarios ensuring compliance

Besides, the following economic added values describe the potential of P3Tech Measurement configuration:

- Mitigates technical risks associated with physical infrastructure acquisition
- Cost and time elimination of the field tests
- Ensures 100% reliable decision-making based on business processes and statistical data within the same AI-driven process
- Improves project efficiency by 40% in terms of time and cost through AI optimization
- Decreases configuration and installation risks by 45% when integrating Legacy Systems' Data Store within AI-driven processes
- Eliminates organization turnover risks with AI-guided decision-making processes
- Cuts down quality improvement project costs by 50%, including ISO and CMMI maturity process levels, through AI implementations
- Eliminates decision-making risks through AI-driven processes aligned with compliance standards defined within the process

The integration of AI in P3Tech's measurement configuration signifies a transformative step toward business excellence. This revolution is characterized by unprecedented precision, enhanced efficiency, and greater adaptability in various business processes. In other words, AI algorithms provide high accuracy in measurements, streamlined processes reduce time and resource expenditure, and AI systems can adjust to new conditions swiftly. This architecture fosters sustainability and prepares organizations for the dynamic business environment.

5.5 *The Power of AI Through P3Tech Machine: Unlocking Business Operational Excellence and Economic Prosperity*

By leveraging AI Technologies in the context of P3Tech Machine configuration, organizations embark on a journey toward unparalleled operational efficiency and economic prosperity. The fusion of cutting-edge AI solutions with machine configuration not only streamlines processes but also propels organizational growth through innovation and enhanced control. This integration heralds a new era

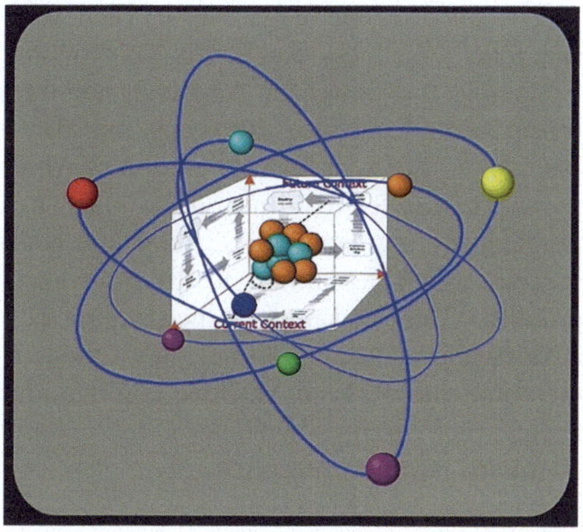

Fig. 11 P3Tech Machine configuration. Source: Elaborated by the authors

where real-time adjustments, seamless service integrations, and advanced problem-solving tools redefine the very essence of operational excellence and economic value creation. Through the lens of AI-driven transformations, P3Tech Machine configuration emerges as a pivotal force driving organizations toward higher levels of efficiency, productivity, and strategic advancement in the digital age. The following technical aspects explore the understanding of the P3Tech Machine configuration potential, as illustrated in Fig. 11:

- AI-driven solution integrating organizational business process definitions and generating information systems
- Real-time process changes based on metrics collected from real-world data
- Generation and integration of Web-based service processes (competencies)
- Web Process Service facilitating seamless processes
- AI tool for identifying and selecting solution alternatives for business process challenges

The following economic aspects also explore the understanding of the P3Tech Machine configuration potential:

- Effortless and cost-free automation of information systems
- Zero effort and cost in computer systems maintenance
- Comprehensive consideration of all aspects to elevate an organization's CMM to level 5
- Generation of work opportunities and income
- Explicit identification and amplification of competencies to drive new business initiatives with AI insights
- Ensuring 100% control over organizational processes with AI precision
- Guaranteeing 100% accuracy in recording organizational process timelines with AI-enabled systems
- A 30% increase in the utilization of best organizational practices facilitated by AI technologies

The convergence of AI with P3Tech Machine configuration marks a significant leap toward business excellence and economic empowerment for organizations. By harnessing the power of AI-driven solutions, businesses can not only automate processes and enhance efficiency but also unlock new avenues for growth and innovation. The seamless integration of AI technologies into machine configuration paves the way for real-time adaptations, streamlined service processes, and robust problem-solving capabilities, ultimately reshaping the landscape of organizational success. As AI continues to drive advancements in machine configuration, the promise of elevated performance, optimized operations, and sustained competitive advantage remains at the forefront of modern business evolution. Embracing AI in the context of P3Tech Machine configuration opens doors to a future where efficiency, profitability, and strategic agility harmoniously coexist, setting the stage for continued progress and prosperity.

6 BVLL Experimentation: Results from Collaborative Projects in the USA and Brazil Since 1972

Several experiments utilizing BVLL with its PRIMETHOD and P3Tech architectures have been conducted in the USA and Brazil since 1972 through collaborative agreements with various institutions worldwide.

The experiences outlined in the timeline span over several decades showcase a remarkable journey of academic and professional growth, innovation, and leadership worldwide. Noteworthy achievements during this period include contributions to the development of the first Brazilian computer alongside the Ministry of the Navy and pioneering work in graph clustering algorithms for cancer analysis and taxonomy of plants.

Subsequent years experiences delve into transdisciplinary research, particularly in Soil Value for Experiential Agriculture Development at EMBRAPA, the most representative agriculture research center in Brazil. This was followed by groundbreaking work in Software Engineering, including involvement in the Star Wars Program and seminal research on Software Evolution Management, and leadership in computer science and management science.

The impact of these experiences extended into the realm of national and international projects, notably as agriculture and systems integration. Projects such as the *Paulista Software Factory*, the Telesp Project, and the Federal Senate's Living Laboratory underscored a commitment to cutting-edge technology implementation and management, earning international recognition and certification.

Between 1995 and 1998, the P3Tech environment emerged as a groundbreaking innovation, consistently ahead of its time. State-of-the-art machines and workstations and construction of physical spaces were carried out to implement living laboratories, as shown in Fig. 12.

Fig. 12 TELESP BVLL facilities. Source: Elaborated by the authors

Its integration with value-based processes yielded remarkable transformations. In June 1998, a team trained in the PRIMEMETHOD methodology spearheaded the implementation of the first integrated P3Tech environment at Telecomunicações de São Paulo S.A. (TELESP), certified by the Society for Design and Process Science (SDPS), as shown in Fig. 13.

This initiative gave birth to the Telesp Software Factory and introduced the living laboratory concept, revolutionizing the Brazilian largest telecommunications company just before its privatization. The factory became a pioneering force, capable of specifying, simulating, and generating software products in real time, setting the stage for the *Fábrica de Software Paulista* project endorsed by São Paulo State Governor, Mário Covas.

This achievement marked the inception of a community comprising scientists, entrepreneurs, and value-based process experts through the BVLL network, as illustrated in Fig. 14.

Their vision is bold: to leverage science and technology for integrated development, reducing risks, ensuring business evolution, enhancing workers' quality of life, and fostering a more equitable, inclusive, and cooperative society, both in Brazil and globally.

In more recent years, the focus shifted toward the coordination and operation of projects for the implementation, development, and training of living laboratories in Brazil and abroad. These include university laboratories at Pontificia Universidade Católica do Paraná (PUC-PR), Texas A&M University-Commerce (TAMUC), the

Fig. 13 SDPS Certifies First International Telecom BVLL (1998), BVLL Project Presentation to Governor Mário Covas (Nov. 1996) & COMDEX Award (Aug. 1997). Source: Elaborated by the authors

University of Alabama at Birmingham (UAB), and Adventist University of São Paulo (UNASP); government innovation projects at the Brazilian Federal Senate, the Brazilian Space Agency (AEB), Caixa Econômica Federal (CAIXA), Bank of Brazil (BB), Embrapa Instrumentation, Brazilian Ministry of Planning (MP), and Brazilian Ministry of Human Rights (MDH); as well as a Brazilian private company learning venture projects at Ambiência Sistemas de Informação [5, 6, 9, 22, 31–33, 37].

Collaborations with these esteemed organizations and various government ministries reflect a continued dedication to innovation and technological advancement on a global scale.

Overall, this timeline encapsulates a journey characterized by visionary leadership, pioneering research, and a profound impact on academia, industry, and society at large.

The following section highlights some of the results obtained from these research and development initiatives.

Fig. 14 TELESP BVLL Inauguration and Results Presentation to C-Level. Source: Elaborated by the authors

6.1 Empowering Business Value: Implementing PRIMETHOD and P3Tech in Research Institutions and Corporate Initiatives

A business value process was defined employing PRIMETHOD, P3Tech Initial, Management, and Process in the research facilities of the institutions described in the previous section of this chapter. The TELESP project initiative enabled the development of their BVLL through the application of its main characteristics shown in Fig. 15. With regard to the banking sector, fifteen employees from BB management and operational team underwent training to establish a BVLL focused on credit recovery. Additionally, the Institute of Exact and Technological Sciences of PUC-PR utilized the PRIMETHOD and P3Tech methodology and architecture to establish the inaugural Web-based digital knowledge ecosystem called LabP3 Network (Labp3.net). This platform was designed for developing modeling and simulation process applications, as well as facilitating distance education for the creation of BVLLs. This initiative gave rise to the university's inaugural business incubator, which concentrated on software development and forged partnerships with private sector entities like Siemens. In collaboration with AEB and the Brazilian Management Center of the Ministry of Science, Technology and Innovation (CGEE), a BVLL was established, involving key institutions within the Brazilian Aerospace

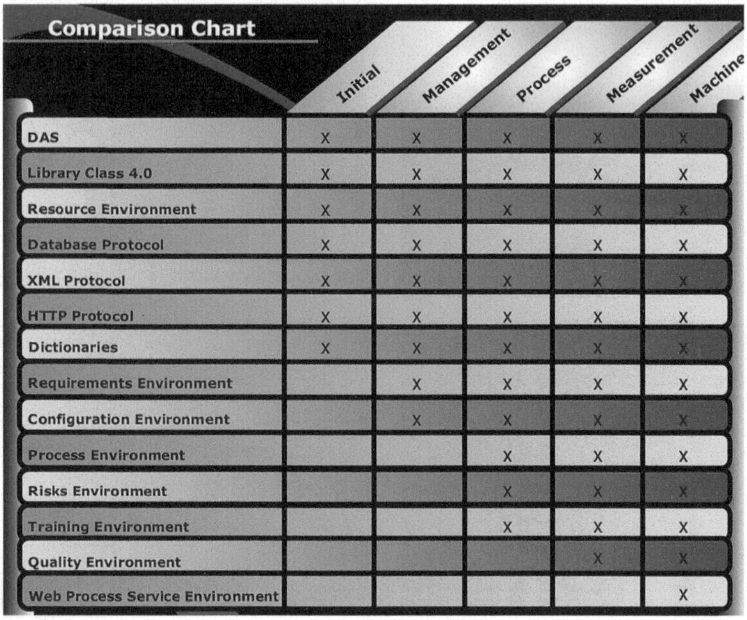

Comparison Chart

	Initial	Management	Process	Measurement	Machine
DAS	X	X	X	X	X
Library Class 4.0	X	X	X	X	X
Resource Environment	X	X	X	X	X
Database Protocol	X	X	X	X	X
XML Protocol	X	X	X	X	X
HTTP Protocol	X	X	X	X	X
Dictionaries	X	X	X	X	X
Requirements Environment		X	X	X	X
Configuration Environment		X	X	X	X
Process Environment			X	X	X
Risks Environment			X	X	X
Training Environment			X	X	X
Quality Environment				X	X
Web Process Service Environment					X

Fig. 15 PRIMETHOD and P3Tech architecture configurations of the BVLL (TELESP). Source: Elaborated by the authors

Sector's science, technology, and innovation (S,T&I) ecosystem. The implementation utilized PRIMETHOD and P3Tech methodologies to model and simulate a multifaceted socioeconomic system, encompassing technical-productive modalities, inter-organizational dynamics, and technological cooperation, influenced by cultural and competitive factors. Recognized as a strategic priority by the Brazilian government, this initiative aimed to develop an inter-organizational cooperation network to propel Brazil's involvement in nanotechnology innovation applied to payloads and satellites. At CEF, the BVLL for Business Development was created to facilitate the exchange of expertise in strategic business management, engaging C-level executives. As a result of this initiative, knowledge and practices gained were extended to the Brazilian Ministry of Planning. Moreover, UNASP utilized P3Tech Machine and currently operates a BVLL while offering an MBA program specializing in BVLL. Furthermore, in collaboration with Embrapa Instrumentation, a BVLL was created to facilitate the dissemination of outcomes related to the coordination, management, and operation of agents within a research and innovation network focused on aerial pesticide application. Assisted by the Ministry of Human Rights, a BVLL focused on urban development for longevity was initiated. It was utilized for training public administrators across 15 Brazilian cities, encompassing all states in the country. The initiative yielded 15 process models emphasizing value, aimed at enhancing regional longevity. The Brazilian Federal Senate is providing courses in PRIMETHOD and

P3Tech Process for its staff, having outlined and developed over two hundred process business values.

Also, the following Human Resources were trained by each respective organization mentioned above:

- TELESP: the initiative engaged the Operational Planning Department, comprising 380 staff members across five divisions: engineers, IT technicians, systems analysts, programmers, and administrators. These teams collaborated closely with the C-suite, influencing corporate decisions at the highest level.
- BB: fifteen employees from management and operational team to establish a new credit recovery department.
- PUC-PR: over 100 graduate and undergraduate students from diverse academic backgrounds participated, along with R&D managers from research institutions collaborating with the university. Additionally, the LabP3 Network reached approximately 1500 individuals.
- CEF: more than 20 C-level staff members for business development.
- UNASP: 66 individuals, including two with a PhD, and 58 with undergraduate degrees.
- UAB: six individuals enrolled in the PhD Multidisciplinary Program.
- TAMUC: three individuals enrolled in the Master Program in Computer Science.
- Brazilian Federal Senate: 61 individuals, with 2 holding an MBA and 59 with undergraduate degrees in various areas of concentration.
- AEB: three individuals with a master's degree. Also, top executives from leading institutions in the aerospace sector such as Department of Aerospace Science and Technology (DCTA), National Institute for Space Research (INPE), Institute of Applied Economic Research (IPEA), Support Program for Scientific and Technological Development (PADCT), and University of Brasilia (UnB).
- Embrapa Instrumentation: three researchers, two with a doctoral degree and the other with a master's degree.
- MDH: 47 public managers from 24 cities.
- Ambiência Sistemas de Informação: 25 individuals, including 8 with a PhD, 7 with a master's degree, and 10 with undergraduate degrees in various areas of concentration.

These experiences underscore outcomes that address critical aspects of social governance, including technical and professional training, employability, and continuity, all while considering their sustainability impact on society and the environment.

In conclusion, the integration of AI into the development and implementation of business value processes has proven to be instrumental in enhancing operational efficiency and strategic decision-making across various institutions in the USA and Brazil. The utilization of BVLL methodology and architectures, in alignment with ESG and SDG frameworks, as well as the training of human resources in these advanced technologies, has resulted in significant advancements in new business processes and new workforce capabilities. The collaborative efforts between academic institutions, government agencies, and private companies have not only

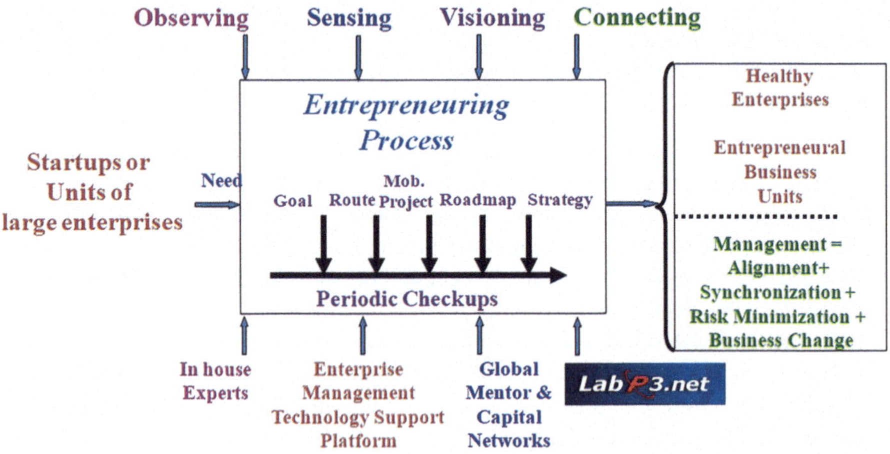

Fig. 16 Learning venture environment. Source: Elaborated by the authors

facilitated the exchange of new knowledge and expertise but have also paved the way for the successful implementation of AI-driven solutions in the business environment applying ESG and SDG principles. Moving forward, continued investment in AI technologies and training programs will be essential to further drive innovation, productivity, and economic prosperity in the rapidly evolving digital landscape.

Also, the utilization of the PRIMETHOD methodology alongside the P3Tech architecture model emerges as a pivotal tool in orchestrating, organizing, and documenting the essential components required for the operation, management, and evolution of any new educational endeavor, regardless of its complexity.

As education undergoes radical transformations, there arises a necessity to reimagine the roles of both educators and learners, harmonizing new technologies with transformative pedagogical strategies. The invaluable insights of Paulo Blikstein serve as guiding lights in this journey, offering a roadmap toward an education system that is not only pertinent but also equitable and empowering.

By amalgamating the principles of PRIMETHOD and the P3Tech architecture model with the philosophies of Blikstein, a pathway to educational innovation becomes apparent. This integration engenders an educational framework that is not only technologically sophisticated but also socially conscious, illustrated in Fig. 16.

Through the fusion of Blikstein's constructionist approach and critical pedagogy, learning environments can be cultivated wherein students not only assimilate technical expertise but also cultivate a discerning comprehension of the world around them.

7 Conclusions and Future Prospects

The convergence of BVLL approach for innovation and learning ventures with the emerging concept of Artificial Intelligence of Things (AIoT), characterized by interconnected AI-driven heterogeneous computing systems and wireless communication networks embedded into the physical environment, has demonstrated significant effectiveness and necessity in the exploration of Web process services handling vast amounts of data distributed across diverse contexts requiring precise synchronizations.

The future avenue of research and development entails the co-evolution of BVLL toward a Cooperative Network of AIoT-enabled BVLLs, aimed at facilitating the sharing of business values experiments in alignment with environmental, social, and governance principles and sustainable development goals for human transformation. Key research challenges include addressing content management, interface design, multiplatform compatibility, and interaction protocols to foster cultural convergence through business values while considering learning venture and ESG and SDG frameworks [28, 55]. Additionally, the seamless integration of Internet of Things and big data principles and technologies in zero time is imperative within a cooperative network of AIoT-enabled BVLLs to drive continuous innovation and efficiency in business processes while advancing ESG and SDG objectives for human transformation.

7.1 Harnessing Artificial Intelligence for Human Transformation

Influenced by a myriad of social, economic, cultural, educational, technological, political, and environmental factors, the co-evolution of BVLL toward a Cooperative Network of AIoT-enabled BVLLs aspires to become a beacon of transformative education and innovation for modeling, simulating, emulating, and enacting self-transformative communities—complex and dynamic socio-economic systems considering the modalities of technical-productive, inter-organizational, and technological cooperation, driven by culture and competitiveness [5, 6, 22, 31–33, 37].

Self-transformative communities are social groups or networks characterized by their inherent capacity for self-transformation and evolution. Unlike traditional communities, which may rely heavily on external influences or hierarchical structures for change, self-transformative communities possess the intrinsic ability to adapt, innovate, and redefine themselves from within. Members of these communities actively engage in processes of reflection, learning, and collective action, driving continuous growth and development. Moreover, self-transformative communities foster a culture of empowerment and autonomy, where individuals are encouraged to take ownership of their personal and collective transformation journeys. By harnessing the collective wisdom and creativity of its members, a self-transformative community becomes a dynamic ecosystem of mutual support, resilience, and innovation, capable of navigating complex challenges and shaping its own destiny [31].

At its core lies a commitment to awakening, inspiring, and educating individuals and organizations from diverse backgrounds, including under-represented minorities and developing countries, within a global and multisectoral context, for human transformation in alignment with ESG and SDG principles.

With the legacy of the experiments described in this chapter as a guiding light, the co-evolution of BVLL toward a cooperative network of AIoT-enabled BVLLs endeavors to propel a purposeful and transcultural education and innovation ethos, fostering ethical, effective, and efficient articulation, operation, and management of innovation initiatives [41]. Central to its mission is the cultivation of significant connections and the facilitation of co-evolution among stakeholders, catalyzing their growth, rehabilitation, and reintegration into society, as well as enhancing their competitiveness and survival in a rapidly evolving landscape.

To realize its overarching vision, the co-evolution of BVLL sets forth specific objectives centered on the utilization and advancement of artificial intelligence frameworks and tools. Through a combination of virtual and face-to-face communication platforms, participants are mobilized across various contexts within learning venture ecosystems (Fig. 16):

- Inspiration: Facilitating discussions on strategic and emerging issues related to the existing BVLL legacy, the co-evolution of BVLL toward a cooperative network of AIoT-enabled BVLLs aims to co-create innovative solutions aligned with real-world needs and demands.
- Training: Offering dynamic courses and certification programs, the co-evolution process of BVLL equips individuals with methods, techniques, and tools that evolve the ethos of purposeful and transcultural education and innovation.
- Sharing: Promoting the utilization of resources, including regulations, norms, laws, and financial, physical, environmental, human, and technological assets, to translate ideas into tangible results that address societal challenges.
- Meaningful connections: Facilitating collaborative efforts among stakeholders to propose and incubate innovative solutions through a global network of innovation BVLLs, leveraging existing infrastructure within the global innovation ecosystem.
- Learning: Establishing observatories to document and disseminate learning from innovative experiences, fostering cultural change, and facilitating the adaptation of successful ideas across diverse contexts. Additionally, the co-evolution of BVLL encourages research dissemination and knowledge sharing to enhance innovation management practices.

In essence, the co-evolution of BVLL toward a Cooperative Network of AIoT-enabled BVLLs envisions a future where artificial intelligence serves as a catalyst for human transformation, enabling individuals and organizations to navigate complex challenges and unlock their full potential in a rapidly evolving world.

Acknowledgments The authors of this chapter express gratitude for the information and assistance extended by the students, professors, and staff members of UnB, EMBRAPA, TELESP, UNASP, UAB, TAMUC, NASA, the Brazilian Federal Senate, MPOG, CAIXA, AEB, Ambiência Sistemas de Informação, and collaborative institutions. Their contributions have been invaluable in shedding light on the intricacies of value-based business processes.

Special thanks are also extended to the researchers who have delved into value-based processes, as cited in the references section, for their valuable insights and contributions to the field.

References

1. Laney, D. (2001). 3D Data management: Controlling data volume, velocity, and variety. *META Group Research Note, 6*(70), 1–4.
2. Boffo, R., & Patalano, R. (2020). *ESG investing: Practices, progress and challenges*. OECD.
3. Mishra, M., Desul, S., Santos, C. A. G., et al. (2024). A bibliometric analysis of sustainable development goals (SDGs): A review of progress, challenges, and opportunities. *Environment, Development and Sustainability, 26*, 11101–11143.
4. Davenport, T. H., Harris, J., & Abney, D. (2017). *Competing on analytics: The new science of winning; With e new introduction*. Harvard Business ReviewPress.
5. Gattaz, C. C., Cruvinel, P. E., & Piscopo, M. R. (2014). Semantic parameters to manage an innovation network using managing as designing approach: The Virtual Innovation Society network case. *International Journal of Innovation, 2*, 45–64.
6. Gattaz, C. C., Cruvinel, P. E., & Bernardes, R. C. (2019). Leveraging digital knowledge ecosystem framework implementation: Case study: Aligning knowledge management and innovation goals for agricultural aerial pest control. *Encyclopedia with Semantic Computing and Robotic Intelligence, 2*, 1950001-1–1950001-10.
7. Gattaz, C. C., Amato Neto, J., & Catharino, M. (2006a). The dynamic cooperation network as an instrument for the technological management and innovation process: The case of the Brazilian aeronautic sector. *Journal of Technology Management and Innovation, 1*, 140–147.
8. Gattaz, C. C., Amato Neto, J., Catharino, M., Techima, K., & Coral, R. (2006b). A dynamic relationship framework for innovation: Implications for the Brazilian aerospace strategy operations. *Journal of Integrated Design and Process Science, 3*, 17–31.
9. Gattaz, C. C. (2001). *Brincando de Processo: Um método de capacitação na metodologia de processo*. Available in http://independent.academia.edu/CristianeGattaz
10. Gattaz Sobrinho, F. (2023). *Value oriented process modeling and simulation*. 158 pgs.
11. Gattaz Sobrinho, F., Gattaz, C. C., & Pacheco, O. P. (2011a). A value-based business process management network model. *Journal of Integrated Design and Process Science, 15*(4), 85–94.
12. Gattaz Sobrinho, F., Gattaz, C. C., & Pacheco, O. P. (2011b). Complexity measures for network process evolution. *Journal of Integrated Design and Process Science, 15*(4), 95–115.
13. Gattaz Sobrinho, F. (2000). *Processo: A máquina contextual nos negócios*. Available in: http://www.labp3.net
14. Chen, M., Mao, S., & Liu, Y. (2012). Big data: A survey. *Mobile Networks and Applications, 19*(2), 171–209.
15. Russom, P. (2011). *Big data analytics. TDWI Best Practices Report*, Fourth Quarter, pp. 1–34.
16. Almirall, E., & Wareham, J. (2009). Contributions of living labs in reducing market-based risk. In *Proceedings of the 15th international conference on concurrent enterprising*. Leiden, NL.
17. Janssen, M., Charalabidis, Y., & Zuiderwijk, A. (2018). Benefits, adoption barriers and myths of open data and open government. *Information Systems Management, 33*(4), 258–268.
18. Pallot, M. (2009). *Engaging users into research and innovation: The living lab approach as a user centred open innovation ecosystem*. Webergence - http://www.cwe-projects.eu/bscw/bscw.cgi/1760838?id=715404_1760838

19. Schwittay, A. (2008). 'A living lab': Corporate delivery of ICTs in rural India. *Science, Technology and Society, 13*(2), 175–209.
20. White, B. J., Martin, B. A. & Wold, R. J. (2021). The integrated value model (IVM): A relational data model of business value. In: Kautish, S. K. (Ed) *Using strategy analytics to measure corporate performance and business value creation.*
21. IOM. (2012). *Information sharing and collaboration: Applications to integrated biosurveillance: Workshop summary*. National Academy Press.
22. Felipe, I. J. S., Mendes-Da-Silva, W., & Gattaz, C. C. (2019). Crowdfunding research agenda: Semantic analysis of the media and geography of investments. *Encyclopedia with Semantic Computing and Robotic Intelligence, 2*, 1930001–1930010.
23. Kiron, D., Prentice, P. K., & Ferguson, R. B. (2012). The benefits of big data: Six ways it can drive decision making. *MIT Sloan Management Review, 55*(2), 1–22.
24. McAfee, A., & Brynjolfsson, E. (2012). Big data: The management revolution. *Harvard Business Review, 90*(10), 60–68.
25. Ertas, A., Maxwell, T., Rainey, V. P., & Tanik, M. M. (2003). Transformation of higher education: The transdisciplinary approach in engineering. *IEEE Transactions on Education, 46*(2), 289–295.
26. Fielder, G., & Gattaz Sobrinho, F. (2015). *Value-based process engineering*. IEEE, vol. TBD, no. TBD, pp. TBD.
27. Fischer, C., Radinger-Peer, V., Krainer, L., et al. (2024). Communication tools and their support for integration in transdisciplinary research projects. *Humanities and Social Sciences Communications, 11*, 120.
28. NRC. (2014). *Convergence: Facilitating transdisciplinary integration of life sciences, physical sciences, engineering and beyond*. The National Academies Press.
29. Zimmerman, B. (2001a). *Ralph Stacey's agreement & certainty matrix*. Page 1. Available in: http://216.119.127.164/edgeware/archive/think/main_aides3.html
30. Zimmerman, B. (2001b). *Ralph Stacey's agreement & certainty matrix*. Page 4. Available in: http://216.119.127.164/edgeware/archive/think/main_aides3.html
31. Gattaz, C. C. (2010). *Um modelo de referência de formação e gestão de redes organizacionais: o caso do sistema de C,T&I do setor aeroespacial brasileiro*. Ph.D. Thesis, Escola Politécnica, University of São Paulo, São Paulo, SP.
32. Gattaz, C.C., Falvo, S.R., Cruvinel, P.E. (2020). Verbal and mathematical literacy education and STEAM in the technopolis of São Carlos, Brazil. In: Zintgraff, C., Suh, S., Kellison, B., & Resta, P. E. (Org.). *STEM in the Technopolis: The power of STEM education in regional technology policy* (1 edn, vol. 1, pp. 225–248). Springer International Publishing.
33. Prado, A. I. F., Marinho, A. K. B. B., Gattaz, C. C., & Mendes-Da-Silva, W. (2021). The COVID-19 pandemic in Brazil: What is happening on the front line. *Transdisciplinary Journal of Engineering and Science, 12*, 1–4.
34. Chesbrough, H. W. (2003). *Open innovation: The new imperative for creating and profiting from technology*. Harvard Business School Press.
35. Hoogerwerf, E. J., Desideri, L., Malavasi, M., Rimondini, M., & Kübler, A. (2013). *Towards a framework for user involvement in research and development of emerging assistive technologies*. AAATE Vilamoura.
36. Hinton, G., Deng, L., Yu, D., Dahl, G. E., Mohamed, A., Jaitly, N., Senior, A., Vanhoucke, V., Nguyen, P., Sainath, T. N., & Kingsbury, B. (2012). Deep neural networks for acoustic modeling in speech recognition: The shared views of four research groups. *IEEE Signal Processing Magazine, 29*(6), 82–97.
37. Gattaz, C. C., Amato Neto, J., Gattaz Sobrinho, F., Boland, M., & Bangalore, R. (2012). Critical factors to explicit required knowledge to manage the virtual innovation society network. *Journal of Integrated Design & Process Science, 15*, 13–26.
38. Mitchell, M. (2009). *Complexity, A guided tour*. Oxford University Press, 349 pgs.
39. Pohl, K. (2010). *Requirements engineering – Fundamentals, principles and techniques*. Springer, 813 pgs.

40. Sidhu, N., Gupta, S., Sharma, R., Mehta, K., Taneja, S. (2024). The transformation of human existence through the integration of artificial intelligence. In: *Innovative technologies for increasing service productivity* (pp. 134–144). IGI Global.
41. Rossetto, D. E., Bernardes, R. C., Borini, F. M., & Gattaz, C. C. (2018). Structure and evolution of innovation research in the last 60 years: Review and future trends in the field of business through the citations and co-citations analysis. *Scientometrics, 115*, 1329–1363.
42. Ofosu-Ampong, K. (2024). Artificial intelligence research: A review on dominant themes, methods, frameworks and future research directions. *Telematics and Informatics Reports, 14*, 100127.
43. Miao, F., Holmes, W., Ronghuai, H., Hui, Z. (2021). *AI and education: Guidance for policy-makers*. UNESCO, 50 pgs.
44. Li, X., Rong, K., & Shi, X. (2024). Situating artificial intelligence in organization: A human-machine relationship perspective. *Journal of Digital Economy*.
45. Yu, H. (2024). The application and challenges of ChatGPT in educational transformation: New demands for teachers' roles. *Heliyon, 10*(2), 1–15.
46. Campos, F. R, & Blikstein, P. (Orgs.). *Inovações radicais na educação brasileira*. Porto Alegre: Penso, 2019. 480 p.
47. Johnson, N. (2007). *Simply complexity*. Oneworld Publications, 236 pgs.
48. Michalski, R. S., Carbonell, J. G., & Mitchell, T. M. (2013). *Machine learning: An artificial intelligence approach*. Springer.
49. Von Hippel, E. (1986). Lead users: A source of novel product concepts. *Management Science, 32*, 791–805.
50. Von Hippel, E. (1988). *Sources of innovation*. Oxford University Press.
51. Yeh, R. T., Pearlson, K. E., Kozmetsky, G. (2000). *Zero time: Providing instant customer value – Every time, All the time!* Wiley. 270 pgs.
52. Simon, H. (1973). The structure of ill structured problems. *Artificial Intelligence, 4*, 181–201.
53. Rahman, H. (Ed.). (2011). *Cases on SMEs and open innovation: Applications and investigations: Applications and investigations*. IGI Global.
54. Wingo, S., & Tanik, M. (2015). *Using an agile software development methodology for a complex problem domain*. IEEE.
55. NRC. (2015). *Enhancing and effectiveness of team science*. The National Academies Press.

The Power of Smart Design: How Intelligence Shapes Custom Digital Products

Michael P. Papazoglou, Bernd J. Krämer, and Amal Elgammal

Abstract Smart manufacturing fundamentally transforms traditional manufacturing into the next generation of data- and knowledge-driven digital manufacturing. This chapter presents a proven digital twin-driven manufacturing approach called manufacturing blueprints. It includes a novel manufacturing knowledge model and a programming approach to rethink and redesign the whole product customization and development process. Manufacturing blueprints is a comprehensive digital twin approach that addresses the entire smart product life cycle, including product design, production, and performance aspects. Manufacturing blueprints promises to realize the vision of smart manufacturing by fully digitizing all physical assets and processes, connecting factory sites and plants to customize outputs, and allocating resources to provide a logical shift between the digital and physical realms of product customization.

Keywords Smart manufacturing · Digital twins · Meta-programming · Manufacturing blueprints · Product customization · Production planning

---

This research is partially funded by the EC Horizon 2020 project Monitoring Multidimensional Aspects of Quality of Life After Cancer Immunotherapy (QUALITOP) under contract number H2020-SC1-DTH-01-2019-875171.

Michael P. Papazoglou is also with Universities of New South Wales and Macquarie University, Sydney.
Amal Elgammal is also with Egypt University of Informatics, Egypt, and on leave from Cairo University, Egypt.

M. P. Papazoglou · B. J. Krämer (✉) · A. Elgammal
Scientific Academy for Service Technology e.V. (ServTech), Potsdam, Germany
e-mail: mikep@servtech.info; kraemer@servtech.info; amal@servtech.info

S. C. Suh (ed.), *Artificial Intelligence for Design and Process Science*,
https://doi.org/10.1007/978-3-031-67886-8_6

1 Introduction

Large Industry 4.0 or smart manufacturing is signaled by a transition toward a physical-to-digital-to-physical connection. Smart manufacturing represents the next industrial revolution, realized through the application of digital technologies in industrial processes. A smart manufacturing ecosystem will interweave all aspects of manufacturing, from plant operations to the supply chain, exhibiting a set of connected machines, process automation, and manufacturing units, enabling virtual tracking of capital assets, processes, and resources. The aim is to create an integrated, automated, and optimized production flow that produces increasingly individualized customer products [1].

The manufacturing paradigm advocated by smart manufacturing allows manufacturing systems (machines, sensors, devices, actuators, valves, and networking technologies) to have both a digital counterpart and a physical interaction with the real world. This results in a *digital twin* model that mirrors the physical and the virtual worlds [2]. This digital-twin approach enables manufacturers to build an intelligent (sensor-equipped) virtual, digital product capturing any physical product at any stage of production. The digital twin approach can analyze the behavior of a digital product and provide actionable insights that guide informed decisions about processes and materials using advanced visualization tools, such as 3D CAD/CAM tools, and simulations that observe the impact on the shape and properties of the physical counterpart of the product.

The digital twin representation shows the evolution of a product and production process in every stage of the product life cycle [3]. This helps product designers and engineers to optimize performance, predict behavior, and gain insights from past design and production experience. Data from the product in the field can be fed back into the digital twin and used as the basis for further innovation and improvement, enabling manufacturers to virtually recreate a product and its production and even simulate its performance in the real world without taking any physical action.

The vision of smart manufacturing and digital twins requires new languages for modeling, sharing, and correlating smart digital product aspects (product, process, supplier, and machine knowledge) while supporting the distributed nature of industrial automation processes.

To address these challenges, this article proposes (i) a novel *digital twin knowledge model* (a semantic model that captures relevant direct and indirect product and production data) and (ii) a *digital twin programming paradigm* that operates on top of the digital twin knowledge model and serves to correlate and manage readily available product/manufacturing information and processes. The work presented in this chapter capitalizes on the smart manufacturing enablers and building blocks in [3] by integrating and synergizing an advanced *model-driven product engineering* approach that leverages the power of meta programming languages. Model-driven engineering has the potential to surmount the complexity of the manufacturing ecosystem to simplify the product design and development processes and drive productivity gains [4, 5]. Meta-programming paradigm can improve the productivity, efficiency, quality, and reliability of software systems.

In the following discussion, Sect. 2 presents related work and compares it with the findings in this chapter. In Sect. 3, we present the requirements for twin-driven product customization and production planning. Section 4 extends traditional model engineering to monitor the requirements of digital twins and digital threads following a novel model-driven product engineering approach. Section 5 presents the proposed DT model and its meta-programming environment. In Sect. 6, the approach is applied to an industrial strength aerospace case study. Finally, Section 7 summarizes the chapter and presents perspectives of our work.

2 Literature Review

The ability to capture, integrate, and process heterogeneous manufacturing knowledge and data is central to supporting the key tenets of smart manufacturing discussed in this chapter: digital twins, customizable products, and meta-programming languages for manufacturing environments.

2.1 Digital Twins

Grieves first introduced the concept of DTs back in 2003 [2]; however, the rapid development of DT-enabling technologies, including simulation, data acquisition, data communication, sensors, visualization, cloud computing, and big data analytics, has only recently emerged. These have triggered the transformation of the DT from being a concept to its application and development in various fields [6].

With the growing attention paid to the concept and development of DTs, several analytical and state-of-the-art articles have been published recently [6–9]. The study in [7] provides a categorical literature review of the concept of DT in manufacturing, distinguishing between Digital Models (DM), Digital Shadow (DS), and DTs. DM is defined as a digital representation of an existing or proposed physical object that does not use automated data exchange between physical and digital objects. DS is another automated one-way data flow between the state of an existing physical object and a digital object. DT also integrates bidirectional data flow between physical and digital objects. The study then concluded that the literature focusing on the highest-level development in the form of DT is rare as compared to DM and DS. The work presented in this article aims to fill this gap.

The authors in [9] present the challenges and revolutionary technologies for the Internet of Things (IoT), artificial intelligence (AI), and DT in the domains of manufacturing, healthcare, and smart cities. They define DT as a simple bidirectional integration of data between physical and virtual machines. In a parallel context, the research in [8] investigates the correlation and differences between cyber-physical systems (CPSs) and DTs and concludes that they are not similar in several aspects considering their origin, development, engineering aspects, CPSs mapping, and base elements.

A state-of-the-art review considering 50 relevant papers and 8 patents has been conducted in [6], which concludes that DT applications in the product design account for 18% of the literature, while 35% address the production process (mainly the execution phase while neglecting production planning), and 47% address the monitoring process (mostly prognostic health monitoring).

In contrast, the DT approach proposed here provides a formal manufacturing knowledge model and an expressive meta-programming environment (see Sect. 2.3) for the seamless translation of validated product designs into efficient and optimized production plans. This approach can be extended to subsequent processes of the product life cycle, from production to monitoring, with rigorous solutions, and concrete IT implementations. However, these are beyond the scope of this article.

2.2 Product Customization

Product customization is the production of goods and services to meet the needs of individual customers with efficiency close to mass production. Critical to the successful implementation of a customization strategy is the concept of product architecture, which is the means to enable the reuse of parts, assemblies, technologies, concepts, and knowledge to achieve both product commonality and variability at the same time [10].

Modularity and commonality in product design ensure customization to bring product costs closer to mass production. Both enable product differentiation/customization by reducing lead times and benefiting from economies of scale. During the design phase, commonality is primarily used to reduce the effort required to create product variants [11]. Giovannini et al. [12] present an innovative approach to rationalize product diversity by associating each product variant with the profile of the customer most likely to be interested in it.

Tian et al. [13] argue that in the case of mass customization, due to the strong similarities between mass customization products and their components, a parameterized approach can be used. Research studies related to product customization are looking at knowledge models that represent the platform of a product family [14, 15]. The study in [14] presents a module-based integrated design scheme to support the creation of a product platform, product family generation, and customized assessment. Nomaguchi et al. [15] propose a knowledge model of product architecture design system that focuses on design repositories that reduce data redundancy and inconsistencies.

The implementation of product customization in the literature primarily focuses on capturing the direct information about the customization process that represents the solution space, including possible parameters of the product and its geometry and structure. However, equally important information that is not directly used to perform personalization, such as information about customers, suppliers, and product quality data, is not considered [16].

In contrast, the DT approach proposed in this work (i) is based on the formal foundation of the blueprints knowledge model; (ii) mitigates usability concerns of modelling languages by employing a meta-programming approach and 3D visualization capabilities, enabling continuous and iterative collaboration between the customer and the designer/engineer; and (iii) extends to subsequent life cycle processes by adopting an integrated data/knowledge approach.

2.3 Product Models, Data Exchange Standards, and Meta-programming Languages

Product model and data exchange standards that can be used in conjunction with product engineering include the ISO-10303 and the MTConnect standards. The ISO10303 standard (www.steptools.com) describes how digital product information is represented and exchanged, enabling companies to unify all product information associated with individual products throughout their life cycle. The MTConnect standard (www.mtconnect.org) defines a semantic vocabulary for manufacturing plants to provide structured contextualized data without their proprietary format. It is clear that product engineering and digital twins require more expressive constructs than those offered by the product model and data exchange standards examined above. Much effort has been put into the development of ontology approaches such as AutomationML (www.automationml.org). It is an open, neutral, XML-based data exchange format that allows the transfer of design data from production systems.

Other efforts have focused on enhancing the complexity of automated systems by proposing programmable logic controllers (PLCs) and domain-specific languages (DSLs) [17] for model-driven development of automated manufacturing processes [18]. DSLs raise the level of abstraction beyond programming by specifying the solution directly in terms of domain concepts. A typical example is the Systems Modeling Language (SysML) [19]. SysML captures PLC functional and non-functional requirements, supports mapping of abstract machine features to factory floor machine operations, and generates code for the appropriate PLC runtime environment. In addition, an orchestration engine has been developed to accommodate the adaptation of automated systems in operation and the physical changes in the production environment [20]. However, till now, little weight has been placed on developing appropriate abstraction mechanisms to bridge the components of the digital and physical worlds.

Significant efforts are reported in [21], where the authors introduced the idea of digital twin-centric control. Here, a rudimentary DT derived from a product version creates assembly plans and synthesizes the resources in a manufacturing cell.

To avoid problems such as those mentioned above, meta-programming languages can be used [22]. A meta-programming language involves writing a program that can operate on other programs or can represent its own code as a data structure of the language itself [23, 24]. Despite the many examples of program generation reported in the literature, most of the proposed systems use ad hoc technology to build program fragments.

To remedy these limitations, multi-level languages have been proposed as intermediate representations for partial evaluation and as a formal basis for runtime code generation, the most prominent early example being MetaML [25], AutomationML [26], NodeRED (nodered.org), and Converge [27]. However, all of the above developments lead to a platform-dependent design and are not suitable for smart manufacturing.

It is clear from the above analysis that product models and DSLs currently have very limited capabilities in the context of product engineering. Almost all efforts focus on very specific aspects of PLCs on the factory floor, where they abstract from the physical processes in the controller environment while not targeting digital twins. In contrast, the meta-programming approach in this chapter provides a canonical model and language that encodes an actionable digital twin to fully represent and simulate the characteristics and performance properties of a physical product, its product line, and associated production processes in the virtual world, before the product is physically produced. In the following section, we present the basics of product customization and production planning and the requirements for twin-driven product customization.

3 Digital Twins for Product Customization and Production Planning

Transdisciplinary research helps develop effective data integration strategies and advanced analytics techniques that can provide actionable insights for decision-making, process optimization, and predictive maintenance. Smart manufacturing requires a transdisciplinary approach in several ways:

(i) Integrated technology development: Smart manufacturing involves the convergence of different technologies such as the Internet of Things (IoT), artificial intelligence (AI), robotics, and data analytics. Transdisciplinary research facilitates collaboration between experts in these fields, leading to the development of integrated technologies that can work together seamlessly in smart manufacturing systems.
(ii) Interdisciplinary problem-solving: Smart manufacturing challenges often require solutions that span several disciplines. Transdisciplinary approaches allow researchers and practitioners from different fields such as engineering, computer science, materials science, and business to work together to solve complex problems related to the automation, optimization, and efficiency of manufacturing processes.

(iii) Data integration and analytics: Smart manufacturing generates huge amounts of data from sensors, machines, and various other sources.
(iv) Supply chain optimization: Smart manufacturing extends beyond individual factories to include supply chain optimization. A comprehensive approach to supply chain management is required, taking into account logistics, information flow, and coordination between different stakeholders, resulting in more efficient and responsive manufacturing networks.

3.1 Digital Twins Facets

To achieve digital product customization, DTs allow product designers to model multiple permutations and provide a holistic view of all aspects of a digital product. They streamline the process of customer demands and implement usage data that will increase customization options across three facets:

Product facet (for efficient design/customization of products)—Allows manufacturers to analyze how a product works under different design conditions, make the necessary adjustments in the digital counterpart, and ensure that the physical product performs as designed. Digital twin product facets allow manufacturers to test proposed product variations before physically prototyping the product.

Production facet (for improved production planning and production)—Helps to verify how the manufacturing process will run before production on the shop floor. It simulates the process using the product facet and analyzes the digital thread to optimize production under a variety of conditions and what-if scenarios. A digital thread is a single seamlessly connected data chain of data captured throughout the life cycle of a single product, designed, modeled, manufactured, used, and delivered from the initial design concept to the finished product. Creating a digital twin replicates the entire manufacturing process. This allows manufacturers to find process errors without affecting the production volume of the manufacturing plant.

Performance facet (for improved quality and performance of products and production)—Supports the collection and analysis of data on the usage and effectiveness of digital products and production processes, providing actionable insights for informed decision-making and continuous optimization of both product and process aspects. The performance facet gathers real-time data from operational products and the production line, enabling manufacturers to identify opportunities to improve the product or production process.

3.2 Requirements for Digital Twin-Driven Product Customization and Production Planning

Manufacturing customization now includes minimal flexibility to change fixed parameters. Additional flexibility requires new modeling and processing languages to express, exchange, and process product and manufacturing knowledge, facilitating the transition from digital to physical products. This goal will require the integration of innovative and disruptive technologies and capabilities focused on DTs that describe the structure and characteristics of a customized product, the shape of the product, the materials, the components, and the behavior of the individual parts and assemblies that make up the product. This technology will use, cross-correlate, and unify large, dispersed product and production-related datasets to provide greater visibility into the state of a product, its various parts, and production processes. The result is a product with smarter, more reliable, safer, and more secure plug-and-play integration of digital and physical components.

Ultimately, development of digital twins will also enable transformative customer-centric product ideation and customization that can optimize the entire product life cycle. This customer-centric vision is revolutionary but highly complex. It requires technologies and tools that focus on large-scale collaboration between different stakeholders, from manufacturer to designer, from designer to end-user, and from end-user to manufacturer. To address such concerns, this article lays the groundwork for how customer-centric companies can collaborate to produce a range of customizable products using the three facets of DTs discussed in Sect. 3.1:

A Digital Twin Knowledge Model (DT-KM): this is a formal digital representation—known as the *Manufacturing Blueprint Knowledge Model*—that collects, stores, and processes "intelligent, actionable data" from all points in the product and production life cycle. This way, an end-to-end, holistic view of a product is achieved. In the DT-KM, each physical product has one unique digital twin that provides a comprehensive accuracy of the product and its production efficiency, linking the facets of product, production, and performance.

A Digital Twin Meta-Programming Language (DT-MPL), known as the *Manufacturing Blueprint Programming Language*, rationalizes, structures, interrelates, and aggregates generic DT-KM knowledge to improve decision-making and create products, solutions, and services that meet customer needs.

The approach outlined above enables a fully programmable digital twin to support highly individualized products, capable of gathering information about actual usage and customer needs, which can be used to design new features based on both direct product feedback and actual usage. As a result, product design and customization provide product components with sufficient compatibility and adaptability to complement "living" products that combine ever-changing physical and digital characteristics.

4 Model-Driven Product Engineering

The complexity of the manufacturing ecosystem shows that advanced model-driven engineering (MDE) approaches have the potential to be used in manufacturing to simplify the product design and development processes and drive productivity gains [4, 5]. Model-based engineering provides a simultaneous, collaborative design process that allows users to identify and define requirements, model solution architectures, validate and share ideas among various stakeholders with different viewpoints, and enable them to trade-off between features and costs. The MDE approach provides a means of linking different engineering processes through artifacts and abstractions that meet the requirements of industry acceptance and enable analytic methods. The Systems Modeling Language (SysML) is a popular choice among MDE practitioners. However, its informal semantics make it poorly suited to rigorous analysis.

To realize the digital twin and digital thread concepts, the conventional MDE approach needs to be specialized and extended to satisfy the requirements of smart manufacturing. In Fig. 1, we illustrate an advanced model-driven engineering approach—the *Model-Driven Manufacturing* (*MDM*) approach. It supports digital thread and digital twin principles and enables a concurrent and collaborative product customization process. The MDM in Fig. 1 contains three layers that enable analysis process.

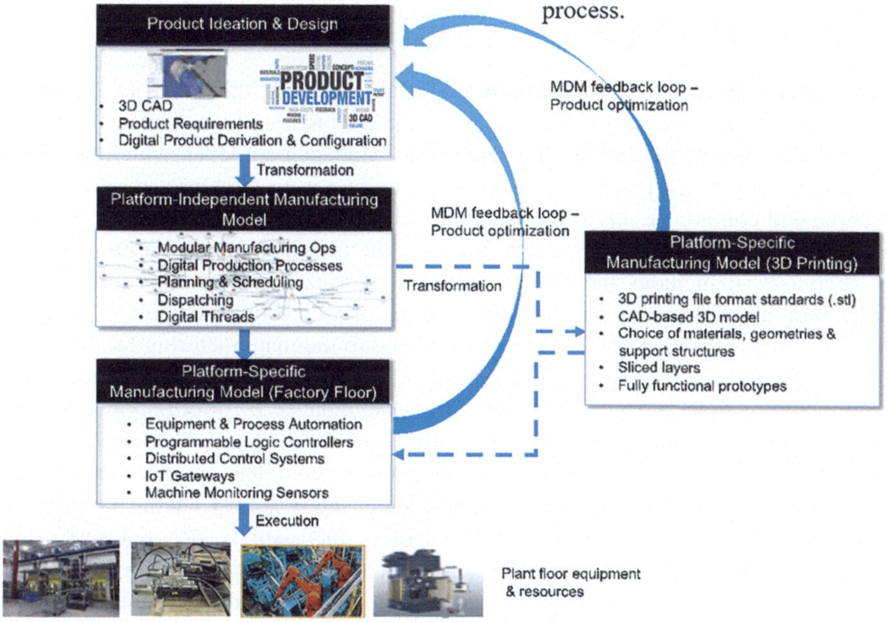

Fig. 1 Model-driven manufacturing activity hierarchy and levels for smart manufacturing and digital Twins

to drive smart manufacturing by collecting, harnessing, and leveraging design, manufacturing, services, IoT, and sensor data.

MDM is an approach that moves away from drawings and other product definition tools, such as natural language descriptions [28] and 3D models, and moves to interactive 3D models. MDM converts the 3D models through model transformation into modular manufacturing operations, digital manufacturing processes, and digital threads that are ultimately realized using additive manufacturing techniques or on the factory floor. Model transformation takes as input the model corresponding to the previous level in the MDM hierarchy and transforms it into the equivalent model of the level immediately below in the MDM hierarchy.

Product Ideation and Design (PID) MDM enables product engineers and customers to imagine, think, and act together on (complex) product development projects. The PID layer of the MDM architecture is essentially a series of sessions that represent a formalized part of the product design phase. Different stakeholders, including designers, developers, engineers, and customers, come together to share their visions, insights, and ideas.

Product ideas take this information and apply it to the design and customization of specific products at the product-agnostic manufacturing model level. At this level, 3D-CAD models interactively capture and visualize all relevant product information in real time for production and quality planning, controlling production processes, work orders generation, and coordination of related processes. In previous R&D efforts, we have designed and implemented a novel approach to realize this level that is formally grounded in the DT blueprints models detailed in Sect. 5, through the 3D interactive product-oriented configuration language (PoCL) [3, 29].

Platform-Independent Manufacturing Model (PIM) At this level, DT controls digital activities, processes, and recipes to create the final product of interest. PIM is rooted in the ISA98 Manufacturing Operations Management level, which provides resources, equipment, materials, personnel, and energy to transform digitized raw material and component descriptions, quality checks, production flows, and production schedules into finished products. It covers the activities to adapt a product.

Therefore, it includes the management of information about schedules, uses, skills, definitions, history, and the current status of all resources (suppliers, personnel, equipment, and materials) within and related to the manufacturing facility. The data collected along with the product design at the PID level can be used to drive the manufacturing flow and provide PIM with an abundance of information that will drive product innovation. PIM combines this automated data with data collected from resources and other processes to provide a more complete real-time view of all manufacturing plants, production lines, and increasingly supply chains. Combined with the analytical power of digital tools, these increasingly rich datasets offer opportunities for innovation that bring unprecedented advantages and benefits.

The digital threads and conclusions derived in this layer are then used to create a fully functional prototype using additive manufacturing (AM) techniques or to instruct machines and robots on the shop floor to carry out product manufacturing functions. AM produces higher-performance designs than traditional manufacturing techniques by enabling multiple design iterations without expensive retooling, allowing for leaner/slimmer manufacturing while enhancing the design quality. AM allows the creation of functional objects on using 3D printer. With AM, manufacturers can reduce assembly time and produce parts that reduce overall manufacturing costs and add value to finished products [30].

The Platform-Specific Manufacturing Model (PSM) transforms production planning decisions for PIM models into control commands for production processes on the factory floor to fulfill the control and monitoring needs of different types of machines and equipment. This type of conversion structures the actual interface between the digital and the physical worlds, resulting in improved production performance, increased uptime, improved resource availability, asset management, and operational speed. Based on factory automation and control systems, PSM includes device control, intelligent devices, work centers, robots, machines, programmable logic controllers, and monitoring sensors such as carbon emission sensors, temperature, and vibration sensors.

To ensure efficiency, high quality, and high throughput, devices typically use different communication protocols that run independently. For these components to work properly, coordination, synchronization, and access to shared resources must be effectively managed. To take advantage of the Factory of Things, manufacturers need to remove the communication barriers between these field devices and connect them to a cloud-based industrial Internet of Things (IIoT), which offer significant advantages for IIoT implementation, including rapid application development, global access to data, and integrated predictive analytics capabilities.

Feedback loop Product manufacturability may depend on functional and non-functional design parameters. This requires a feedback loop in MDM. As shown in Fig. 1, there is a feedback loop between product design and manufacturing process design, manufacturing, and ultimately product delivery and maintenance. Data from the product conception/ideation and design process (and the subsequent use of the DTs and the corresponding physical product manufacturing) is captured and continuously updated, triggering a continuous cycle between the digital and physical domains.

MDM feedback loops can provide not only product improvements but also the ability to reconfigure, improve, and modify production lines, processes, and machines. Real-time operational data can also be collected and analyzed to optimize production processes and predict demand, downtime, and future value. During implementation and deployment on the PSM platform, feedback drives product optimization through quality assurance testing, ensuring that product defects are identified and fixed as soon as they are discovered. In this chapter, we focus mainly on the product independent manufacturing model level and demonstrate how it supports the activities of digital twins and digital threads on the basis of the manufacturing blueprints and its meta-programming environment discussed in the next section.

5 Platform Independent Manufacturing Model: Manufacturing Blueprints and Meta-programming Environment

The Digital Twin Knowledge Model and Meta-Programming Language are a manufacturing-specific DT model and lightweight programmable language that establishes digital threads. They encompass manufacturing domain knowledge together with the regulations of what kind of knowledge should be recorded about each manufacturing element, how these factors can be related, and how this knowledge can be aggregated and reused. In essence, the DT-KM and MPL realize the PIM model.

5.1 Manufacturing Blueprints: Essential Characteristics of Self-Describing Products and Production Processes

Digital Twin in this chapter amalgamates artificial intelligence, machine learning, big data, and Internet of Things technologies that are essential for smart manufacturing. The core element is DT-KM. This is essentially a knowledge-centric model that combines products, services, components, and programs by composing and analyzing product/manufacturing data to create knowledge for data-driven and fact-based decision-making. The DT-KM programmable abstraction type is called the manufacturing blueprint type (or simply blueprint). They transform traditional products into self-describing products by storing, linking, combining, and analyzing data collected throughout the product life cycle. Blueprints rely on model engineering paradigm to manage and link product data and information, including content and context, product portfolios and product families, and manufacturing assets (people, plants, machinery, production line equipment), helping to meet the constraints and requirements (features, quality, performance, time, cost, etc.) of the entire manufacturing ecosystem.

This information can be placed in a broader operational context, forming the basis for generating actionable "intelligence" and the steps to more factual data-driven decision-making. The DT-KM encapsulates supplier, product, and production knowledge into five interrelated and extensible abstract knowledge types, illustrated in Fig. 2. These support the three DT facets outlined in Sect. 3 as follows:

Product facet—captures relevant direct and indirect information about products and services through the following blueprint types:

Supplier blueprint type: Defines the business and technical details of the partner company, such as production capacity details and production capabilities.

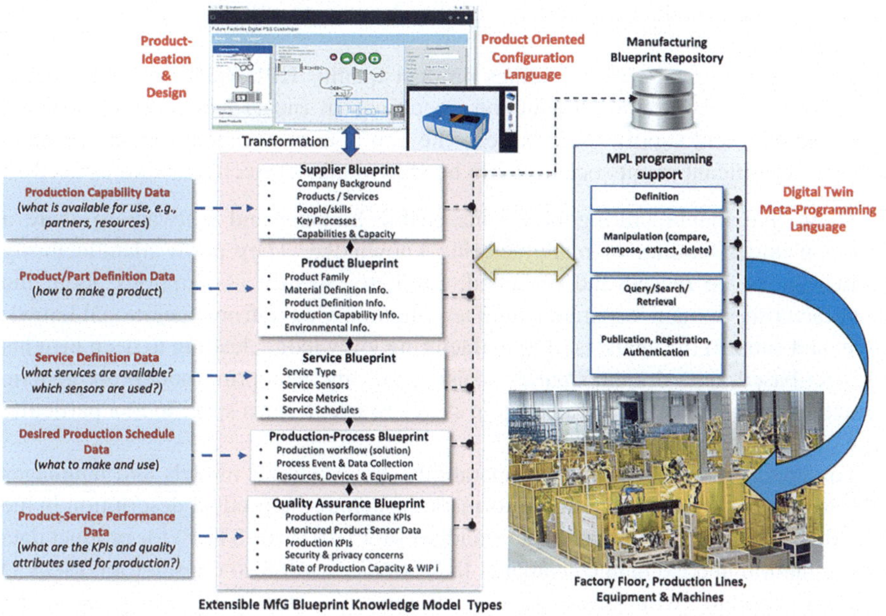

Fig. 2 Manufacturing blueprint types and its meta-programming environment

Product blueprint type: Represents the specifics of standard or configurable products, product parts, and/or materials. This information is combined with other pertinent data such as product characteristics or order information, machine information, and any entities needed to accurately represent the product and facilitate production work. It also contains product family definitions and links them to products, components, and materials.

Service blueprint type: Represents the properties and attributes of services combined with the physical product (as captured in the Product blueprint), to meet the requirements of manufacturers and customers. This includes service types, service metrics, service plans, service scopes, sensors, orders constructed from service plans, compliance standards, service history data, and cost estimates.

Production facet—the production planning process integrates the customized product facet into optimized and efficient production processes and schedules. This knowledge is modeled by the following:

Production process blueprint type: Exhibits manufacturing solutions and standard assemblies associated with optimal manufacturing execution plans that embed integrated business processes into workflows and connect the events/actions of activities related to all elements of actual manufacturing on the factory floor. This facet supports digital threads.

Performance facet: the performance facet is linked to the production facet to achieve production performance characteristics to analyze operational data/information and enhance product and service quality leading to efficient production. This facet comprises:

Quality assurance blueprint: Defines product quality KPIs (metrics) and process performance to monitor production operations in (near) real time and resolve operational and supply chain issues. The aim is to notify/alert human operators when significant events occur and to be able to take corrective action as needed.

These five manufacturing blueprints enable humans and software to share a common understanding of manufacturing knowledge. They allow manufacturing knowledge to be reused and extended, explicitly specify assumptions about the manufacturing domain, separate manufacturing knowledge from operational knowledge, and support the analysis of manufacturing knowledge, leading to deep insights and fact-based, data-driven, smarter decision-making. Blueprint models are generic by nature but can easily be scaled up in stages to take a form specific to a particular type of industry structure.

To support versatility and interoperability, the blueprint models and languages rely on industry-wide production information, such as the product description in the EXPRESS data modelling language standard ISO 10303 (or STEP) for product data representation and exchange standards ISA-88/95. It will also consider the ISO/CD 23247-1 digital twin manufacturing framework standard, which is under development.

The implementation of the blueprinting detailed conceptual model and its meta-programming language (discussed in detail in the following subsection) is based on the Ontology Web Language[1] (OWL) and SPARQL,[2] respectively, which are formally based on Description Logic [31]. This enables the application of diverse types of reasoning; the verification of properties, preferences, and constraints; and the checking of the consistency of the manufacturing knowledge. The blueprinting detailed conceptual model is outside the scope of this article.

5.2 Blueprint Meta-programming Language

The blueprint meta-programming language launches digital threads by allowing developers to define custom behavior for fundamental language operations using the abstraction mechanisms in the DT-KM. To that end, we provide programming support, use fact-based and data-driven decision-making processes, and connect all stakeholders to a centralized, searchable knowledge base. It shapes the digital twin by capturing context-specific knowledge (structure, manufacturing, quality, and sensor-specific information) about the appropriate configurations and combinations of parts, components, and materials that can be linked to the required processes that

[1]OWL 2: https://www.w3.org/TR/owl-features/

[2]SPARQL 1.1 Query Language: https://www.w3.org/TR/sparql11-query/

are to be performed in its production. The blueprint meta-programming language is implemented as a graphical DSL; however, in the following discussion, the language is presented textually. To this end, the blueprint meta-programming language provides programming support through high-level operators that process the five blueprints:

Blueprint definition operators—These provide the notations needed to define the five blueprints listed. In particular, this operator is represented textually as *insertIndvidual*(p), which inserts an instance of a specific class into the DT-KM.

Blueprint manipulation operators—These provide a set of operators to save and retrieve existing blueprints maintained in the DT-KM and compare and assemble/compose products from product parts and subassemblies. A product assembly/composition consists of an assembly of individual parts and a production plan for each assembled/composed part. Blueprint assemblies use a "compose" operator to connect a set of compatible blueprints end to end (e.g., product-to-product or service-to-service combinations). In particular:

retrieve(A) returns all blueprint instances that satisfy the criteria/conditions in predicate A.
compose(p, q) takes two blueprint instances of the same type and returns a new composed blueprint instance pq.
compare(p, q) compares two blueprint instances p, q of the same type and returns T if the two instances are equivalent and F, otherwise. Two blueprints are equivalent if their components, parts, characteristics, and materials are identical.
diff(p, q) returns the difference between two blueprints instances of the same type p, q.

Query services—query blueprints or zoom in on individual blueprints to extract valuable information for data-driven smart decision-making. In particular: *query*(A) returns T if query request captured by predicate A is satisfied and false otherwise. Expressive classes of query patterns are identified and formalized to capture requiring query patterns. This is outside the scope of this chapter.

6 Application of the Manufacturing Programming Environment on a Pilot Case

To demonstrate the DT approach in this chapter, we present a real-life "made-to-order" pilot case provided by PRIMA Industries (a leading company manufacturing laser and sheet metal machinery). The pilot case deals with "distributed production on demand," which is a scenario in which the DT approach can enable a smart manufacturing ecosystem that is formed when different manufacturing units work together to meet customers' needs.

This pilot case assumes that a turbine engine manufacturer orders a multi-axis 3D cutting, drilling, and welding laser system to process parts of a turbofan engine used

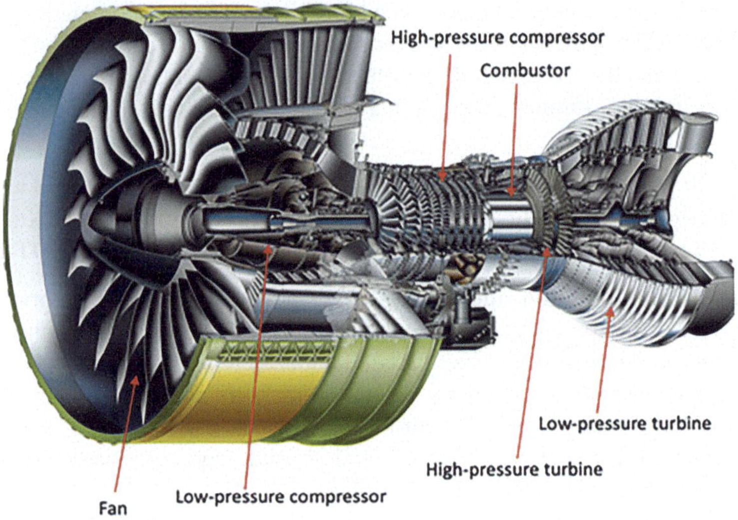

Fig. 3 A diagram of the components of a turbofan engine (source Engine Alliance)

in the Airbus A318. The engine is a two-spool, axial-flow, high-bypass ratio, turbofan powerplant for subsonic service with a thrust range of 311–340 kN and a fan blade tip diameter of 2.96 m. The main modules of the engine are as shown in Fig. 3 and consist of a compressor section (low- and high-pressure compressor), a combustion section, a turbine section (high- and low-pressure turbine), and gearbox as an accessory drive.

The pilot targets for operations using a large number of applications of high-precision 3D laser cutting, welding, and drilling and high-power fiber-laser applications. It has to provide much flexibility and a variety of configurations for processing parts in the aerospace market segment, which requires manufacturing flexibility, rapid prototyping, and quick changeovers.

OEMs expect to contract with many Tier 2 suppliers that supply special components for laser processing systems such as Angle torches, acetylene valves, plasma cutters, and optical focus control components in the manufacturing ecosystem. We assume that descriptions of these parts are represented in DT-KM using the five blueprint types and are stored in the DT-KM.

6.1 *Product Customization*

Customization begins with the customer, in collaboration with a product designer searching and querying the blueprint repository to find a base product or variant that is close enough to the customer's requirements. For this purpose, the stakeholders in product design invoke the *retrieve* operator presented in Sect. 5.2. For example, a customer may be looking for a laser processing machine that incorporates high-accuracy rotary table motion combined with a new generation beam director laser positioning capability to support new manufacturing processes and also improve existing processes. The beam director needs to provide a rotary axis motion of 800o, tilt axis motion of 400o, and an axis speed of 80 rpm. This is expressed using the *retrieve* operator of the blueprint meta-programming language and represented textually[3] as:

$$S = \textbf{\textit{retrieve}}(LaserProcessingMachine,$$

$$hasHighAccuracyRotaryTable, hasBeamDirector(800,400,80))$$

We assume that *retrieve* returns the three products $S = \{p_1, p_2, p_3\}$. Assume further that after inspecting the set of returned products and comparing them using the *compare* operator, the stakeholders decide to choose p_1 as the base product for customization.

Scenario 1: Parameterized customization When the customer selects a product, say p_1, a new product variant, say p_{11}, is created that inherits all the characteristics of its root p_1, such as components, parts, assemblies, and their properties. In its simplest form, consider a scenario where the customer might require that the work area of p_{11} should be X 650 mm, Y 650 mm, and Z 650 mm. Now, assume that p_1 has its working area as X 750 mm, Y 550 mm, and Z 650. This results in a branching mechanism that creates new products/variants from base products or existing variants by means of parameterization, after performing consistency checks (enabled by the ontology reasoner) to ensure that values of product p_{11} are valid. This is expressed textually as:

$$\boldsymbol{p_{11}} \equiv \boldsymbol{p_1}$$

$$\boldsymbol{p_{11}}(workingArea(650,650,650))$$

$$\textbf{\textit{insertIndvidual}}(\boldsymbol{p_{11}})$$

Scenario 2: Adaptive customization Assume now the customer wants to augment the laser machine of p_{11} with a cross-jet element, which allows a high-velocity gas barrier. In addition, the current version uses conventional Nd:YAG laser, and the customer wants to replace it with a fiber laser to improve the quality of drilling and micromachining and cutting of different materials and improve the quality, including the divergence and energy distribution of the laser beam. This is expressed textually as (*replacePart* is a function that replaces one *Part* instance by another *Part* instance after checking the logical consistency of the composition and the overall consistency of the DT-KM):

[3]The textual representations in this section are simplified for presentation purpose.

$$\boldsymbol{CrossJet}(crossJet_{11})$$

$$\boldsymbol{hasPart}(\boldsymbol{p_{11}}, crossJet_{11})$$

$$\boldsymbol{FiberLaser}(fiberLaser_{11})$$

$$\boldsymbol{replacePart}(hasPart(p_{11}, YAGLaser_{11}, fiberLaser_{11}))$$

Scenario 3: Service customization Suppose the customer demands an advanced failure predictive maintenance service to process high-temperature materials more effectively. The service coupling is supported by the service blueprint in Sect. 5.1. This service provides early signs of an imminent failure and provides the urgency of calibration or repair when the machine is worn out and needs calibration. It also provides guidance to laser operators and maintenance personnel to reduce risk and prolong operation. For simplicity, assume that this service already exists in the blueprint repository and is identified as s_1. Then s_1 is added to p_{11} by creating an instance of *hasService* association relationship:

$$\boldsymbol{hasService}(p_{11}, s_1).$$

For example, the included service requires three instances of temperature sensors and IoT meters to be attached to the machine. This can be configured by the customer to select, for example, a specific sensor vendor or specific sensor configurations. This can be specified (representing only sensors) as follows (($\bigwedge$ is the "And" logical operator)):

$\boldsymbol{TempSensor}(tempSensor_1) \bigwedge \boldsymbol{TempSensor}(tempSensor_2) \bigwedge$

$$\boldsymbol{TempSensor}(tempSensor_3)$$

$$\boldsymbol{tempSensorOf}(tempSensor_1, s_1)$$

$$\boldsymbol{tempSensorOf}(tempSensor_2, s_1)$$

$$\boldsymbol{tempSensorOf}(tempSensor_3, s_1)$$

$$\boldsymbol{hasPart}(p_{11}, tempSensor_1) \bigwedge \boldsymbol{hasPart}(p_{11}, tempSensor_2) \bigwedge$$

$$\bigwedge \boldsymbol{hasPart}(p_{11}, tempSensor_3)$$

The customer may then request a cost estimate of her new customized product variant based on information captured in the blueprint instances of the requested customized product. This feature addresses the problem of long cycles to calculate the cost of a new customized product. This enables the customer to make an informed decision on whether to accept the current design or tweak the design to meet her cost constraints.

The above scenario mainly addresses product DTs. In addition, multi-axis laser machine performance and usage data enables new value-added products and service offerings in terms of predictive maintenance, equipment efficiency, quality control, and customer engagement to solve DT performance issues.

6.2 Digital Product Production Planning

The Production Process Blueprint shows the production solution and the corresponding Production Execution Plan operating on the Production DTs examined in Scenarios 1, 2, and 3. They implement workflows that link people, processes, "things," and manufacturing data with activity events to enable actual production in the factory floor, such as the customized product variant p_{11}. When working with partners in the manufacturing ecosystem, a clear definition of the digital production process (i.e., the target production process) and who will perform them is critical to a smooth production operation. To this end, the MPL is based on industry standard SCOR processes. In Fig. 4, the digital production process is shown as a simplified version of two interrelated SCOR Level 4 subprocesses. One is for "production planning," and the other is for "production control."

Figure 4 shows how the laser-cutting and welder manufacturing process is linked to other target OEM blueprints. The figure also illustrates how the second-tier supplier *blueprints* produced by Angle Torch ($Supp_1$), Acetylene Valve ($Supp_2$), Plasma Cutter ($Supp_3$), and Optical Focus Control parts ($Supp_4$) suppliers are combined with those of the OEM to create the final product, viz., p_{11}. The use of the *compose* operator (+ symbol in Fig. 4) combines Tier 2 supplier blueprint types in a compatible pairwise manner to create a complete manufacturing solution.

The products/parts supplied by each of the four suppliers are denoted p_{sx}, where $x \in \{1, 2, 3, 4\}$ stands for supplier number; similarly, production processes are denoted pP_{sx}, quality assurances are denoted QA_{sx}, and *comp* denotes the *compose* operation (denoted as *comp* below):

$$\boldsymbol{targetSupplier} = comp(comp(comp(supp_1, supp_2), supp_3), supp_4)$$

$$\boldsymbol{targetProduct} = (comp(comp(p_{s1}, p_{s2}), p_{s3}), p_{s4})$$

$$\boldsymbol{targetService} =$$

$$comp\left(comp\left(comp\left(\underset{(spareParts,\, maintenance)}{comp}, repair \right), overhaul \right), failurePredictionMaintenance \right)$$

$$\boldsymbol{targetProductionProcess} = (comp(comp(pP_{s1}, pP_{s2}), pP_{s3}), pP_{s4})$$

$$\boldsymbol{targetQA} = (comp(comp(QA_{s1}, QA_{s2}), QA_{s3}), QA_{s4})$$

This interlinking of the overall target OEM blueprint and supplier blueprint brings the end-to-end visibility beneficial for an OEM to gear effective performance

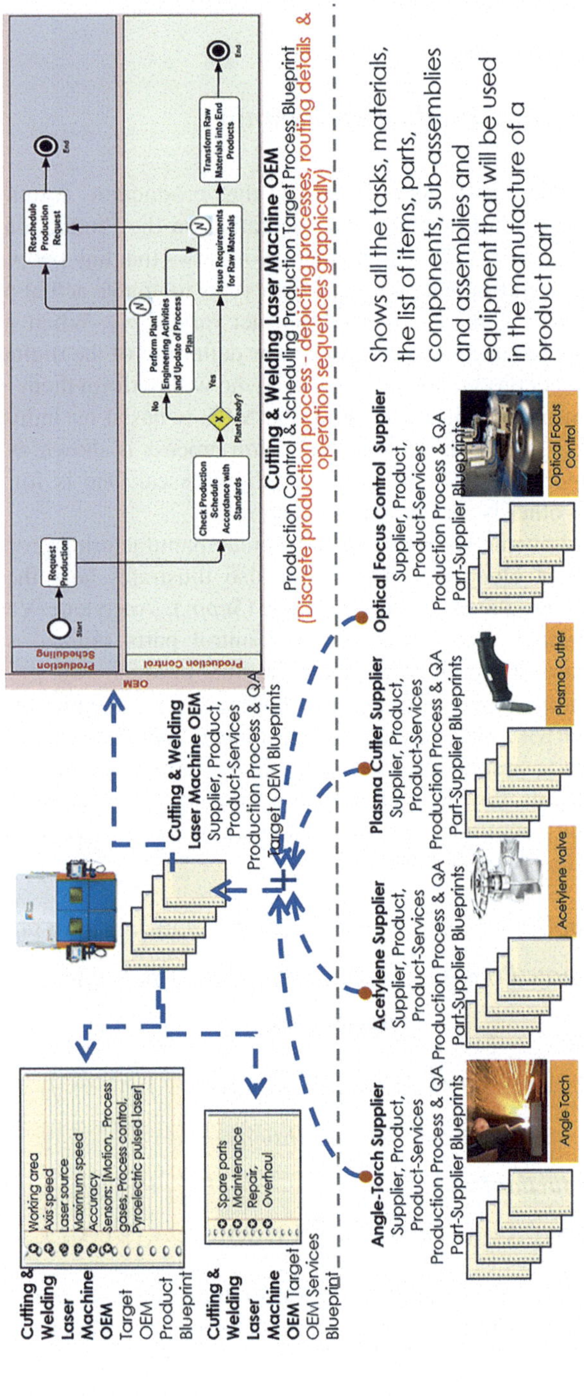

Fig. 4 Merging blueprints into a full manufacturing solution

of supply chain and operational effectiveness improvement across the entire manufacturing ecosystem.

7 Summary and Future Prospects

This chapter presents a novel digital twin approach that provides a set of high-level abstract knowledge types that can be assembled and programmed via a purpose-built meta-programming language to formally represent, assemble, cross-correlate, and process knowledge regarding all aspects of a customized product, services, production processes, and quality assurance. By leveraging digital twins, the manufacturing model and its programming environment can help manufacturers to (i) gain insights to improve digital models; (ii) capture, aggregate, and analyze operational data; and (iii) improve product quality and production system efficiency.

Current and future work concentrates on extending blueprints with AI and machine learning techniques to improve situational awareness and enable validation and improvement of product designs, processes, and analysis of performance characteristics and, critically, identify more opportunities for product innovation. This will help DTs to recreate potential real-world conditions that can be experimented in a virtual environment. We expect to explore AI- and machine learning-based customization algorithms to automatically generate multiple alternatives from customization requirements.

Future work will also consider AI- and machine learning-based planning and scheduling algorithms to improve manufacturing process synchronization, increase transparency, and reduce the utilization and delivery times of customized products by providing track-and-trace visibility across the entire production chain. Throughout the product development phase, the designer will be able to review and validate these manufacturing process plans by walking through the complete production sequence and directly visualize the corresponding product assembly, including associated tooling and resources.

Acknowledgments The authors would like to thank PRIMA INDUSTRIE S.p.A. (https://www.primaindustrie.com/) for providing the main elements of the pilot study for this chapter.

References

1. *Digital Industry 4.0: How to navigate digitization of the manufacturing sector*. 2016.
2. Grieves, M. (2014). *Digital twin: Manufacturing excellence through virtual factory replication (While paper)*. University of Michigan.
3. Papazoglou, M. P., Elgammal, A., & Krämer, B. J. (2020). Collaborative on-demand product-service systems customization lifecycle. *CIRP Journal of Manufacturing Science and Technology, 29*, 205–219. https://doi.org/10.1016/j.cirpj.2018.08.003

4. Söderberg, R., Wärmefjord, K., Carlson, J. S., & Lindkvist, L. (2017). Toward a digital twin for real-time geometry assurance in individualized production. *CIRP Annals, 66*(1), 137–140. https://doi.org/10.1016/j.cirp.2017.04.038
5. Frechette S. Model based enterprise for manufacturing. 2011.
6. Tao, F., Zhang, H., Liu, A., & Nee, A. Y. C. (2019). Digital twin in industry: state-of-the-art. *IEEE Transactions on Industrial Informatics, 15*(4), 2405–2415. https://doi.org/10.1109/TII.2018.2873186
7. Kritzinger, W., Karner, M., Traar, G., Henjes, J., & Sihn, W. (2018). Digital twin in manufacturing: A categorical literature review and classification. *IFAC-PapersOnLine, 51*(11), 1016–1022. https://doi.org/10.1016/j.ifacol.2018.08.474
8. Tao, F., Qi, Q., Wang, L., & Nee, A. Y. C. (2019). Digital twins and cyber–physical systems toward smart manufacturing and industry 4.0: Correlation and comparison. *Engineering, 5*(4), 653–661. https://doi.org/10.1016/j.eng.2019.01.014
9. Fuller, A., Fan, Z., Day, C., & Barlow, C. (2020). Digital twin: Enabling technologies, challenges and open research. *IEEE Access, 8*, 108952–108971. https://doi.org/10.1109/ACCESS.2020.2998358
10. Pine, B. J. (1999). *Mass customization: The new frontier in business competition*. Harvard Business School Press.
11. Johnson, M. D., & Kirchain, R. (2010). Developing and assessing commonality metrics for product families: A process-based cost-modeling approach. *IEEE Transactions on Engineering Management, 57*(4), 634–648. https://doi.org/10.1109/TEM.2009.2034642
12. Giovannini A. (2014). Approach for the rationalisation of product lines variety. *Preprints of the 19th world congress: The international federation of automatic control South Africa* (pp. 3280–91).
13. Tian, X., Huang, L., Jia, X., & Zhang, Z. (2008). Exploring parameterised process planning for mass customisation. In X.-T. Yan, C. Jiang, & B. Eynard (Eds.), *Advanced design and manufacture to gain a competitive edge* (pp. 643–652). Springer.
14. Zha, X., & Sriram, R. D. (2006). Platform-based product design and development: A knowledge intensive support approach. *International Journal of Uncertainty, Fuzziness and Knowledge-Based Systems, 19*(7), 524–543.
15. Nomaguchi, Y. (2006). Proposal of knowledge model for designing product architecture and product family. *IJCC workshop 2006 on digital engineering*.
16. Papazoglou, M., Heuvel, W. J. V. D., & Mascolo, J. (2015). Reference architecture and knowledge-based structures for smart manufacturing networks. *IEEE Software, 99*, 1. https://doi.org/10.1109/MS.2015.79
17. Wąsowski, A., & Berger, T. (2023). *Domain-specific languages: Effective modeling, automation, and reuse*. Springer.
18. Kandare, G., Strmčnik, S., & Godena, G. (2010). Domain specific model-based development of software for programmable logic controllers. *Computers in Industry, 61*(5), 419–431. https://doi.org/10.1016/j.compind.2009.10.001
19. Vogel-Heuser, B., Schütz, D., Frank, T., & Legat, C. (2014). Model-driven engineering of manufacturing automation software projects – A SysML-based approach. *Mechatronics, 24*(7), 883–897. https://doi.org/10.1016/j.mechatronics.2014.05.003
20. Bührer, U. T., Legat, C., & Vogel-Heuser, B. (2015). Changeability of manufacturing automation systems using an orchestration engine for programmable logic controllers. *IFAC-PapersOnLine, 48*(3), 1573–1579. https://doi.org/10.1016/j.ifacol.2015.06.310
21. Sierla, S., Kyrki, V., Aarnio, P., & Vyatkin, V. (2018). Automatic assembly planning based on digital product descriptions. *Computers in Industry, 97*, 34–46. https://doi.org/10.1016/j.compind.2018.01.013
22. Papazoglou, M. P. (2018). Metaprogramming environment for industry 4.0. *2018 sixth international conference on enterprise systems (ES)* (pp. 1–8).
23. Bartlett, J. (2005). *Introduction to metaprogramming*. IBM developerWorks.

24. Kelechi, C., & Iwuji, A. (2018). A meta goal programming model with weighted achievement function and mixed-integer variables for multi-product manufacturing systems. *Annuals of Statistical Theory and Applications, 2*, 1–8.
25. Taha, W., & Sheard, T. (2000). MetaML and multi-stage programming with explicit annotations. *Theoretical Computer Science, 248*(1), 211–242. https://doi.org/10.1016/S0304-3975(00)00053-0
26. Schroeder, G. N., Steinmetz, C., Pereira, C. E., & Espindola, D. B. (2016). Digital twin data modeling with automationML and a communication methodology for data exchange. *IFAC-PapersOnLine, 49*(30), 12–17. https://doi.org/10.1016/j.ifacol.2016.11.115
27. Tratt, L. (2004). *Compile-time meta-programming in converge*. King's College London, Department of Computer Science.
28. Chen, Z., Yao, S., Lin, J., Zeng, Y., & Eberlein, A. (2007). Formalisation of product requirements: From natural language descriptions to formal specifications. *International Journal of Manufacturing Research, 2*, 362–387.
29. Elgammal, A., Papazoglou, M., Krämer, B., & Constantinescu, C. (2017). Design for customization: A new paradigm for product-service system development. *The 9th CIRP IPSS conference: Circular perspectives on product/service-systems*. Elsevier.
30. Michalik, J., Joyce, J., Barney, R., & McCune, G. (2015). In Deloitte (Ed.), *3D opportunity for product design: Additive manufacturing and the early stage*. Deloitte University Press.
31. Markus, K., Frantisek, S., & Ian, H. (2012). *A description logic primer*. eprint arXiv:1201.4089: Cornell University.

Compound Noun Phrase Similarity in Bidirectional Transformer Language Models

Rey A. Gonzalez and Julia Rayz

Abstract The evolution of language models, particularly transformer-based architectures like BERT and Sentence-BERT, has significantly impacted natural language processing (NLP), introducing advancements in text analysis, translation, and content generation. These models excel in understanding the subtle nuances of language, including multi-word expressions (MWEs) like compound nouns, which are known for their complex semantic properties. Our research investigates the ability of transformer encoder models to discern and interpret the distinct meanings of compositional compound nouns, crucial for tasks such as semantic analysis and information retrieval. By conducting a systematic comparison of similarity scores among compound nouns and exploring the effects of modifier and head-noun manipulation, we uncover insights into the models' capabilities to comprehend the semantic depth of these expressions. Our findings suggest that transformer encoders can capture the nuances of compound nouns. Our work highlights the potential of these models to advance our understanding and processing of natural language, promising significant improvements in search technologies and the broader domain of NLP.

Keywords NLU · Compound nouns · Noun phrases · Transformer models · Semantic similarity

1 Introduction

The development of language models has markedly influenced the domain of natural language processing (NLP), introducing advancements in areas such as text analysis, translation, and content generation. Transformer-based architectures, such as BERT (Bidirectional Encoder Representations from Transformers) and Sentence-BERT (sBERT), have demonstrating success in text similarity measurement capabilities [1, 2]. These models are characterized by their bidirectional training strategy, which

R. A. Gonzalez (✉) · J. Rayz
Purdue University, West Lafayette, IN, USA
e-mail: gonza736@purdue.edu; jtaylor1@purdue.edu

S. C. Suh (ed.), *Artificial Intelligence for Design and Process Science*,
https://doi.org/10.1007/978-3-031-67886-8_7

represents a difference from autoregressive models, which predict tokens in a sequence solely based on preceding context [3].

Multi-word expressions (MWEs)—including compound nouns and phrasal verbs—may present features such as complex non-compositionality [4, 5] and context-dependent usage [6, 7]. Compound nouns, for example, often exhibit a semantic richness that surpasses the sum of their parts. Consider the terms *fig leaf* and *orange juice*. At first glance, these appear to be straightforward compositions, a leaf from a fig tree and juice from an orange, respectively. However, the former has also come to symbolize a covering for something embarrassing or shameful. While the meaning of orange juice can be determined from its individual parts, the meaning of fig leaf cannot for all cases. It should be noted that orange juice is also ambiguous, but the ambiguity stems from orange being a color or a fruit, and thus, while ambiguous, orange juice is still compositional.

Our work suggests that transformer encoders are capable of observing distinct and accurate meanings of compositional compound nouns. This observation is significant, albeit based on a limited number of examples, indicating that these models can grasp the subtle semantic distinctions that compound nouns convey. The ability to accurately interpret these nuances is crucial for tasks such as semantic analysis, machine translation, and information retrieval, where understanding the precise meaning of compound nouns can greatly affect the accuracy and relevance of the results. The successful interpretation of such compositional compound nouns by transformer encoders further underscores the potential of these models to enhance our understanding and processing of natural language, offering promising avenues for future research and application in NLP.

Moreover, the ability to identify and understand compositional compound nouns has profound implications for improving search functionalities. In search contexts, recognizing the compositional nature of compound nouns enables more sophisticated query processing. For example, when a search involves a compositional compound noun, it is vital to discern which component of the compound noun is variable and which is fixed to generate relevant search results. This distinction allows for the dynamic adaptation of search queries to find entities similar to the target concept. For instance, in a search for apple juice, understanding that apple can be replaced with other fruits like orange or grape to find similar entities—while maintaining juice as a fixed term—enhances the search experience by providing diverse but relevant alternatives.

This nuanced understanding and manipulation of language elements are pivotal in advancing search technologies. It allows for more refined searches that consider the semantic relationships between words, rather than relying solely on keyword matching. Such advancements could significantly improve the precision of information retrieval systems, making them more responsive to the actual intent behind users' queries. Consequently, the application of transformer encoders to discern and manipulate the structure of compositional compound nouns not only benefits linguistic analysis and translation tasks but also elevates the capabilities of search engines and information retrieval systems to understand and cater to the complex nuances of human language.

We contribute to the field by:

- Systematically comparing similarity scores of compound nouns and corresponding manipulations of modifier and head nouns
- Discussing results supporting transformer-encoder models' capabilities in observing distinct meaning of compound nouns, supporting findings in previous studies

2 Background

2.1 Multi-word Expressions

English compound nouns exemplify some potential challenges faced by non-large language model NLP systems employed to process MWEs. Such constructions are difficult to interpret as there may be multiple meaning relations between the nouns involved [7]. For instance, the compound *IBM Lecture* could imply a lecture about, by, at, or sponsored by IBM [7]. This ambiguity requires contextual knowledge for correct interpretation, as no syntactic analysis alone can differentiate among the various possible semantic relations in a basic noun compound. This complexity makes compound nouns an excellent test case for assessing the semantic capabilities of current transformer encoder model NLP systems.

Recent research has delved into how pretrained transformer models grasp the semantics of multi-word expressions (MWEs), even without targeted optimization for these complex expressions [6]. These studies have scrutinized the models' ability to comprehend MWEs and their semantic attributes, including their level of compositionality [6], highlighting the models' inherent capacity to decode the nuanced meanings of such phrases. Our findings seem to support a similar conclusion, as they show success in transformer encoder models accurately observing semantic distance between similar compound nouns.

2.2 Language Models

The choice of a language model is crucial for the success of any NLP task, especially in complex areas such as multi-word expression (MWE) analysis. Large language models, particularly transformer-based models like GPT-4, have gained attention for their generative capabilities. Pioneered by Vaswani et al. [8], different transformer models excel in different tasks such as retrieving semantically similar text and producing convincing, contextually relevant text.

Encoder-only models, such as BERT and sBERT, have shown capability in our specific focus of semantic similarity of phrases. Unlike GPT-based models that process text unidirectionally, BERT processes text in a bidirectional manner, allowing for a richer understanding of context [9]. sBERT, an adaptation of BERT, further refines this approach by producing single-vector sentence embeddings [10]. These embeddings are critical for our study's objective: comparing semantic similarities in phrases (that can be treated as short sentences), particularly in the context of noun phrase modifications within MWEs.

3 Methods

In this section, we present our methodology for evaluating the semantic similarity between compound noun phrases leveraging transformer-based encoder models. Our objective is to quantify the extent to which these models discern semantic resemblances across various utterances, despite differences in expression. Specifically, we focus on the impact of substituting different nouns within a multi-word expression (MWE) on its conveyed meaning. Our analysis revolves around sequences of nouns, denoted as $N_1 + N_2$, where we alter either N_1 or N_2 with a semantically akin noun (i.e., another noun representing an edible fruit such as from strawberry to apple).

Our first hypothesis is that substituting N_1 with N_3 (where the similarity between N_1 and N_3, denoted as sim(N_1, N_3), is high) will yield a higher semantic similarity between the compound phrases $N_1 + N_2$ and $N_3 + N_2$ compared to replacing N_2 with N_4 (where sim(N_2, N_4) is comparably high). In essence, with both sim(N_1, N_3) and sim(N_2, N_4) being significant, we hypothesize that the semantic similarity of ($N_1 + N_2$, $N_3 + N_2$) is greater than that of ($N_1 + N_2$, $N_1 + N_4$).

For instance, kiwi smoothie is expected to exhibit a closer semantic proximity to strawberry smoothie than strawberry drink to strawberry smoothie, assuming the similarity between strawberry and kiwi surpasses that between smoothie and drink.

Our second hypothesis is that if the similarity between N_1 and N_3 (sim(N_1, N_3)) is greater than between N_1 and N_5 (sim(N_1, N_5)), then the semantic similarity of the compound phrases ($N_1 + N_2$, $N_3 + N_2$) will surpass that of (N_1

- N_2, $N_5 + N_2$). This hypothesis underlines the significance of the similarity degree between the original noun and its substitute in determining the overall semantic resemblance of the compound noun phrase.

For example, if kiwi is more semantically akin to strawberry than apple is to strawberry, then kiwi smoothie would be deemed more semantically similar to strawberry smoothie than apple smoothie is to strawberry smoothie. This highlights the role of noun substitution's similarity degree in influencing the semantic coherence of the compound noun phrase.

This methodology section outlines our approach and establishes a foundation for our experimental design, enhancing understanding of transformer encoder models' processing of semantic similarity in compound nouns.

3.1 Generating Compound Noun Phrases and Analysis of Uncommon Phrases

Our research methodology was designed to focus on generating and analyzing compound noun phrases, aiming to delve into the nuances of semantic relationships within these phrases. We began by selecting a set of base nouns related to common culinary items, specifically drink, salad, smoothie, chicken, and duck. These were chosen to cover a diverse range of food categories, ensuring a comprehensive examination of semantic interactions. To modify these nouns, we chose a variety of modifier nouns, starting with those that were closely related (e.g., edible fruits such as kiwi, strawberry, orange, apple) and then expanding to include modifiers with a broader semantic scope (green and chocolate). This selection strategy aimed to explore a wide semantic field, from modifiers with direct relevance (e.g., orange with apple) to those with more abstract associations (e.g., chocolate with kiwi). By systematically varying the semantic scope between the base nouns and their modifiers, we enabled a detailed exploration of how semantic proximity and diversity influence the formation and interpretation of compound noun phrases.

In the analysis phase, we excluded compound noun phrases deemed extremely uncommon, such as apple chicken, apple duck, chocolate salad, green chicken, green duck, kiwi chicken, kiwi duck, strawberry chicken, and strawberry duck, to maintain a focus on more commonly encountered combinations. However, we chose to include chocolate chicken and chocolate duck to explore their capabilities to capture meaning along different semantic dimensions. In order to evaluate the models' capability to grasp nuanced semantic changes resulting from modifier substitution, we measured the cosine similarities between compound noun phrases and their modified versions. Through this methodology, we aim to offer an exploration of semantic similarity within compound noun phrases, enhancing our insights into the cognitive processing of language and the potential of transformer encoder models in capturing complex semantic relationships.

4 Results and Discussion

In this study, we examined the effects of modifications on noun phrases, specifically focusing on two types of phrases labeled as N_1 and N_2, to test two main hypotheses. Our analysis uncovered that modifications made to the first noun typically resulted in a greater degree of similarity compared to changes made to the second noun in the noun phrase, which lends support to our first hypothesis. This trend is demonstrated in various contexts, as shown in Fig. 1.

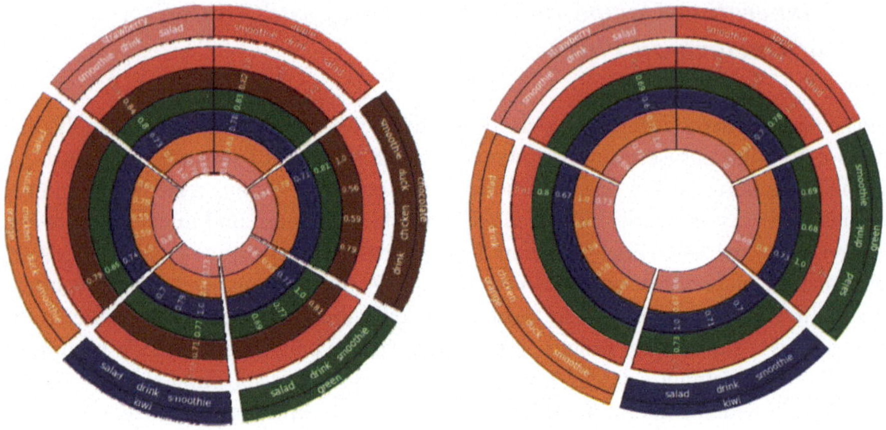

(a) Smoothie (b) Salad

Fig. 1 Comparative analysis of N_1 vs. N_2 changes across categories Smoothie and Salad. This overview illustrates the significant shifts and trends observed in the consumption patterns and preferences across these categories. (**a**) Smoothie. (**b**) Salad

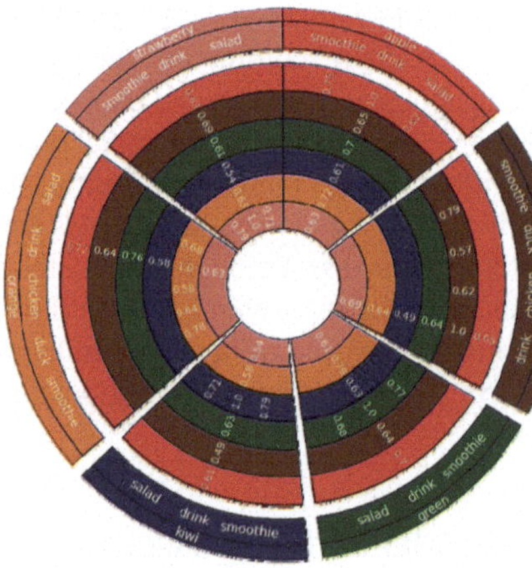

Fig. 2 Comparative analysis of N_1 vs. N_2 changes across category Drink. This overview illustrates the significant shifts and trends observed in the consumption patterns and preferences in this category.

To further elucidate this phenomenon, Figs. 1, 2, and 3 present the findings of our cosine similarity analysis. This analysis measures the semantic distances between the base compound nouns and their modified counterparts across different thematic tracks, depicted as follows:

- Red track: modifications with apple + N_2
- Brown track: modifications with chocolate + N_2

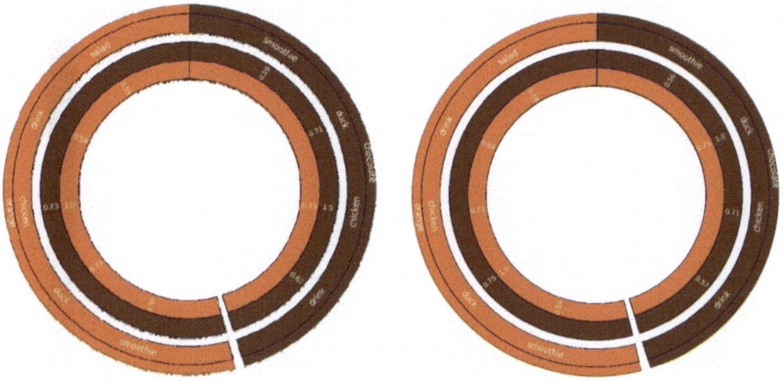

(a) Chicken (b) Duck

Fig. 3 Comparative analysis of N_1 vs. N_2 changes across different categories: Chicken and Duck. This overview illustrates the significant shifts and trends observed in the consumption patterns and preferences across these categories. (**a**) Chicken. (**b**) Duck

- Green track: modifications with green + N_2
- Blue track: modifications with kiwi + N_2
- Orange track: modifications with orange + N_2
- Pink track: modifications with strawberry + N_2

Each track in Fig. 1a, for instance, represents the variation in the smoothie dish resulting from altering the initial noun (N_1) to one of these specified fruits or colors, thereby providing a tangible demonstration of the nuanced effects of noun phrase modification on semantic similarity.

Notably, a remarkable observation emerged when comparing noun phrases involving strawberry and chocolate, with these combinations showing a surprisingly high level of similarity, more so than when strawberry was paired with other fruits. This observation suggests a unique semantic interaction between strawberry and chocolate, potentially due to their common association in culinary contexts and popular culture, highlighting a fascinating aspect of language where cultural and contextual factors significantly influence semantic relationships.

Furthermore, an anomaly was observed in the context involving the modifier drink, as depicted in Fig. 2. Unlike other categories, drink combinations deviated from expected similarity patterns, suggesting an underlying complexity in how beverages are semantically processed compared to solid food items. This deviation warrants further exploration, as it may reveal insights into the distinct cognitive categorizations of food and beverages in language.

Intriguingly, while analyzing the effects of various fruit modifiers on dish nomenclature and their resultant cosine similarities, an unexpected pattern emerged specifically with kiwi-based modifications, as highlighted in Figs. 1, 2, and 3. Contrary to Hypothesis 1, which anticipated a uniform influence of fruit modifiers on semantic similarity, kiwi modifications exhibited a notably lower cosine similarity with other fruits. This deviation is particularly perplexing considering the broadly analogous culinary applications and sensory profiles shared among fruits. The

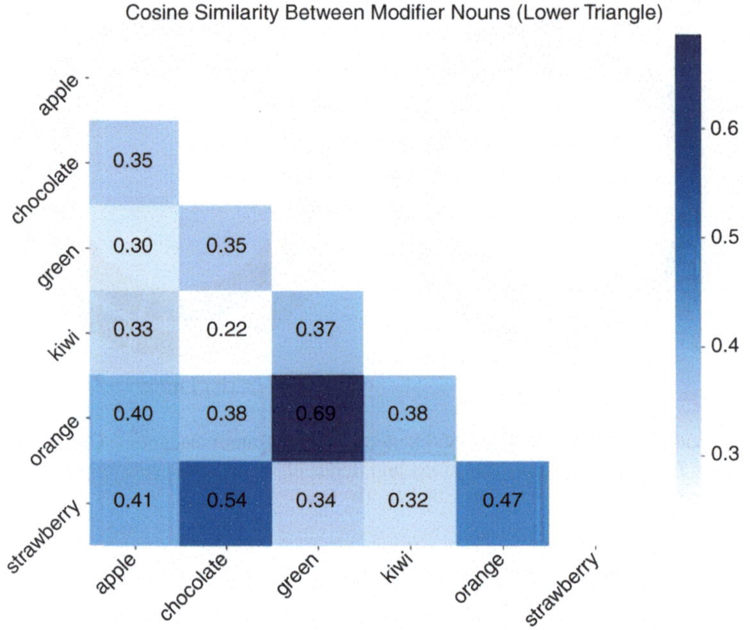

Fig. 4 Modifier noun cosine similarity adjacency matrix

anomaly raises questions about the underlying semantic mechanisms at play and suggests that the integration of kiwi into dishes may invoke unique cognitive associations or semantic fields distinct from other fruits. This phenomenon warrants further investigation to discern whether the lower similarity scores are attributable to cultural, lexical, or perhaps cognitive distinctions associated with kiwi and its culinary uses.

These findings, especially the high similarity between strawberry and chocolate and the drink anomaly, underscore the intricate interplay of cultural, contextual, and cognitive factors in shaping semantic similarity. They invite further investigation into how specific combinations of modifiers and nouns transcend straightforward semantic relations, suggesting that our understanding of language is profoundly influenced by a myriad of factors beyond mere lexical or syntactic considerations.

Overall, our results support the notion that the similarity between modified noun phrases is influenced by a complex interplay of factors, including the specific modifiers used and the context in which they appear. While our findings affirm the initial hypotheses in several respects, they also underscore the nuanced and context-dependent nature of language and meaning construction.

The evidence, particularly the anomalies presented in Fig. 1 and the unexpected findings in Fig. 2a, b, underscores the complexity of noun phrase modification and its impact on semantic similarity. These findings not only support our initial hypotheses to a degree but also reveal the nuanced influence of context and modifier semantics. Further, our results align with those of previous work in transformer model processing of MWEs [6] (Figs. 4 and 5).

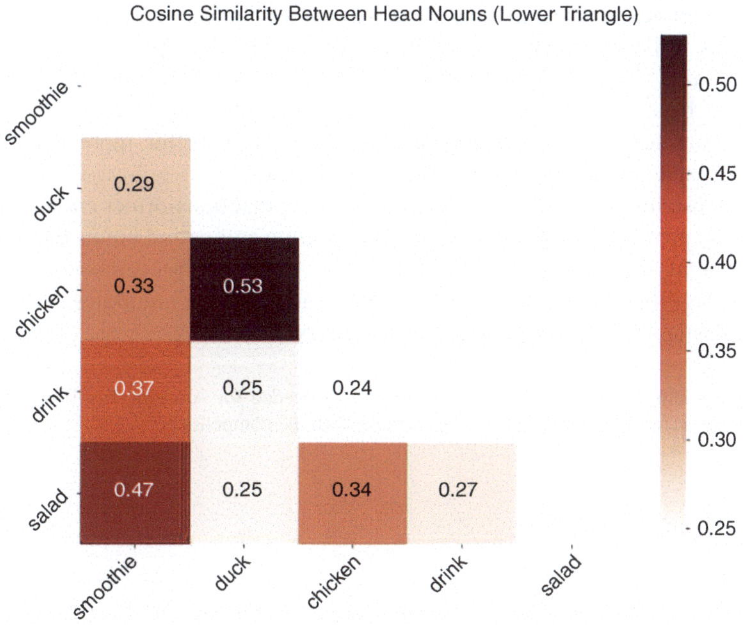

Fig. 5 Head noun cosine similarity adjacency matrix

5 Conclusion

This research delved into the intricate realm of semantic similarity within compound noun phrases, employing the advanced capabilities of bidirectional transformer language models. Our systematic investigation yielded findings that not only corroborate the efficacy of transformer encoder models, such as BERT and sBERT, in processing compound nouns despite their challenging linguistic features but also enrich our understanding of semantic dynamics in natural language processing (NLP). Our study substantiated the hypothesis that alterations to the first noun in compound phrases generally produce higher semantic similarity scores than modifications to the second noun, thereby emphasizing the pivotal role of the head noun in determining the semantic essence of the phrase. This observation underscores the fundamental principle of head-driven semantic interpretation within compound noun constructs.

However, our analysis revealed notable exceptions, accentuating the context-dependent nature of semantic similarity and the profound influence of modifier semantics on phrase interpretation. Particularly striking were the unexpected similarity scores in instances involving modifiers such as chocolate and strawberry, pointing to a sophisticated interplay between lexical semantics and contextual usage in dictating phrase meaning. These nuances hint at the underlying complexity of language comprehension and the significance of cultural and cognitive factors in semantic association.

Future avenues of research should extend beyond the current scope of multi-word expressions (MWEs) analyzed, to encompass a broader spectrum of linguistic structures and delve into additional languages. Moreover, integrating external knowledge bases or ontologies could offer substantial enhancements in models' grasp of complex semantic relationships, paving the way for more nuanced and contextually aware language processing capabilities.

In synthesizing our findings, it becomes evident that transformer encoder models are not only proficient in identifying and interpreting compound nouns but also offer pivotal insights into the nuanced and dynamic nature of linguistic semantics. This capability signifies a considerable advancement in search technologies, allowing for more sophisticated and semantically aware query processing.

Acknowledgments This work was inspired by tasks needed for Amazon TaskBot competition [11]. No data or models were used that overlapped with the competition.

References

1. Gamallo, P., Garcia, M., & de Dios-Flores, I. (2022). Evaluating contextualized vectors from both large language models and compositional strategies. *Procesamiento del Lenguaje Natural, 69*, 153–164.
2. Gamallo, P., de Prada Corral, M., Garcia, M. (2021). Comparing dependency-based compositional models with contextualized word embeddings. In: *ICAART* (2) (pp. 1258–1265).
3. Radford, A., Wu, J., Child, R., Luan, D., Amodei, D., Sutskever, I., et al. (2019). Language models are unsupervised multitask learners. *OpenAI blog, 1*(8), 9.
4. Balwin, T., & Nam, K. S. (2010). *Multiword expressions, Chap. 12* (pp. 267–292). Chapman and Hall/CRC.
5. Farahmand, M., Smith, A., Nivre, J. A multiword expression data set: An-notating non-compositionality and conventionalization for English noun com-pounds. In: *Proceedings of the 11th workshop on multiword expressions* (pp. 29–33). Association for Computational Linguistics, Denver, Colorado (Jun 2015). https://doi.org/10.3115/v1/W15-0904. https://aclanthology.org/W15-0904
6. Miletić, F., & Im Walde, S.S. (2024). *Semantics of multiword expressions in transformer-based models: A survey*.
7. Taylor, J. M., Raskin, V., Petrenko, M. S., Hempelmann, C. F. (2010). Multiple noun analysis: An implementation ontologic semantic technology. In *Proceedings of the multiconference international computer science and information technology* (pp. 517–524).
8. Vaswani, A., Shazeer, N., Parmar, N., Uszkoreit, J., Jones, L., Gomez, A. N., Kaiser, Ł., & Polosukhin, I. (2017). Attention is all you need. *Advances in Neural Information Processing Systems, 30*.
9. Devlin, J., Chang, M.W., Lee, K., Toutanova, K.: *Bert: Pre-training of deep bidirectional transformers for language understanding*. arXiv preprint arXiv:1810.04805 (2018).
10. Reimers, N., Gurevych, I. (2019). *Sentence-bert: Sentence embeddings using Siamese bert-networks*. arXiv preprint arXiv:1908.10084.
11. Hu, Y., Setpal, J., Zhang, D., Zietek, J., Lambert, J., Gonzalez, R., Rayz, J. (2023). Boilerbot: A reliable task-oriented chatbot enhanced with large language models. In: *Alexa prize TaskBot challenge 2 proceedings*. https://www.amazon.science/alexa-prize/proceedings/boilerbot-a-reliable-task-oriented-chatbot-enhanced-with-large-language-models

A Reinforcement Learning Framework for Transferable Neural Architecture Optimization

Raghav Vadhera and Manfred Huber

Abstract Historically, deep learning has proven increasingly useful and has become a frequently used tool for a wide range of applications. However, the sensitivity of deep learning systems to the specific network architecture, both in terms of learning ability and performance, has made them difficult to utilize for non-experts and emphasized the need for automatic network architecture optimization. Previous work largely optimizes a network for one specific problem using architecture search, requiring significant amounts of time training different architectures during optimization. To alleviate this, the approach proposed here learns a network optimization policy on an abstract problem and architecture embedding those transfers across problems and thus permits the optimization of networks for new problems without excessive additional training. Siamese networks here learn an effective, coherent embedding of the network architecture space, which, together with a problem-specific feature vector to capture the complexity of the problem, serve as a basis for a reinforcement learning agent to acquire a transferable policy to derive high-performing network architectures for a large array of problems. To demonstrate the feasibility and potential of the approach, initial experiments with a set of standard classification problems and an architecture space comprising a limited range of fully connected networks are performed, showing the ability of the approach to learn a policy that optimizes the architecture even for new problems that were not part of policy training. In summary, we employed a novel RL approach to successfully learn a policy for network optimization in a derived architecture embedding space that incrementally optimized the network.

Keywords RL · NAO · TD3 · Actor · Critic

R. Vadhera (✉) · M. Huber
University of Texas, Arlington, TX, USA
e-mail: bvadhera@post.harvard.edu; huber@cse.uta.edu

S. C. Suh (ed.), *Artificial Intelligence for Design and Process Science*,
https://doi.org/10.1007/978-3-031-67886-8_8

1 Introduction

Deep neural networks have become a versatile tool for a range of problems [1] with successes in many challenging applications, such as speech recognition [2], image recognition [3, 4], and machine translation [5–7]. Along with this success is a paradigm shift from feature designing to architecture designing, e.g., from SIFT [8] and HOG [9] to AlexNet [4], VGGNet [10], GoogleNet [11], and ResNet [12]. However, the performance of these systems tends to be highly sensitive to the specific network architecture and the available dataset. Although the advent of many tools has made their implementation easier, designing architectures still requires expert knowledge and time. Even seemingly simple choices such as the architecture hyperparameters for multilayer perceptrons (MLP), i.e., the number of hidden layers and units, are complex decisions with significant impact on performance on a specific dataset [13]. This difficulty of designing good architectures emphasizes the need for techniques for Automatic Neural Architecture (ANA) design [14].

Despite the fact that ANA design has been a topic of research for many years, current approaches tend to suffer from limitations in terms of their ability to either address larger network architecture spaces [15, 16] or to transfer across problems within a problem domain without requiring complete re-training on the new target problem [17–19]. The former is here usually due to the use of a discrete, type-specific set of network transformations that can be used during optimization, while the latter stems from the use of a local architecture search procedure that relies on frequent re-evaluation and retraining during the local optimization process.

The goal in this chapter is to develop a more general framework that uses reinforcement learning with a flexible architecture modification action space that allows to represent a broader task domain through architecture embedding and that facilitates planning through a performance prediction [20] component to learn a transferable policy for architecture optimization. Initial experiments in this chapter show that the framework, trained on a set of classification problems, can successfully learn a policy that results in an optimized target architecture on a new problem without the need for retraining.

2 Related Work

Different aspects of the Automatic Neural Architecture (ANA) modelling procedure have been studied, from training data collection and pre/post-processing to elaborate training schemes and algorithms. Increased attention has been directed to systematic ways to establish an appropriate architecture in contrast to the current common practice of repetitive trial and error, which is time-consuming and produces uncertain results [17]. Reinforcement learning (RL) has been effectively used to learn a policy to incrementally build neural network classifiers for a specific problem

[17, 18]. In reinforcement learning [21]–based methods, the choice of a component of the architecture is regarded as an action. A sequence of actions defines an architecture of a neural network, whose performance is used as the reward. Many of these techniques use a small, pre-defined set of architecture modification actions [15, 17], which limits their applicability to specific architecture types. One approach to attempt to address this is the use of an architecture embedding space to permit a general, continuous action space [18, 19]. However, target network performance over this embedding space tends to be highly non-convex and leads to many local extrema, limiting the optimization in this approach to single problems, requiring intensive retraining for each target problem and extensive evaluation training for each individual architecture optimization.

Generalization over target problems has been the focus of Bose [15], where a generic policy for network optimization is learned. This approach, however is limited by its simple action space with ensembles of small fully connected networks and cannot be applied to the wider range of problems.

In this chapter, an approach is proposed that combines the concepts of a network embedding space with target problem features and the learning of a transferable policy to allow for more general architecture spaces and to limit the need for extensive retraining for new problems. To address the challenges of complex dynamics of network performance under architecture transformations in an embedding space, the approach condenses and organizes legal network embeddings using Siamese networks and utilizes a reinforcement learning framework for complex policy formation that permits the system to more reliably achieve high-performing final architectures in the presence of significant local extrema for task performance. Taking inspiration from previous work using network embeddings [15, 18, 19, 22] and various approaches to network architecture search [14, 17, 23, 24], we propose an architecture that provides the promise to extend to various network types as well as to transfer optimization strategies across problems.

3 Background

We are presenting an approach that uses reinforcement learning on a network embedding space to learn a policy that can yield an optimized network architecture. The embedding space here converts the space of network architectures into a lower-dimensional continuous space and defines a continuous action space for the RL agent. To permit generalization across target problems and to facilitate planning, the system also utilizes a feature vector encoding target problem complexity and a derived performance prediction [20] component.

3.1 Embedding Space

Network architecture optimization needs to represent the space of applicable networks and, if using RL, an action space of network modifications. To efficiently represent the set of networks for a deep learning system, much like Luo [18], we map a network description language into an embedding space using an encoder-decoder component. This lower-dimensional latent embedding also defines a continuous action space as displacement vectors in the embedding space. The network embedding vector, augmented with a feature vector encoding the problem for which the network architecture is to be optimized, forms the state for the RL problem, while displacements in the embedding space provide the RL learner's action space.

One problem with such a derived embedding space is that it can fracture the space of legal network embeddings into disconnected regions.

While this does not affect local optimization using gradient ascent as in [18], it makes learning RL policies for optimization more difficult as they need to cross regions of the embedding space that do not decode to valid network architectures. To address this and condense the space of legal networks, a Siamese neural network (SNN) [b31] is used here in the encoder structure to organize the embedding space into coherent legal network regions.

3.2 Reinforcement Learning

RL [25] is used here as it allows to learn from quantitative feedback and thus addresses the problem in network architecture optimization that optimal network configurations for the target problems generally are not known. Utilizing the network embedding space, RL operates here by executing actions in embedding space to modify the network architecture and observing resulting reward in the form of changes in actual or predicted network performance. Based on this, a value function is estimated, and a policy is learned that optimizes the obtained rewards. Figure 1 shows this basic operation of the RL learning agent.

1. *Value function:* The Q-Value estimates performance as the expected utility of the learning agent in state **s** when performing action **a** and otherwise following policy (π). This value function not only considers immediate reward feedback, *r(s,a)* but also takes into account future payoffs.

$$Q_\pi(s,a) = \sum_{s'} P^a_{ss'}\left(r(s,a) + \gamma \sum_{a'} \pi(a'|s').Q_\pi(s',a')\right) \tag{1}$$

The Bellman equation \cite{b14} provides the basis for performance estimation and policy learning.

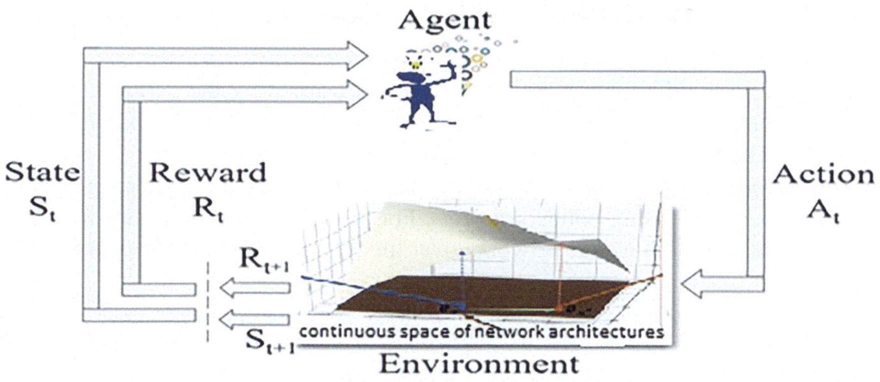

Fig. 1 Overview of reinforcement learning agent

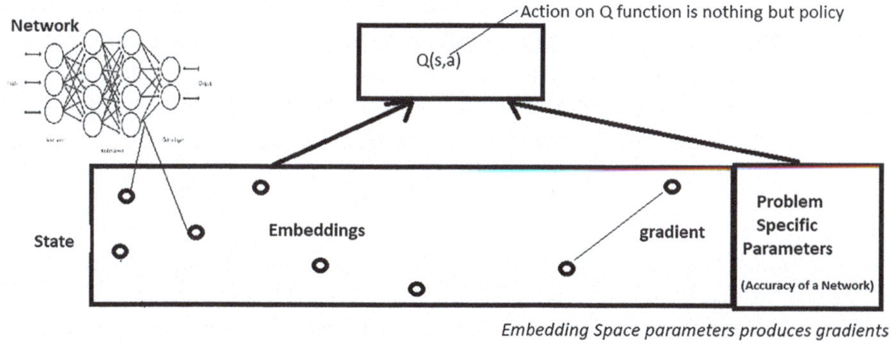

Fig. 2 Network embedding space (left) and problem features (right) as State and Action Space for RL (top)

In the network optimization problem considered here, reward represents increase in performance achieved by a network modification action, and the Q-value tries to predict expected improvements achievable by policy π. The state is provided by concatenating the embedding vector (representing the current network architecture) and a problem specific feature vector (capturing problem complexity related information), while possible actions are continuous displacement vectors in the embedding space. Figure 2 shows the connection of the embedding space and the value function.

2. *Policy learning:* As we use a continuous embedding space augmented with a continuous action space in the form of embedding space displacement vectors, the approach presented here utilizes an actor-critic RL approach [26, 27] to perform policy and value function learning.

3.3 Actor-Critic Methods and Policy Gradient

In the used actor-critic approach, the Q value is learned by the "critic network," which estimates the value function in form of the state-value Eq. (2) and the action-value Eq. (3).

The "actor network" updates the policy distribution in the direction suggested by the "critic network" using policy gradients. For this, both critic and actor functions are parameterized with neural networks over the augmented embedding space.

$$V_\pi(s) = \sum_a \pi(a|s).\sum_{s'} P^a_{ss'}(r(s,a) + \gamma.V_\pi(s')) \tag{2}$$

$$Q_\pi(s,a) = \sum_{s'} P^a_{ss'}\left(r(s,a) + \gamma \sum_{a'} \pi(a'|s').Q_\pi(s',a')\right) \tag{3}$$

Policy gradients [28] are used to optimize the actor's probability distribution of embedding space displacement actions. The goal is to learn a policy (π) that maximizes the cumulative future reward from current time *t* to terminal time *T*. If *r(t + 1)* is the reward for performing action *a(t)* at state *s(t)*, then:

$$r(t+1) = R(s(t), a(t))$$

1. *Reward and performance prediction:* To learn a network optimization policy, the reward has to capture the incremental improvement achieved when modifying the network. For a target domain of supervised classification, a direct way to capture reward is in terms of the expected accuracy gain of the target network after modification. To reduce the need for re-training target networks and to allow planning, the architecture includes a performance prediction [20] component that predicts network performance using previously trained problems. To limit task-specific training, the input to this network again contains, besides the network embedding, problem specific features to facilitate generalization across tasks.

3.4 Twin-Delayed Deep Deterministic Policy Gradient (TD3)

The twin-delayed deep deterministic policy gradient (TD3, 5] algorithm is a model-free, online, off-policy reinforcement learning method. It is an extension of the DDPG (Deep Deterministic Policy Gradient) algorithm [29] and reduces value function overestimation bias and overfitting spikes by including two value function learners and utilizing delayed actor updates. The basic operation of TD3 is shown in Fig. 3.

TD3 agents use a deterministic policy actor π(S) and one or more Q-value function critics Q(S, A). During training, a TD3 agent utilizes a circular experience

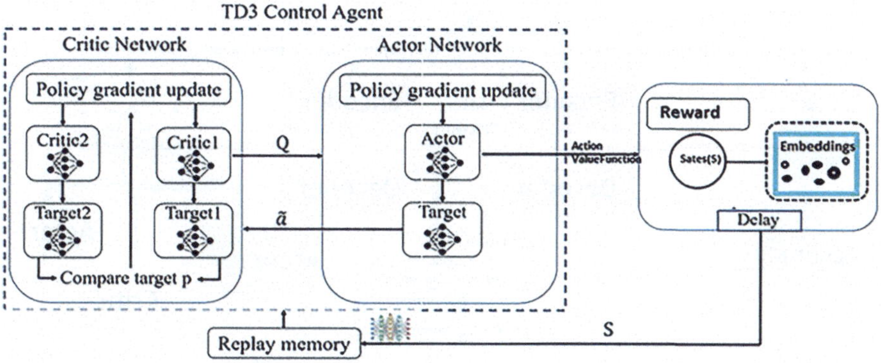

Fig. 3 Internal structure diagram of the td3 policy gradient controller

replay buffer to increase the number of actor and critic updates and perturbs the policy action using a stochastic noise model.

4 Approach and Implementation

To address automatic network optimization, the approach in this chapter utilizes reinforcement learning on top of a network embedding space. The embedding space is learned using an encoder-decoder network and provides a compact representation of all network architectures for the problem task as well as a corresponding fixed-dimensional, continuous network modification action space. To further organize the embedding space, it utilizes a Siamese network [30] to co-locate embeddings of valid network architectures and adds a loss term representing the precision of target problem accuracy prediction. To allow generalization across both the reinforcement learning components and the accuracy prediction network, an additional feature vector that abstractly encodes the complexity of the target problem is utilized.

For learning the network architecture modification policy, TD3 actor-critic networks are used. To further reduce the need for target network retraining and facilitate planning, the RL approach here uses the abovementioned accuracy prediction network to generate reward predictions. The accuracy prediction network uses the network embedding as well as the target problem feature vector to predict the achievable classification accuracy for the target problem as well as whether the embedding corresponds to a legal decoded network.

The architecture diagram in Fig. 4 takes the "network architecture description" and the "problem description" as input. The former represents the network characteristics, such as number of layers and nodes, and the latter represents features reflecting the complexity of the target problem, such as dimensionality, data size, feature correlations, or accuracy achieved by baseline architectures.

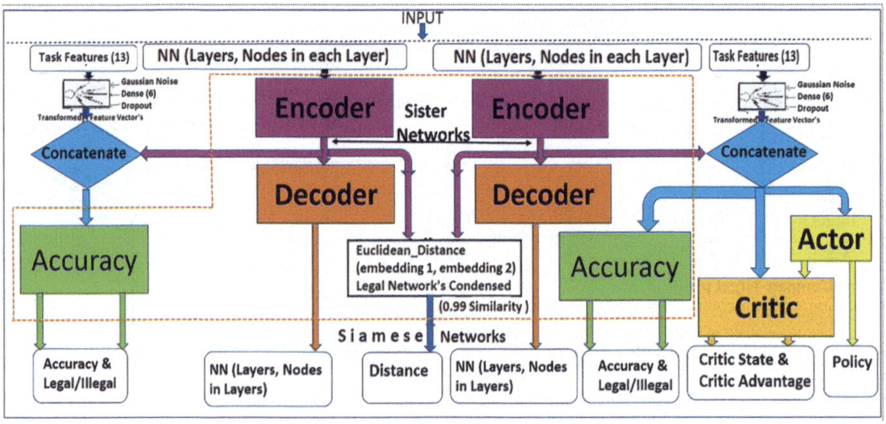

Fig. 4 Architecture overview

The "encoder" model transforms the network description into an embedding space, which, with the problem description, serves as input to the "accuracy" prediction, "actor," and "critic" networks. The "decoder" model is used to translate the embedding back to a corresponding network architecture for use on the target task. To improve the organization of the embedding space, a Siamese network [30] was also used encapsulating the encoder-decoder and action prediction networks as indicated as a dashed box in Fig. 4, where an embedding space is derived using an encoder-decoder and Siamese to focus on learning embeddings to place legal networks together and augmented with problem features to form the state. On this, an accuracy and legal embedding prediction network (center) predicts reward, and an actor-critic pair (right) learns the value function and network modification policy.

4.1 Encoder and Decoder Model

The encoder learns to transform the "network architecture description" into a continuous embedding space. The decoder model performs the reverse, translating an embedding point back into a network description as shown in Fig. 5.

To better organize the embedding space, this autoencoder is augmented with loss terms from the "accuracy prediction" network and arranged in a Siamese network to co-locate embeddings that decode into legal network descriptions. The effect of this is an embedding space that is easier to traverse by the actor as shown in the embedding space image in Fig. 6, where blue regions correspond to legally decodable network architectures, while red regions decode to illegal descriptions.

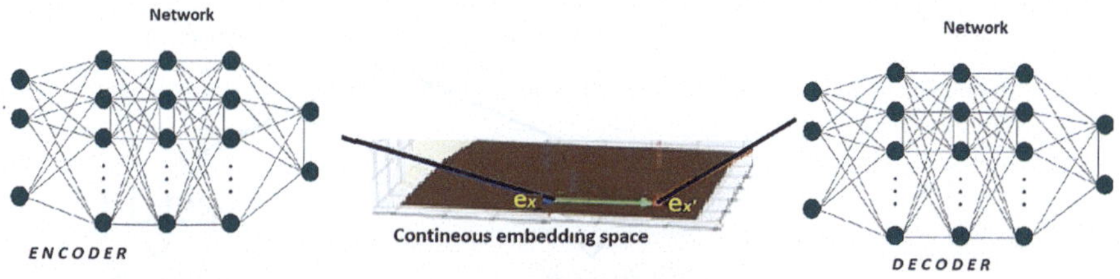

Fig. 5 Encoder-decoder

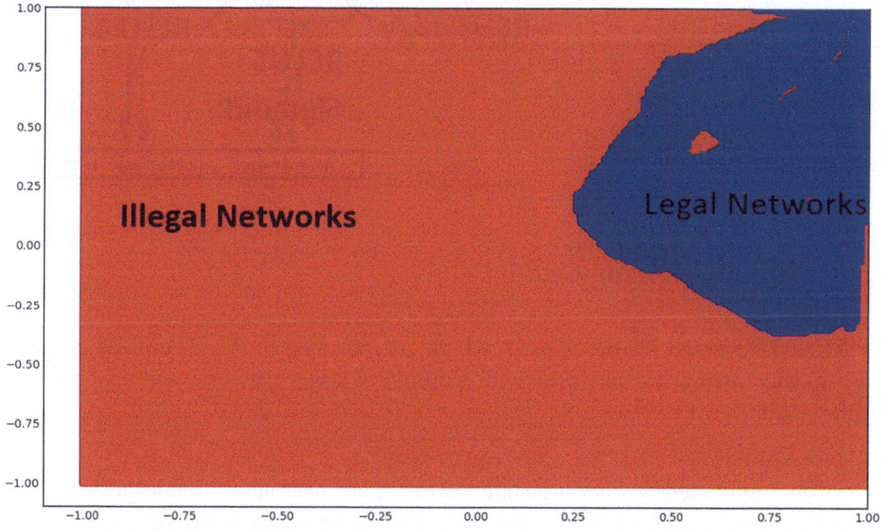

Fig. 6 Co-located legal and illegal networks

4.2 Accuracy Model

As accuracy prediction is problem specific, the accuracy model's input is comprised of the concatenation of the embedding and a "problem description" feature vector. Using this, it predicts a performance measure of the network for the target problem as well as whether the embedding state corresponds to a legal architecture. It serves to help organize the embedding space and to generate simulated rewards in order to minimize the amount of network training. The example layered architecture used in the experiments presented later is shown in Fig. 7.

During the first training phase encoder-decoder and accuracy models are trained together using a loss function that includes reconstruction loss as MSE, embedding consistency loss from the Siamese network, as well as accuracy prediction and legal network identification losses.

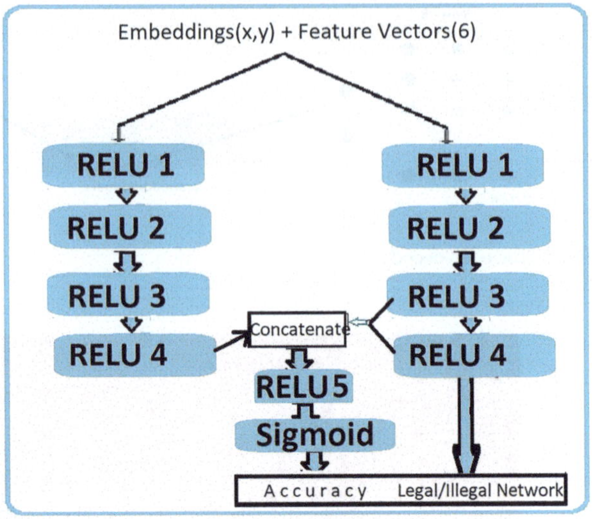

Fig. 7 Accuracy network layers

4.3 *TD3-Based Actor-Critic*

For RL, a TD3 based learner is used, which, as indicated in Fig. 3, utilizes delayed actor updates, two critic networks with a common target network, and action noise regularization.

1. Actor Model:
   The augmented embedding state also feeds to the "actor" model to learn the policy. Shown as the rightmost output in Fig. 4, the "actor network" provides the policy to optimize a target network. It computes the policy (π) used to select the next step (action "a") in the embedding space to obtain the embedding of the new, modified network.
2. Critic Model
   The "critic" model evaluates actions taken by the actor in the context of the augmented embedding state and learns the utility function to output state values, $V(s)$, and advantage values, $A(s,a) = Q(s,a)\text{-}V(s)$. Internally, this critic maintains two separate value function estimates for both utility functions and a common target network that achieves an action update delay and function smoothing. For the actor critic component, the reward function is derived as the actual (for online learning) or predicted (for planning) improvement of the performance prediction of the "accuracy" model, leading to policy trajectories as shown in Fig. 8.

To train the actor and critic components, the system generates new embedding space trajectories, which serve as training data together with the reward extracted from the accuracy network's performance predictions. As the policy changes over time, it is essential that old trajectories are discounted and new ones generated continuously.

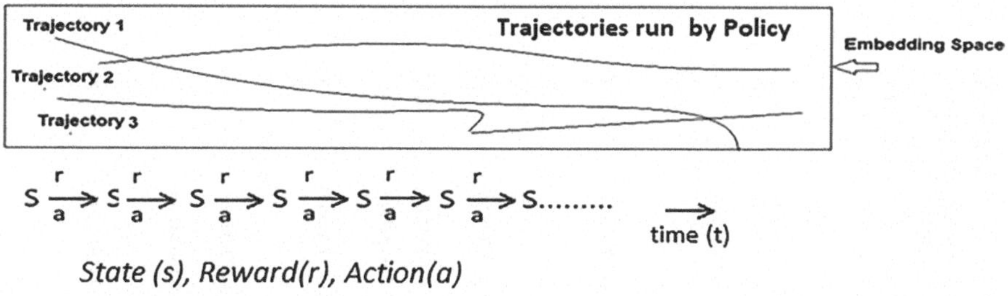

Fig. 8 State-action-reward sequence for policy

5 Training and Results

Like the NOA architecture in [18], the initial training here was focused on small, fully connected networks, along with some performance data (network accuracy) and network status (legal/illegal) to help construct a simpler modification space. To perform initial proof-of-concept experiments, this resulted here in defining the network space as fully connected networks with up to two hidden layers and at most 24 units per hidden layer and a target problem space of 12 classification problems from the UCI dataset [31]. This permits the input network specification to be supplied in terms of layers and unit numbers per layer and provides an easy means of generating initial training data by training 300 random networks [32], on each of the 12 target problems. Since the network architecture input formulation allows for illegal inputs, an additional 300 illegal network descriptions were generated and assigned accuracy values of 0 to allow the system to learn the demarcations of the embedding space. To evaluate the ability of the learned policy to generalize, the set of classification problems was divided into a training set consisting of nine and a test set with the remaining three problems, and only data from training problems was used during all stages of the training process.

To characterize the complexity of target problems, a problem description feature vector with 13 problem attributes was designed. Apart from "No of Classes," "Data Set Size", "Attribute Type," it also includes Entropy of dataset labels, average Entropy of dataset features, as well as the accuracy for three fixed baseline architectures. The resulting feature vectors for the used problems are shown in Fig. 9.

To be able to study and evaluate the individual components of the proposed architecture and to determine appropriate network layouts for the components, the proposed system is trained using a sequence of pre-training stages.

To be able to study and evaluate the individual components of the proposed architecture and to determine appropriate network layouts for the components, the proposed system is trained using a sequence of pre-training stages. First, the encoder-decoder networks are trained together with the accuracy and legal network predictions using supervised learning.

After this, the critic is pre-trained using random actions and a discount value of $\Upsilon = 0$ to predict the reward of the system. Similarly, the actor is trained subsequently

Problems (From UCI DATASET)	FEATURE VECTORS (Normalized)												
Features ⇒ Problems ⇓	NoOf Attributes	NoOf Classes	Data SetSize	Attribute Type	Entropy Label	AvgEntrophy Features	AvgCorelationBetFeatures	2_6_8_TrainingAccuracy	2_6_8_TestAccuracy	1_5_0_Training Accuracy	1_5_0_Test Accuracy	2_6_20_Training Accuracy	2_6_20_Test Accuracy
FV1 (AreM)	0.75	0.625	0.5621	0	0.933	0.42884418	0.49610	0.71918	0.7223	0.68524545	0.6914062	0.73545754	0.75
FV2 (Somerville Happiness)	0.75	0	0.0017	1	0.997	0	0.73455	0.85294	0.4482	0.71568626	0.6551724	0.9607843	0.75
FV3 (Activity_Recognition_Healthy_older_People)	1	0.25	1	0	0	0.15927052	0.21455	0.96969	0.9715	0.9657799	0.9657261	0.9748202	1
FV4 (Banknote_Authentication)	0.25	0	0.0180	0	0.984	0.44379607	0	1	1	0.9888551	0.9854545	1	0.25
FV5 (Basketball)	1	0.375	0.7042	0	0.915	0.5844241	0.28445	0.68732	0.6949	0.56217027	0.5677974	0.7537864	1
FV6 (BloodTransfusion)	0.25	0	0.0097	0	0.438	1	1	0.80669	0.8	0.7936803	0.78	0.7936803	0.25
FV7(Caesarian)	0.5	0	0.0008	1	0.723	0.1499662	0.48148	0.89473	0.75	0.7894737	0.4375	0.9122807	0.5
FV8(ContainerCraneController)	0	1	0	0	0.938	0.335498	0.28777	0.9	0	0.9	0	0.27728313	0
FV9(Cryotherapy)	0.75	0	0.0009	0.5	1.008	0.31014156	0.54376	1	0.9444	1	0.9444444	1	0.75
FV10 (Test 1)-(Ecoli)	1	0.75	0.0042	0	0.268	0.35927358	0.61289	0.91286	0.8088	0.917012453	0.7647058	0.92116183	1
FV11 (Test 2)-(Car)	0.75	0.25	0.02280	1	1.008	0.161037415	0.28777	0.90265	0.8843	0.853580058	0.8063583	0.946098149	0.75
FV12 (Test 3)-(VertebralColumn)	0.75	0	0.0039	0	0.783	0.816133676	0.93418	0.86547	0.8870	0.838565052	0.9032257	0.856502235	0.75

Fig. 9 Problem selection attributes

to reflect the pre-trained critic. After this, the critic is pre-trained one more time using the learned actor, but a discount value of $\Upsilon = 0.9$ to represent modification trajectories before the standard TD3 training learns the final actor and critic values by training the entire actor-training network.

5.1 Siamese Network Encoder-Decoder-Accuracy Training

1. *Encoder-decoder design*: Encoder and decoder models are designed with four dense layers as shown in Fig. 10. The use of a tanh activation function at the encoder output here yields a size-limited embedding space, which is easier to organize as an unlimited space.
   The encoder and decoder models are trained together with the accuracy and legal network prediction model to better organize the embedding space. To achieve this, the encoder-decoder-accuracy architecture is organized in a Siamese network that attempts to co-locate legal networks and separate legal and illegal network embeddings.
2. *Accuracy/legal model design*: The chosen architecture for the accuracy model was nine dense layers and two output layers using sigmoid activation function to output accuracy and status (legal/illegal) of the network.
   Since the accuracy predictions depend on the target problem, this model uses the augmented embedding, which combines the network embedding with the target problem feature vector. As the number of target problems in the training set is relatively small here, it is important to address overfitting. For this, the problem feature vector was transformed into a compressed, lossy embedding using Gaussian Noise, a dense layer of size 6, and a dropout layer with 20% dropout, to obtain noisy problem feature vectors of size 6 during training. Figure 11 shows the used problem feature embedding network.

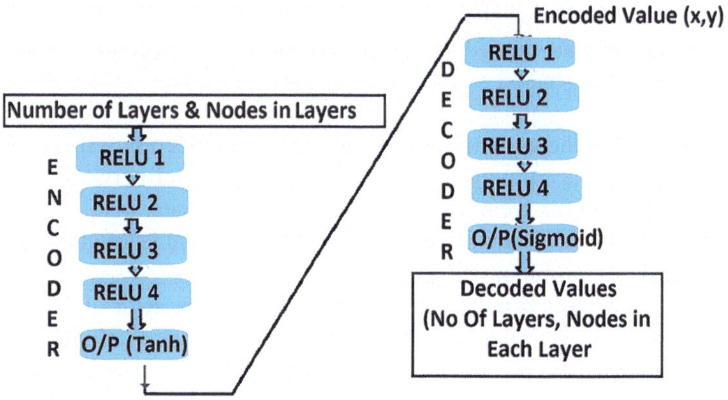

Fig. 10 Encoder-decoder layered diagram

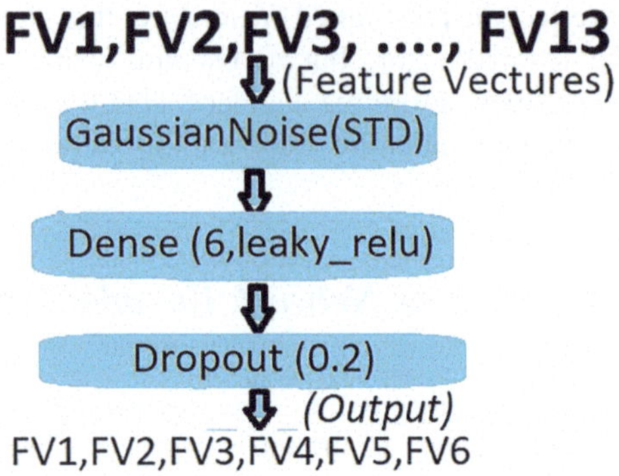

Fig. 11 Feature vector transformation

3. *Encoder-decoder-accuracy training:* To train the components, a custom loss consisting of decoder_loss, accuracy_loss, legal_loss, and distance_loss is used:

$$\text{custom\_loss} = w_D{}^*(\text{decoder\_loss}) + w_A{}^*(\text{accracy\_loss}) + w_L{}^*\text{legal\_loss} + w_{Dist}{}^*\text{distance\_loss}$$

where *legal_loss* is the **MSE** of the network reconstruction, accuracy_loss is the **MSE** of the accuracy prediction, *legal_loss* is binary cross-entropy of legal network prediction, and *distance_loss* is the distance error of the Siamese network.

Weights were determined experimentally, and the learned components were evaluated for consistency of the embedding space, accuracy of network architecture reconstruction, and precision of the accuracy and legal network predictions. After training, the encoder-decoder network achieved a reconstruction accuracy on legal networks of 99%.

To validate the spatial consistency of the encoding space, the locations of legal and illegal network descriptions were evaluated and compared to the legal predictions. Figure 12 shows the results where blue points indicate valid networks, while red dots indicate embedding points that do not correspond to legal network configurations. The shaded region indicates the area for which the system predicts legal networks.

This shows that the system is able to organize the embedding space coherently and can relatively accurately demarcate the area of legal network embeddings with a legal prediction accuracy of 98% on validation data.

To evaluate the accuracy prediction, Fig. 13 shows the learned predictions for a specific training problem (FV 5).

The accuracy prediction here achieved a mean square error of 4.5×10^{-5}, on validation data across all training problems, indicating its ability to learn to predict accuracy across a range of problems. Note that the system is only trained on a small region of the embedding space for illegal networks, and thus accuracy predictions in illegal areas are hard to interpret.

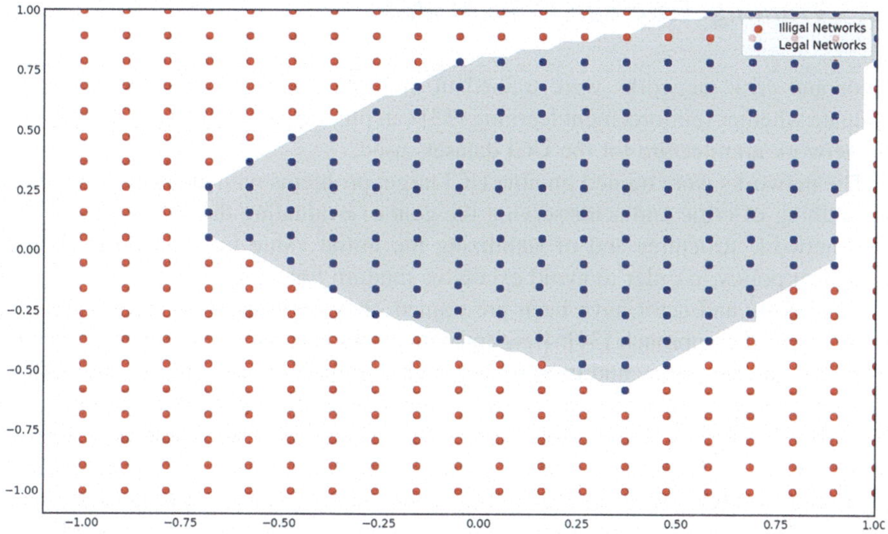

Fig. 12 Embedding space representation for legal (blue) and illegal (red) network configurations

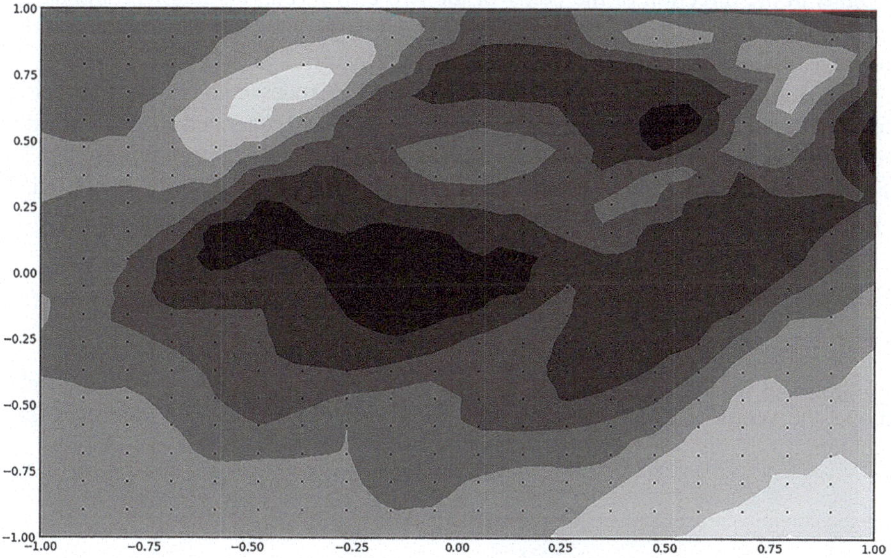

Fig. 13 Accuracy network prediction over embedding

5.2 Training Actor and Critic Models

Actor and critic networks were trained in multiple stages as indicated before to evaluate whether reinforcement learning [33] can produce a policy that will optimize the network architecture for the UCI datasets used.

The networks were trained on nine UCI target problems with alternate individual pre-training of critic and actor serving the goal of evaluating the sufficiency of the used network structures and of stabilizing the initial value function estimate and consistent policy in order to avoid excessive random trajectory generation.

Once critic and actor have been pre-trained, they are trained together using the TD3 actor-critic approach [34]. Here trajectory data is constructed online using the perturbed current policy and used to augment a temporally decaying replay buffer. This buffer stores states, actions, rewards, and new states, and random sampling on the buffer is used to obtain sufficient training examples to allow the networks to converge. Rewards are predicted by passing next state to the accuracy model and computing the reward as the difference to the accuracy of the current state. This eliminates the need for further target problem training. The two critic networks are here trained using a loss obtained from the Bellman Eq. (1) that provides separate losses for V(s) and A(s, a), and the target critic network is updated by updating its weights in the direction of the better of the two critics (i.e., the one with the larger value). The actor is trained using policy gradient by propagating the gradient of the negative advantage value as a loss back through the critic network.

The actor-critic network was trained for 5000 episodes with a new step being generated and 300 samples trained per episode. Actions generated by the actor are here displacement vectors in the two-dimensional embedding space represented as the sine and cosine of the direction and a length between 0 and 1 and are multiplied by a scaling factor of δ =0.005 to result in steps in the embedding space as:

$$next\_state = state + \delta * length * \begin{pmatrix} cos\,(dir) \\ \sin\,(dir) \end{pmatrix} \tag{5}$$

Figure 14 on the left shows the learned target critic V(s) values, while the right shows the vector field representing the policy actions for a specific training target problem.

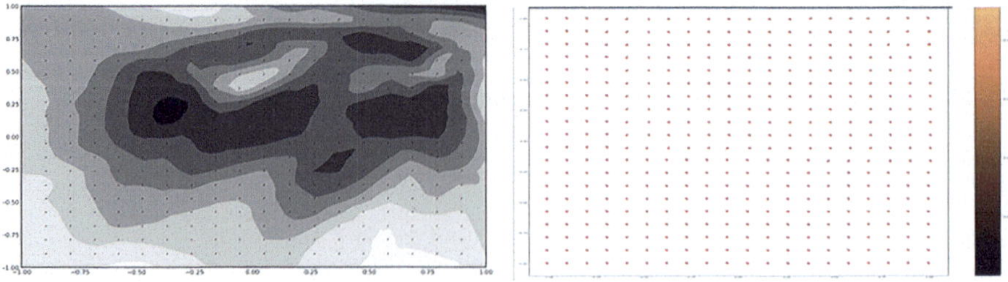

Fig. 14 Critic value (left) and learned policy actions (right) over embeddings of legal and illegal networks

Figure 14 on the left shows the learned target critic V(s) values, while the right shows the vector field representing the policy actions for a specific training target problem.

Examining the policy reveals a strategy that converts random starting networks to a small number of final networks which correspond closely to local maxima in the accuracy space. Once the training is finished, we evaluate the learned policy to see if it is able to transform the random start network into a high accuracy final network for UCI classification problem from the test set and thus if it is able to generalize network architecture optimization across target problems. Figure 15 shows eight policy trajectories generated by the policy from random start networks for one of the test problems.

These trajectories show that the policy manages to transform random networks into high-performing networks that match or exceed the performance of the best of the 300 initial random networks even for problems that were never seen during training. The policy here cannot follow a straight line but has to traverse accuracy "valleys," effectively leaving local maxima in favor of better, more globally optimal networks.

Figure 16 validates our results by comparing the accuracy achieved by the learned policy on the eight training and three test problems during ten policy executions from random start networks. Here, the rightmost column displays the ratio of the accuracy achieved by the network optimized by the learned policy and the best among the 300 initial random networks and shows that the networks found by the

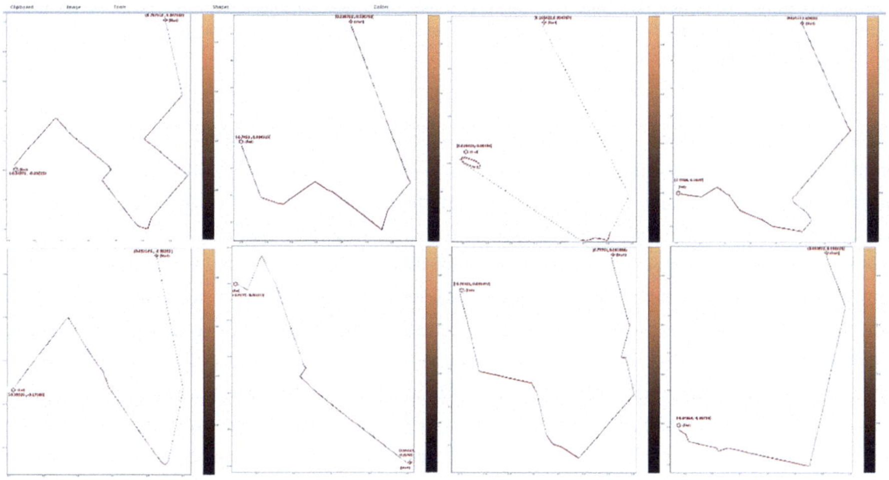

Fig. 15 Policy trajectories on random starting networks

Problem (Feature Vector)	Test NN1	Test NN2	Test NN3	Test NN4	Test NN5	Test NN6	Test NN7	Test NN8	Test NN9	Test NN10	Avg. Accuracy	Std Deviation	Best Accuracy from Orig. Network	Accuracy Found / Best Network Accuracy (Ratio)
FV1 (2,8,24)	0.722	0.7116	0.7038	0.7129	0.7098	0.70549	0.7176	0.7106	0.7089	0.71342	0.711419	0.0055146	0.72029	0.98768687
FV2 (2,8,24)	0.6209	0.6557	0.6209	0.5514	0.5869	0.68962	0.5869	0.5869	0.5171	0.5514	0.596551	0.0515316	0.58621	1.017647977
FV3 (2,8,24)	0.9061	0.9131	0.9151	0.9147	0.9144	0.91488	0.9132	0.9147	0.9153	0.9153	0.913829	0.002618	0.97065	0.941460043
FV4 (2,8,24)	1	1	1	0.9922	1	1	1	1	0.9927	1	0.998545	0.003047	1	0.998545448
FV5 (2,8,24)	0.6369	0.6529	0.6809	0.6369	0.6877	0.69986	0.7032	0.6782	0.6435		0.668954	0.02667	0.74327	0.900017454
FV6 (2,8,24)	0.8466	0.8399	0.8533	0.8399	0.8466	0.86	0.86	0.833	0.86	0.85333	0.849298	0.0095955	0.83333	1.019162229
FV7(2,8, 24)	0.7562	0.5934	0.9012	0.8463	0.5721	0.91512	0.8016	1.1874	1.0121	0.64217	0.822767	0.1934122	0.75	1.097023292
FV8	1	0.9444	0.9444	0.9444	0.9444	0.94444	0.9444	0.9444	0.8888	0.88888	0.938887	0.0315393	0.94444	0.9941162
Test – FV10	0.8829	0.8829	0.8823	0.8383	0.8383	0.82354	0.7946	0.8083	0.8083	0.80885	0.836765	0.034278	0.82353	1.016071784
Test – FV11	0.9597	0.9564	0.9598	0.9593	0.9738	0.96821		0.9593		0.95722	0.961818	0.0060283	0.96243	0.999366232
Test – FV12		0.8387	0.8876	0.8548	0.8706	0.91939		0.9149			0.881717	0.0333108	0.87097	1.012342062

Fig. 16 Performance matrix or accuracy between initial network vs network's discovered by policy

learned optimization policy achieve better or equivalent accuracies even for the never-before-seen test problems.

6 Conclusions

Finding good network architectures is essential for the success of deep learning systems. This chapter proposes a novel deep learning framework that uses reinforcement learning to learn a network architecture modification policy that transfers across target problems without the need for significant re-training.

The proposed approach optimizes network architectures in a learned network embedding space constructed using an autoencoder and Siamese network. Using this and a performance predictor, an actor-critic RL component is trained, which uses the embedding vector as a network representation as well as problem specific features to learn a policy for network architecture modification over the continuous action space of embedding space moves. Initial experiments using classification datasets from the UCI repository show that the proposed system is able to successfully learn an embedding space as well as a policy that derives network architectures that are close to optimal even for not-before-seen test problems.

References

1. Ma, J., Sheridan, R. P., Liaw, A., Dahl, G. E., & Svetnik, V. (2015). Deep neural nets as a method for quantitative structure-activity relationships. *Journal of Chemical Information and Modeling, 55*, 263–274.
2. G. Hinton, L. Deng, D. Yu, G. E. Dahl (2012), A.-R. Mohamed, N. Jaitly, A. Senior, V. Vanhoucke, P. Nguyen, T. N. Sainath, et al., "Deep neural networks for acoustic modeling in speech recognition: The shared views of four research groups," IEEE Signal Processing Magazine, vol. 29, no. 6, pp. 82–97.
3. Lecun, Y., Bottou, L., Bengio, Y., & Haffner, P. (1998). Gradient-based learning applied to document recognition. *Proceedings of the IEEE, 86*(11), 2278–2324.
4. Krizhevsky, A., Sutskever, I., & Hinton, G. E. (2016). ImageNet classification with deep convolutional neural networks. In F. Pereira, C. Burges, L. Bottou, & K. Weinberger (Eds.), *Advances in neural information processing systems* (Vol. 25, pp. 1097–1105). Curran Associates, Inc. Available: https://papers.nips.cc/paperfiles/paper/2012/hash/c399862d3b9d6b76c8436e924a68c45b-Abstract.html
5. Sutskever, I., Vinyals, O., & Le, Q. V. (2014). Sequence to sequence learning with neural networks. *Advances in neural information processing systems* (vol. 27).
6. Bahdanau, D., Cho, K., & Bengio, Y. (2014). Neural machine translation by jointly learning to align and translate. *CoRR, abs/1409.0473*.
7. Wu, Y., Schuster, M., Chen, Z., Le, Q. V., Norouzi, M., Macherey, W., Krikun, M., Cao, Y., Gao, Q., Macherey, K., et al. (2016). Google's neural machine translation system: Bridging the gap between human and machine translation. *arXiv preprint* arXiv:1609.08144.
8. Lowe, D. G. (1999). Object recognition from local scale-invariant features. In *Proceedings of the seventh IEEE international conference on computer vision* (vol. 2, pp. 1150–1157). IEEE.
9. Dalal, N., & Triggs, B. (2005). Histograms of oriented gradients for human detection. In *2005 IEEE computer society conference on computer vision and pattern recognition (CVPR'05)* (vol. 1, pp. 886–893).
10. Simonyan, K. & Zisserman, A. (2014) Very deep convolutional networks for large-scale image recognition. *arXiv preprint* arXiv:1409.1556.
11. Szegedy, C., Liu, W., Jia, Y., Sermanet, P., Reed, S., Anguelov, D., Erhan, D., Vanhoucke, V., & Rabinovich, A. (2015) Going deeper with convolutions. In *Proceedings of the IEEE conference on computer vision and pattern recognition* (pp. 1–9).
12. He, K., Zhang, X., Ren, S., & Sun, J. (2016). Deep residual learning for image recognition. In *Proceedings of the IEEE Conference on Computer Vision and Pattern Recognition (CVPR).*
13. Gaurav, M. (2019). *How to find the optimum number of hidden layers and nodes in a neural network model?* https://datagraphi.com/blog/post/2019/12/17/how-to-find-the-optimum-number-of-hidden-layers-and-nodes-in-a-neural-network-model
14. Kapanova, K. G., Dimov, I., & Sellier, J. M. (2018). A genetic approach to automatic neural network architecture optimization. *Neural Computing and Applications, 29*(5), 1481–1492.
15. Bose, S., & Huber, M. (2016). Incremental learning of neural network classifiers using reinforcement learning. In *IEEE international conference on systems, man, and cybernetics (SMC)*. IEEE.
16. Zoph, B., & Le, Q. V (2016). Neural architecture search with reinforcement learning. *arXiv preprint* arXiv:1611.01578.
17. Baker, B., Gupta, O., Naik, N., et al. (2016) Designing neural network architectures using reinforcement learning. In: *arXiv preprint* arXiv:1611.02167, vol. A247, pp. 529–551.
18. Luo, R., Tian, F., Qin, T., Chen, E., & Liu, T.-Y. (2018). Neural architecture optimization. *Advances in neural information processing systems* (vol. 31).
19. Zhou, Z.-H., Jianxin, W., & Tang, W. (2002). Ensembling neural networks: Many could be better than all. *Artificial intelligence, 137.1 2*, 239–263.
20. Baker, B., Gupta, O., Raskar, R., et al. (2017). Accelerating neural architecture search using performance prediction. *arXiv preprint arXiv, 1705*, 10823.

21. Kaelbling, L. P., Littman, M. L., & Moore, A. W. (1996). Reinforcement learning: A survey. *Journal of Artificial Intelligence Research, 4*, 237–285.
22. Granitto, P. M., Verdes, P. F., & Alejandro Ceccatto, H. (2005). Neural network ensembles: Evaluation of aggregation algorithms. *Artificial Intelligence, 163*(2), 139–162.
23. Brock, A. et al. (2017). Smash: One-shot model architecture search through hypernetworks. In: *arXiv preprint* arXiv:1708.05344.
24. Cai, H. et al. (2017). Reinforcement learning for architecture search by network transformation. In: *arXiv preprint* arXiv:1707.04873.
25. Sutton, R. S., & Barto, A. G. (2018). *Reinforcement learning: An introduction*. MIT Press.
26. Konda, V., & Tsitsiklis, J. (1999). Actor-critic algorithms. *Advances in neural information processing systems* (vol. 12).
27. Fujimoto, S., van Hoof, H., & Meger, D. (2018). Addressing function approximation error in actor-critic methods. In Dy, J., & Krause, A. (Eds) *Proceedings of the 35th international conference on machine learning, ser. Proceedings of machine learning research* (2016) (vol. 80, pp. 1587–1596). PMLR. [Online]. https://proceedings.mlr.press/v80/fujimoto18a.html
28. Yoon, C. (2018). Deriving policy gradients and implementing REINFORCE. https://medium.com/@thechrisyoon/deriving-policy-gradients-and-implementing-reinforce-f887949bd63.
29. *Deep Deterministic Policy Gradients Explained*. (2019). https://towardsdatascience.com/understanding-actor-critic-methods931b97b6df3f
30. Benhur, S. (2022). A friendly introduction to Siamese networks. *Data Science and Machine Learning*. [Online]. https://builtin.com/machine-learning/siamese-network
31. Dua, D., & Graff, C. (2017). *UCI machine learning repository*. http://archive.ics.uci.edu/ml, University of California, Irvine, School of Information and Computer Sciences.
32. Sutton, R. S., Whitehead, S. D., et al. (2014). Online learning with random representations. In *Proceedings of the tenth international conference on machine learning* (pp. 314–321).
33. Likas, A. (1999). A reinforcement learning approach to online clustering. *Neural Computation, 11*(8), 1915–1932.
34. Byrne, D. (2019). *TD3: Learning to run with AI*. https://towardsdatascience.com/td3-learning-to-run-with-ai-40dfc512f93.

Learning Shortcuts: On the Misleading Promise of NLU in Language Models

Geetanjali Bihani and Julia Rayz

Abstract The advent of large language models (LLMs) has enabled significant performance gains in the field of natural language processing. However, recent studies have found that LLMs often resort to shortcuts when performing tasks, creating an illusion of enhanced performance while lacking generalizability in their decision rules. This phenomenon introduces challenges in accurately assessing natural language understanding in LLMs. Our chapter provides a concise survey of relevant research in this area and puts forth a perspective on the implications of shortcut learning in the evaluation of language models, specifically for natural language understanding (NLU) tasks. This chapter urges more research efforts to be put toward deepening our comprehension of shortcut learning, contributing to the development of more robust language models, and raising the standards of NLU evaluation in real-world scenarios.

Keywords Large language models · Natural language understanding · Shortcut learning · NLU · Generalization

1 Introduction

Large language models (LLMs) have become the convention in the field of natural language processing in recent years. The preference for LLMs can be attributed to their performance gains in a wide variety of NLP tasks, including question answering, textual entailment, sentiment analysis, and commonsense reasoning [1–3]. As LLMs scale up, their performance gains not only compete with but also exceed human performance on language understanding benchmarks [4, 5]. Whether such performance gains are meaningful depends on the quality of the evaluation metrics and the relevance of benchmarking schemes [6, 7].

G. Bihani (✉) · J. Rayz
Purdue University, West Lafayette, IN, USA
e-mail: gbihani@purdue.edu; jtaylor@purdue.edu

S. C. Suh (ed.), *Artificial Intelligence for Design and Process Science*,
https://doi.org/10.1007/978-3-031-67886-8_9

Unfortunately, LLMs have been shown to exploit spurious associations and dataset biases as "shortcuts," achieving inflated scores on NLU benchmarks while lacking reliability and generalization on out-of-distribution samples. Recent works have shown that LLMs tend to learn shortcuts based on statistical cues to make predictions, e.g., the word "not" [8], keywords [9, 10], and cues related to language variations [11]. This behavior, also known as *shortcut learning*, leads the model to learn non-generalizable decision rules that do not perform well on out-of-distribution data [10, 12] but continues to give state-of-the-art results on independent and identically distributed (IID) samples. Thus, PLM performance gains on NLU benchmarks do not necessarily portray improvement in the semantic and reasoning capabilities of language models.

This chapter delineates the challenges in enhancing NLU capabilities within pre-trained language models amidst the presence of shortcut learning. We survey recent research on quantifying and mitigating shortcut learning and examine their implications for language understanding in language models. Finally, we suggest potential research directions and guidelines that can help develop robust and reliable language models.

2 What Is Shortcut Learning?

Shortcut learning refers to the phenomenon where models rely on superficial cues in the training data to make predictions instead of learning the underlying semantics to perform an NLU task. This overreliance on specific features or biases results in poor generalization in out-of-distribution settings. Identifying shortcut learning in language models is an ongoing research area, with recent works utilizing model attention, dataset statistics, and human-annotated samples to identify spurious correlations [10, 13].

General-purpose neural language models have demonstrated learning incidental patterns present in natural language text, owing to the diverse linguistic cues embedded in their training corpora [8, 11]. While prior research asserted the robustness of LLMs in out-of-distribution detection and cross-domain generalization [14], recent studies have revealed that both LLMs and their fine-tuned versions rely on specific keyword-based shortcuts for classification [10]. In an examination of fact verification classifiers, it was shown that claim-only models achieved comparable performance to evidence-aware models. This phenomenon was due to the former model's reliance on idiosyncrasies within the claims, which did not incorporate evidence in its predictions [15]. Empirical analyses of LLMs highlight their dependence on spurious unigram and bigram cues to enhance natural language inference (NLI) task performance [8], as well as the utilization of syntactic heuristics for NLI tasks [16].

2.1 Identifying Shortcuts

Research dedicated to automatically identifying and mitigating spurious cues within training and fine-tuning data has been proposed in recent years [13, 17, 18]. The understanding of shortcut learning behaviors in LLMs was recently extended by leveraging the long-tailed phenomenon [9]. This work observed that LLMs tend to focus on the head of the word distribution, neglecting the poorly learned tail of the distribution. Furthermore, their findings indicate that shortcuts are predominantly learned in the early training iterations, impeding potential learning enhancements in later iterations.

While most works do not differentiate between spurious and genuine tokens, [19] addresses this distinction by employing a human attention-guided approach to detect and alleviate shortcut learning. This mechanism identifies both model and dataset biases, utilizing human attention as a supervisory signal to compel the model to allocate more attention to "relevant" tokens. Their approach enhances robustness on out-of-distribution data and maintains performance on IID data.

3 Implications on NLU Evaluation

3.1 Examining the Impacts

Inflated NLU Performance Scores The performance gains of pre-trained language models on NLU tasks have been the subject of extensive scrutiny within the natural language processing domain. In several recent works, the performance of BERT-like models is shown to be entirely attributable to the exploitation of statistical cues. One work demonstrated that BERT uses the word "not" as a shortcut in several NLU tasks, and the removal of such cues leads to a significant drop in model performance, plummeting from near human baseline to a random score [8]. Similarly, a drop of over 20% in BERT-based NLU model performance was observed when evaluated on out-of-distribution datasets [9]. Another study showed that PLM accuracy scores are inflated by 20% due to most samples containing high levels of superficial information [20].

Moreover, [16] established that training and evaluating models using standard natural language inference (NLI) datasets such as MNLI [21] result in models primarily relying on heuristics. When assessed on a curated dataset lacking such heuristics, model performance dropped below chance performance for examples without heuristics. This highlights that NLI models may not inherently learn the correct rules for inference. Similarly, [15] shows that even with a complete vocabulary overlap, the performance of fact verification models declined by 20% when employing distinct language—devoid of shortcuts—while maintaining consistent claim and evidence relations (*support* or *refute*). [19] also revealed a substantial decline of 40%–60% in BERT-based model performance on NLI and fact verification tasks upon the removal of shortcuts. These studies underscore the pronounced dependence of LLMs on superficial information within the datasets, and the inflated NLU performance reported due to the same.

Overconfidence in LLM Decisions Examining model performance extends beyond task accuracy metrics. Recent works also include a scrutiny of model confidence scores for incorrect predictions. [19] demonstrated that models tend to produce overconfident predictions for data samples with shortcut or trigger patterns, irrespective of the ground truth. This mismatch between model confidence and actual accuracy leads to the phenomenon known as miscalibration, impacting the reliability of models in real-world applications. Ideally, a well-calibrated model assigns high probabilities to correct predictions and low probabilities to incorrect decisions, aligning predicted probabilities with observed event frequencies.

The rising deployment of neural network architectures in high-risk real-world scenarios has prompted extensive research into their calibration [14, 22, 23]. Evaluations of neural network reliability indicate that their confidence predictions are often poorly calibrated and overconfident [24, 25]. Recent studies have extended these findings to pre-trained language models and found that fine-tuning exacerbates miscalibration [26–29]. This is attributed to the excessive parameterization of the models, leading to overfitting on the training data. The attention garnered by pre-trained language models stems from their inclination to exhibit increasing confidence during training, regardless of prediction accuracy [30]. However, these models showcase calibration deterioration in out-of-domain scenarios [27]. Notably, smaller models demonstrate improved calibration on in-domain data, while larger models exhibit better calibration on out-of-domain data [31]. These findings underscore the current inadequacies of pre-trained language models in terms of confidence calibration and reliability in decision-making.

3.2 *Improving NLU amid Shortcut Learning*

The current focal paradigm in improving natural language understanding and evaluation in LLMs revolves around alleviating shortcut learning to prevent inflated NLU task scores. Strategies such as ensemble learning and adversarial datasets are employed to diminish the impact of shortcuts, followed by the assessment of NLU task performance. More robust evaluations extend to measuring model generalization by assessing performance on out-of-distribution datasets.

Data-Centric Approaches Recent approaches to enhance model robustness and mitigate the impact of spurious cues involve the creation of datasets containing curated examples that reduce model reliance on shortcuts during task learning. Incorporating adversarial data points during both training and evaluation, such as mirroring linguistic artifacts around labels, has also been shown to diminish the impact of spurious cues on model learning [8, 15]. [15] demonstrated a notable decrease in model performance when assessed on an adversarial test set, underscoring the necessity for NLU evaluations to incorporate considerations for shortcut learning in language models. Additional efforts in this domain involve the development of adversarial datasets, such as HANS, which assesses whether natural language inference (NLI) models rely on syntactic heuristics to accomplish the task [16].

More recently, novel data generation techniques have been proposed for mitigating spurious correlations and promoting generalization [32]. This technique involves training data generators to create and filter data points that exacerbate spurious correlations but yield significant performance drops in task accuracy. Moreover, even though data augmentation for bias removal reduces the model's dependence on spurious cues, it does not completely eliminate it [33]. This persistence of lexical data biases emphasizes the ongoing challenges in effectively mitigating the impact of spurious cues in NLP models.

Model-Centric Approaches Various strategies centered on models to address shortcuts involve debiasing LLMs at the representation level [34]. This encompasses the creation of adversarial and Product of Expert (PoE)–style ensembles, integrating both biased and robust models [20, 35, 36]. In cases where prior knowledge about dataset biases is lacking, [37] suggests that mitigating spurious cues is more effective when focusing on the model's predictive features. Thus, rather than debiasing input embeddings themselves, they achieve improved robustness by debiasing based on how the model utilizes embeddings. In this scenario, the authors employ a simple Bag-of-Words (BoW) model to first capture superficial cues in the training data and then project the primary model embeddings into a space orthogonal to the BoW cue model. This orthogonality to superficial cue embeddings results in better debiasing. [9] utilize a generalizable shortcut degree measurement, extracted from the dataset statistics, to smoothen SoftMax scores. This discourages the model from generating overly confident predictions for samples with higher shortcut degrees—indicative of the increased presence of shortcuts in a sample.

While these methods enhance performance on out-of-distribution samples, they have been shown to compromise the task accuracy on IID samples [36]. Furthermore, studies have highlighted that these methods inadvertently encode more biases into the inner representations of LMs [34], creating newer shortcuts to deal with.

4 Delving Deeper

4.1 Language and Vocabulary Variation

Accurately identifying and eliminating specific shortcuts used by LLMs poses a significant challenge. Successfully addressing this challenge requires nuanced strategies for pinpointing and mitigating such linguistic cues. Addressing the impact of shortcuts becomes complex when variations in language and vocabulary are introduced. Despite incorporating long-range context, encoding intricate lexical semantic phenomena for improved natural language understanding remains an ongoing endeavor [38–40]. Even when the vocabulary overlap is significant, maintaining consistent performance poses a challenge. This raises questions regarding the broader applicability of current state-of-the-art LLMs across different language contexts and the necessity for models to exhibit resilience and adaptability in the face of varied linguistic expressions.

A way forward It is important to design robust methods capable of identifying and mitigating a diverse range of shortcut cues, both known and unknown. A pivotal focus of research in this domain should be on enhancing the adaptability of state-of-the-art language models in diverse contexts. This involves addressing tasks associated with language and vocabulary variations while categorizing different types of shortcuts across various contexts and task definitions. The emphasis must extend to mitigating challenges linked to unknown dataset biases and instances of incomplete task-specific knowledge during model training. Furthermore, these strategies need extension to navigate effectively through scenarios marked by limited information or unknown biases.

4.2 *Out-of-Distribution Generalization*

Mitigating the impact of shortcuts becomes particularly challenging when LLMs are assessed on out-of-distribution datasets. The reliance on heuristics in NLI models, particularly when trained and evaluated on standard NLI datasets like MNLI [21], poses a challenge to achieving robust inference capabilities. This is highlighted by a significant drop in performance when assessed on curated datasets lacking such heuristics, portraying difficulty in achieving generalization beyond the training distribution. Strategies and datasets need to be devised for the existing variety of NLU tasks, to enhance model robustness and adaptability to diverse data distributions.

A way forward To enhance the overall generalization of language models on out-of-distribution datasets, it is crucial to formulate effective strategies and curate datasets specifically designed for this purpose. This necessitates a focused effort on defining specific robust inference capabilities, facilitating generalization beyond the confines of the training distribution. Furthermore, an in-depth exploration of methodologies that quantify the impact of shortcut removal on LLM performance is essential. Given the intricacies of datasets containing substantial amounts of superficial information, there is a need to develop nuanced approaches for comprehending the consequences of shortcut mitigation strategies. This involves a careful examination of trade-offs to ensure that performance does not experience significant deterioration. The aim is to strike a balance between addressing heuristics reliance and maintaining optimal model performance in the face of diverse and challenging datasets.

4.3 *Impact of Shortcut Removal*

Understanding the magnitude of the impact of shortcut removal on LLM performance is a crucial challenge. The decline in LLM performance in the absence of a handful of such shortcuts underscores the need for a nuanced understanding of the consequences of shortcut mitigation strategies.

Du et al. [9] also showed that model training exacerbates learning of superficial cues due to incentivizing reduction of training loss, which rapidly reduces when the model focuses on the head of word distribution, containing many shortcut features instead of the tail. This is reiterated in [20], i.e., since the majority of training examples are not representative of the real-world data distribution (including the challenge data), minimizing the average training loss is not a legitimate objective. They solve this problem by modifying loss for known dataset biases but maintain that it is a challenge for unknown dataset biases and cases with incomplete task-specific knowledge.

A way forward We need more works that contribute toward measuring the impact of shortcut removal on LLM performance on NLU tasks. While most prior works utilize out-of-distribution accuracy, the types of datasets and the hardness of samples need to be systematized and defined to understand how different distribution shifts impact model learning behaviors.

4.4 *The Caveats of Incentivizing Training Loss*

Understanding the impact of model training on the learning of superficial cues is crucial in the realm of natural language processing. Recent research demonstrated that model training exacerbates the learning of superficial cues [9, 20] because the optimization process incentivizes the reduction of training loss, which rapidly decreases when the model prioritizes the head of the word distribution, rich in shortcut features. Consequently, minimizing the average training loss may not be a legitimate objective. To address this issue, prior works propose modifying the loss function for known dataset biases. However, dealing with unknown dataset biases and cases with incomplete task-specific knowledge remains a challenge.

A way forward There is an imperative need for the reevaluation of the incentives linked to training loss reduction in LLMs. We must delve into alternative training and post-processing strategies that prioritize the acquisition of meaningful linguistic patterns, rather than incentivizing the incorporation of shortcut features. This involves a fundamental shift in training objectives to better align with the actual distribution of real-world data. To ensure the reliability and accuracy of LLMs across diverse language tasks, it is important to investigate the interplay between model generalization and calibration. This exploration will contribute to the development of language models that generalize well and exhibit robustness against challenging samples within datasets.

5 Conclusion

This chapter underscores the interplay between natural language understanding evaluation and shortcut learning within language models. We shed light on the distortions introduced by shortcut learning on NLU evaluation and emphasize the need for a nuanced understanding of its impacts. It is necessary to actively address the challenges posed by shortcut learning, both in terms of identifying and mitigating shortcuts and refining evaluation methodologies. Neglecting these issues jeopardizes the reliability and fairness of NLU assessments. As we move forward, collaborative efforts within the NLP community are essential to advance our comprehension of shortcut learning, fostering the development of more robust language models and elevating the standards of NLU evaluation in real-world contexts.

References

1. Devlin, J., Chang, M. W., Lee, K., & Toutanova, K. BERT: Pre-training of deep bidirectional transformers for language understanding. In: *Proceedings of the 2019 conference of the North American chapter of the association for computational linguistics: Human language technologies*, Volume 1 (Long and Short Papers) (pp. 4171–4186). Association for Computational Linguistics, Minneapolis, Minnesota (Jun 2019). https://doi.org/10.18653/v1/N19-1423. https://aclanthology.org/N19-1423
2. Peters, M. E., Neumann, M., Iyyer, M., Gardner, M., Clark, C., Lee, K., Zettlemoyer, L. Deep contextualized word representations. In: *Proceedings of the 2018 conference of the North American chapter of the association for computational linguistics: Human language technologies*, Volume 1 (Long Papers) (pp. 2227–2237). Association for Computational Linguistics, New Orleans, Louisiana (Jun 2018). https://doi.org/10.18653/v1/N18-1202. https://aclanthology.org/N18-1202
3. Sap, M., Shwartz, V., Bosselut, A., Choi, Y., Roth, D. Common-sense reasoning for natural language processing. In: *Proceedings of the 58th annual meeting of the association for computational linguistics: Tutorial abstracts* (pp. 27–33). Association for Computational Linguistics, Online (Jul 2020). https://doi.org/10.18653/v1/2020.acl-tutorials.7. https://aclanthology.org/2020.acl-tutorials.7
4. Chowdhery, A., Narang, S., Devlin, J., Bosma, M., Mishra, G., Roberts, A., Barham, P., Chung, H. W., Sutton, C., Gehrmann, S., et al. (2023). Palm: Scaling language modeling with pathways. *Journal of Machine Learning Research, 24*(240), 1–113.
5. He, P., Gao, J., & Chen, W. (2022). DeBERTaV3: Improving DeBERTa using ELECTRA-style pre-training with gradient-disentangled embedding sharing. In: *The eleventh international conference on learning representations.*
6. Bommasani, R., Hudson, D. A., Adeli, E., Altman, R., Arora, S., von Arx, S., Bernstein, M. S., Bohg, J., Bosselut, A., Brunskill, E., Brynjolfsson, E., Buch, S., Card, D., Castellon, R., Chatterji, N. S., Chen, A. S., Creel, K. A., Davis, J., Demszky, D., Donahue, C., Doumbouya, M., Durmus, E., Ermon, S., Etchemendy, J., Ethayarajh, K., Fei-Fei, L., Finn, C., Gale, T.,

Gillespie, L. E., Goel, K., Goodman, N. D., Grossman, S., Guha, N., Hashimoto, T., Henderson, P., Hewitt, J., Ho, D. E., Hong, J., Hsu, K., Huang, J., Icard, T. F., Jain, S., Jurafsky, D., Kalluri, P., Karamcheti, S., Keeling, G., Khani, F., Khattab, O., Koh, P. W., Krass, M. S., Krishna, R., Kuditipudi, R., Kumar, A., Ladhak, F., Lee, M., Lee, T., Leskovec, J., Levent, I., Li, X. L., Li, X., Ma, T., Malik, A., Manning, C. D., Mirchandani, S. P., Mitchell, E., Munyikwa, Z., Nair, S., Narayan, A., Narayanan, D., Newman, B., Nie, A., Niebles, J. C., Nilforoshan, H., Nyarko, J. F., Ogut, G., Orr, L., Papadimitriou, I., Park, J. S., Piech, C., Portelance, E., Potts, C., Raghunathan, A., Reich, R., Ren, H., Rong, F., Roohani, Y. H., Ruiz, C., Ryan, J., R'e, C., Sadigh, D., Sagawa, S., Santhanam, K., Shih, A., Srinivasan, K. P., Tamkin, A., Taori, R., Thomas, A. W., Tram'er, F., Wang, R. E., Wang, W., Wu, B., Wu, J., Wu, Y., Xie, S. M., Yasunaga, M., You, J., Zaharia, M. A., Zhang, M., Zhang, T., Zhang, X., Zhang, Y., Zheng, L., Zhou, K., & Liang, P. (2021). On the opportunities and risks of foundation models. *ArXiv*. https://crfm.stanford.edu/assets/r

7. Marie, B., Fujita, A., Rubino, R. (2021). Scientific credibility of machine translation re- search: A meta-evaluation of 769 papers. In: *Proceedings of the 59th annual meeting of the association for computational linguistics and the 11th international joint conference on natural language processing* (Volume 1: Long Papers) (pp. 7297–7306).
8. Niven, T., & Kao, H. Y. (2019). Probing neural network comprehension of natural language arguments. *Proceedings of the 57th annual meeting of the association for computational linguistics* (pp. 4658–4664). https://doi.org/10.18653/v1/P19-1459. https://www.aclweb.org/anthology/P19-1459, conference Name: *Proceedings of the 57th annual meeting of the association for computational linguistics*. Association for Computational Linguistics.
9. Du, M., Manjunatha, V., Jain, R., Deshpande, R., Dernoncourt, F., Gu, J., Sun, T., Hu, X. Towards interpreting and mitigating shortcut learning behavior of NLU models. In: *Proceedings of the 2021 conference of the North American chapter of the association for computational linguistics: Human language technologies* (pp. 915–929). Association for Computational Linguistics, Online (2021). https://doi.org/10.18653/v1/2021.naacl-main.71. https://aclanthology.org/2021.naacl-main.71
10. Moon, S.J., Mo, S., Lee, K., Lee, J., Shin, J. MASKER: Masked keyword regularization for reliable text classification. Proceedings of the AAAI Conference on Artificial Intelligence 35(15), 13578–13586 (May 2021). https://doi.org/10.1609/aaai.v35i15.17601. https://ojs.aaai.org/index.php/AAAI/article/view/17601, number: 15
11. Nguyen, D., Rosseel, L., Grieve, J. On learning and representing social meaning in NLP: A sociolinguistic perspective. In: *Proceedings of the 2021 conference of the North American chapter of the association for computational linguistics: Human language technologies* (pp. 603–612). Association for Computational Linguistics, Online (Jun 2021). https://doi.org/10.18653/v1/2021.naacl-main.50. https://aclanthology.org/2021.naacl-main.50
12. Du, M., He, F., Zou, N., Tao, D., & Hu, X. Shortcut learning of large language models in natural language understanding. *Communications of the ACM, 67*(1), 11.
13. Wang, T., Sridhar, R., Yang, D., Wang, X. Identifying and mitigating spurious correlations for improving robustness in NLP models. In: *Findings of the association for computational linguistics: NAACL 2022* (pp. 1719–1729). Association for Computational Linguistics, Seattle, WA (Jul 2022). https://doi.org/10.18653/v1/2022.findings-naacl.130. https://aclanthology.org/2022.findings-naacl.130
14. Hendrycks, D., Liu, X., Wallace, E., Dziedzic, A., Krishnan, R., Song, D. Pretrained transformers improve out-of-distribution robustness. In: *Proceedings of the 58th annual meeting of the association for computational linguistics* (pp. 2744–2751). Association for Computational Linguistics, Online (Jul 2020). https://doi.org/10.18653/v1/2020.acl-main.244. https://aclanthology.org/2020.acl-main.244
15. Schuster, T., Shah, D., Yeo, Y. J. S., Roberto Filizzola Ortiz, D., Santus, E., Barzilay, R. Towards debiasing fact verification models. In: Inui, K., Jiang, J., Ng, V., Wan, X. (eds.) *Proceedings of the 2019 conference on empirical methods in natural language processing and the 9th international joint conference on natural language processing (EMNLP-IJCNLP)*

(pp. 3419–3425). Association for Computational Linguistics, Hong Kong (Nov 2019). https://doi.org/10.18653/v1/D19-1341. https://aclanthology.org/D19-1341

16. McCoy, T., Pavlick, E., Linzen, T. Right for the wrong reasons: Diagnosing syntactic heuristics in natural language inference. In: *Proceedings of the 57th annual meeting of the association for computational linguistics* (pp. 3428–3448). Association for Computational Linguistics, Florence (Jul 2019). https://doi.org/10.18653/v1/P19-1334. https://aclanthology.org/P19-1334
17. Tu, L., Lalwani, G., Gella, S., & He, H. (2020). An empirical study on robustness to spurious correlations using pre-trained language models. *Transactions of the Association for Computational Linguistics, 8*, 621–633. https://doi.org/10.1162/tacl_a_00335
18. Wang, Z., & Culotta, A. Identifying spurious correlations for robust text classification. In: *Findings of the association for computational linguistics: EMNLP 2020* (pp. 3431–3440). Association for Computational Linguistics, Online (Nov 2020). https://doi.org/10.18653/v1/2020.findings-emnlp.308. https://aclanthology.org/2020.findings-emnlp.308
19. Ren, Y., & Xiong, D. (2023). HuaSLIM: Human attention motivated short- cut learning identification and mitigation for large language models. In *Findings of the association for computational linguistics: ACL 2023* (pp. 12350–12365). Association for Computational Linguistics. https://doi.org/10.18653/v1/2023.findings-acl.781. https://aclanthology.org/2023.findings-acl.781
20. He, H., Zha, S., & Wang, H. (2019). Unlearn dataset bias in natural language inference by fitting the residual. *Proceedings of the 2nd workshop on deep learning approaches for low-resource NLP (DeepLo 2019)* (pp. 132–142). https://doi.org/10.18653/v1/D19-6115. https://www.aclweb.org/anthology/D19-6115, conference Name: *Proceedings of the 2nd workshop on deep learning approaches for low-resource NLP (DeepLo 2019).* Association for Computational Linguistics.
21. Williams, A., Nangia, N., & Bowman, S. (2018). A broad-coverage challenge corpus for sentence understanding through inference. In: *Proceedings of the 2018 conference of the North American chapter of the association for computational linguistics: Human language technologies*, Volume 1 (Long Papers) (pp. 1112–1122). Association for Computational Linguistics, http://aclweb.org/anthology/N18-1101
22. Malinin, A., & Gales, M. (2018). Predictive uncertainty estimation via prior networks. *Advances in Neural Information Processing Systems, 31.*
23. Thulasidasan, S., Chennupati, G., Bilmes, J. A., Bhattacharya, T., Michalak, S. (2019). On mixup training: Improved calibration and predictive un-certainty for deep neural networks. In: *Advances in neural information processing systems* (vol. 32). Curran Associates, Inc. https://proceedings.neurips.cc/paper/2019/hash/36ad8b5f42db492827016448975cc22d-Abstract.html
24. Guo, C., Pleiss, G., Sun, Y., Weinberger, K. Q. On calibration of modern neural networks. In: *Proceedings of the 34th international conference on machine learning* (pp. 1321–1330). PMLR (Jul 2017), https://proceedings.mlr.press/v70/guo17a.html, ISSN: 2640-3498.
25. Nixon, J., Dusenberry, M. W., Zhang, L., Jerfel, G., Tran, D. (2019). Measuring calibration in deep learning. In: *CVPR workshops* (vol. 2).
26. Bihani, G., Rayz, J. T. (2023). Calibration error estimation using fuzzy binning. In: Cohen, K., Ernest, N., Bede, B., Kreinovich, V. (Eds.) *Fuzzy information processing 2023. NAFIPS 2023.* Lecture Notes in Networks and Systems, vol. 751. Springer. https://doi.org/10.1007/978-3-031-46778-3_9.
27. Desai, S., & Durrett, G. Calibration of pre-trained transformers. In: Webber, B., Cohn, T., He, Y., Liu, Y. (Eds.) *Proceedings of the 2020 conference on empirical methods in natural language processing (EMNLP)* (pp. 295–302). Association for Computational Linguistics, Online (Nov 2020). https://doi.org/10.18653/v1/2020.emnlp-main.21. https://aclanthology.org/2020.emnlp-main.21
28. Jiang, Z., Araki, J., Ding, H., & Neubig, G. (2021). How can we know when language models know? On the calibration of language models for question answering. *Transactions of the Association for Computational Linguistics, 9*, 962–977. https://doi.org/10.1162/tacl_a_00407

29. Kong, L., Jiang, H., Zhuang, Y., Lyu, J., Zhao, T., Zhang, C. (2020). Calibrated language model fine-tuning for in-and-out-of distribution data. ArXiv. https://doi.org/10.18653/v1/2020.emnlp-main.102. https://www.semanticscholar.org/reader/05ef3566499e24888a8c50094433661 6f8f418a4. Kong, L., Jiang, H., Zhuang, Y., Lyu, J., Zhao, T., Zhang, C.: Calibrated language model fine-tuning for in-and out-of-distribution data. In: Webber, B., Cohn, T., He, Y., Liu, Y. (eds.) *Proceedings of the 2020 conference on empirical methods in natural language processing (EMNLP)* (pp. 1326–1340). Association for Computational Linguistics, Online (Nov 2020). https://doi.org/10.18653/v1/2020.emnlp-main.102. https://aclanthology.org/2020.emnlp-main.102
30. Chen, Y., Yuan, L., Cui, G., Liu, Z., Ji, H. A close look into the calibration of pre-trained language models (Nov 2022). http://arxiv.org/abs/2211.00151, arXiv:2211.00151 [cs] Chen, Y., Yuan, L., Cui, G., Liu, Z., Ji, H.: A close look into the calibration of pre-trained language models. In: Rogers, A., Boyd-Graber, J., Okazaki, N. (eds.) Proceedings of the 61st Annual Meeting of the Association for Computational Linguistics (Volume 1: Long Papers). pp. 1343–1367. Association for Computational Linguistics, Toronto (Jul 2023). https://doi.org/10.18653/v1/2023.acl-long.75. https://aclanthology.org/2023.acl
31. Dan, S., Roth, D. On the effects of transformer size on in-and out-of-domain calibration. In: *Findings of the Association for Computational Linguistics: EMNLP 2021* (pp. 2096–2101). Association for Computational Linguistics, Punta Cana, Dominican Republic (Nov 2021). https://doi.org/10.18653/v1/2021.findings-emnlp.180. https://aclanthology.org/2021.findings-emnlp.180
32. Wu, Y., Gardner, M., Stenetorp, P., Dasigi, P. Generating data to mitigate spurious correlations in natural language inference datasets. In: Muresan, S., Nakov, P., & Villavicencio, A. (Eds.) *Proceedings of the 60th annual meeting of the association for computational linguistics* (Volume 1: Long Papers). pp. 2660 2676. Association for Computational Linguistics, Dublin (May 2022). https://doi.org/10.18653/v1/2022.acl-long.190. https://aclanthology.org/2022.acl-long.190
33. Zhou, X., Bansal, M. (2020). Towards robustifying NLI models against lexical dataset biases. *Proceedings of the 58th annual meeting of the association for computational linguistics* (pp. 8759–8771). https://doi.org/10.18653/v1/2020.acl-main.773. https://www.aclweb.org/anthology/2020.acl-main.773
34. Karimi Mahabadi, R., Belinkov, Y., Henderson, J. End-to-end bias mitigation by modelling biases in corpora. In: Jurafsky, D., Chai, J., Schluter, N., Tetreault, J. (Eds.) *Proceedings of the 58th annual meeting of the association for computational linguistics* (pp. 8706–8716). Association for Computational Linguistics, Online (Jul 2020). https://doi.org/10.18653/v1/2020.acl-main.769. https://aclanthology.org/2020.acl-main.769
35. Stacey, J., Minervini, P., Dubossarsky, H., Riedel, S., Rocktäschel, T. Avoiding the hypothesis-only bias in natural language inference via ensemble adversarial training. In: Webber, B., Cohn, T., He, Y., Liu, Y. (Eds.) *Proceedings of the 2020 conference on empirical methods in natural language processing (EMNLP)* (pp. 8281–8291). Association for Computational Linguistics, Online (Nov 2020). https://doi.org/10.18653/v1/2020.emnlp-main.665. https://aclanthology.org/2020.emnlp-main.665
36. Utama, P. A., Moosavi, N. S., & Gurevych, I. (2020). Mind the trade-off: Debiasing NLU models without degrading the in-distribution performance. In: *Proceedings of the 58th annual meeting of the association for computational linguistics* (pp. 8717–8729). Association for Computational Linguistics, Online. https://doi.org/10.18653/v1/2020.acl-main.770. https://www.aclweb.org/anthology/2020.acl-main.770
37. Zhou, W., Liu, F., Chen, M. Contrastive out-of-distribution detection for pretrained transformers. In: *Proceedings of the 2021 conference on empirical methods in natural language processing* (pp. 1100–1111). Association for Computational Linguistics, Online and Punta Cana, Dominican Republic (Nov 2021). https://doi.org/10.18653/v1/2021.emnlp-main.84. https://aclanthology.org/2021.emnlp-main.84

38. Bihani, G., Rayz, J. (2021). Low anisotropy sense retrofitting (laser): Towards isotropic and sense enriched representations. In: *Proceedings of deep learning inside out (DeeLIO): The 2nd workshop on knowledge extraction and integration for deep learning architectures* (pp. 81–95).
39. Fei, H., Ren, Y., Ji, D. (2020). Retrofitting structure-aware transformer language model for end tasks. In: *Proceedings of the 2020 conference on empirical methods in natural language processing* (EMNLP) (pp. 2151–2161).
40. Vulić, I., Ponti, E. M., Korhonen, A., Glavaš, G. LexFit: Lexical fine-tuning of pretrained language models. In: Zong, C., Xia, F., Li, W., Navigli, R. (Eds.) *Proceedings of the 59th annual meeting of the association for computational linguistics and the 11th international joint conference on natural language processing (Volume 1: Long Papers)* (pp. 5269–5283). Association for Computational Linguistics, Online (Aug 2021). https://doi.org/10.18653/v1/2021.acl-long.410. https://aclanthology.org/2021.acl-long.410

The Philosophy of Intelligenticism and Its Implications on Potential Future Directions for IS Research and Practice

Francis Joseph Costello and Kung Chang Lee

Abstract In light of recent impressive developments in AI and the proliferation of large language models, this chapter proposes the novel philosophical concept of "Intelligenticism" as a response to these developments. With a new lens through which to observe and navigate the ever-shifting landscape of AI, it aims to reevaluate our proposed novel philosophical notion named "intellectualism" in light of these revolutionary advances. In this sense, we propose and define that the Intelligenticism consists of four philosophical components such as anthroposia, telopolarity, virtuodymica, and temporal bifusion. Then, this study delves into the effects of AI's widespread adoption, specifically as they pertain to IS/IT study. It provides the IS field with a novel philosophical perspective on the topic. A conceptual framework that accounts for the unique challenges and issues of deploying and supervising intelligent devices that communicate with humans is also addressed in the study. Intelligenticism will serve as the jumping-off point for our philosophical exploration.

Keywords Intelligenticism · Anthroposia · Telopolarity · Virtuodymica · Temporal bifusion

1 Introduction

Artificial intelligence (AI) has advanced in ways that are nothing short of astounding [1, 2], especially with the rise of large language model (LLM) AI. Technology and society have undergone a dramatic change as a result of these innovations, posing complex problems with unique solutions that call into question preexisting philosophical paradigms [3]. We suggest an innovative philosophical idea known as *Intelligenticism* in order to understand and effectively respond to the complexity brought about by this technological revolution. With a new lens to view and negotiate the quickly changing environment of AI, this chapter seeks to rethink intellectualism in the wake of these profound breakthroughs in intelligent machines.

F. J. Costello · K. C. Lee (✉)
Sungkyunkwan University, Seoul, South Korea

S. C. Suh (ed.), *Artificial Intelligence for Design and Process Science*,
https://doi.org/10.1007/978-3-031-67886-8_10

Intellectualism has traditionally been a human-centered ideology that places a strong emphasis on human intelligence, reason, and information acquisition. Intellectualism's foundation was laid by influential intellectuals like Socrates and Plato, who emphasized the importance of human reason and knowledge in understanding and reshaping the world [4]. The importance of rational comprehension and the categorical imperative in making ethical decisions was then highlighted by Kant, who strengthened this philosophy [5]. These individuals' ideologies have provided important insights into human cognition and decision-making, advancing our knowledge of the complex web of human mind.

Heidegger's idea of technology as "enframing" [6] underlines both the possible problems that may arise with the development of intelligent robots while also providing insightful perspectives on how technology affects society. We must be aware of the ethical and societal ramifications of these technologies as we continue to create and use AI-powered intelligent devices, making sure they are used to improve human welfare and defend our core values and rights [7]. This criticism challenges us to reconsider and broaden the traditionally human-centric intellectualism's boundaries as well as investigate this brand-new intellectual relationship between humans and machines. With this in mind, we suggest examining Intelligenticism using the ANT (actor-network theory) guiding principles. The unique and insightful perspective offered by ANT recognizes the importance of non-human entities in influencing our socio-technical environment. ANT can assist us in comprehending how AI is changing our understanding of the world by taking into account non-human entities as important participants in the socio-technical network [8].

The rapid advancement of technology, particularly in the field of artificial intelligence, is providing a potential change in how we gather information and make decisions as we head into a new era. With their outstanding deep learning and excellent pattern recognition abilities, LLMs are more than simply tools; they are intelligent beings that could potentially change established standards of intellectualism. These sophisticated machines are capable of digesting enormous volumes of data and producing insights on their own, which has substantial effects outside of academia and research facilities. The discipline of IS, where the convergence of AI and IS is becoming increasingly visible, is one where the pervasive influence of AI's broad use is particularly clear [1, 9]. We provide a novel conceptual approach to this idea within the IS discipline in light of this intersectionality. This perspective expands on earlier theories put forward by philosophers of the past and promotes novel strategies that help people comprehend the peaceful cohabitation between humans and technology that is currently required.

Establishing a conceptual framework that addresses the particular difficulties and factors involved in this scenario is crucial for effectively comprehending, deploying, and managing intelligent devices that interact with people. Our strategy is to provide a more comprehensive view of AI by including Intelligenticism into future IS concerns. Our method considers the challenges of controlling intelligence, including the degree to which machines are intelligently similar to humans (*anthroposia*; Greek *anthropos*, meaning "human"; Latin *ia*, meaning "stage of"), potential conflicts in outcomes (*telopolarity*; Greek *telo*, meaning "end" or "goal"), and moral concerns about the potential consequences of machine advancement (*virtuodynamica*; Latin *virtus*, meaning "virtue"; Greek *dynamis*, meaning "power" or "force"), and the role of temporal elements (*temporal bifusion*; Latin *tempus*, meaning "time"). The likelihood that these computers may surpass human intelligence rises as they continue to develop at an unprecedented rate [10, 11]. These viewpoints must be taken into account when we carefully analyze the philosophical ramifications and future interactions between humans and intelligent beings. By tackling this subject from a philosophical angle, we intend to draw attention to the pressing need to consider how intelligent robots will fit into our future society [12].

Intellectualism is a school of thought that emphasizes information gain, rational thought, and human intelligence. Notable thinkers like Socrates, Plato, and Kant, who highlighted the value of human reason and knowledge in comprehending and influencing the universe, have had an influence on it. The "transcendental idealism" approach, which Kant popularized, sees human mind as an active maker of knowledge rather than a passive recipient. Therefore, understanding and navigating the environment using actively created mental models, or "Erkenntnis," is what Kant defines as intelligence [13].

In reaction to the rapid development of intelligent robots, a novel philosophical idea known as *Intelligenticism* has developed. It provides a novel viewpoint for navigating the shifting terrain of AI. By considering the place of AI-powered robots in our intellectual framework, this idea goes beyond the confines of conventional human-centric intellectualism. Intelligenticism pushes us to develop a thorough grasp of these complex systems while exercising caution when giving computers the ability to make decisions. It highlights how crucial it is to strike a balance between AI's potential and human intelligence. It also emphasizes the need to reconsider how we perceive intelligence, its role in society, and the moral ramifications of empowering artificial intelligence. In essence, Intelligenticism expands the definition of intellectualism to take into account the function and significance of AI in our philosophical framework.

Due to the widespread use of AI and its increasing dominance in information and communication technologies (ICT), the IS discipline is in a unique position to adopt the concepts discussed in this chapter [1, 2, 12]. We believe that this study will serve as a springboard for a deeper and more reflective investigation of the function of AI and the complex relationships that will influence humankind's destiny. We intend to advance a future in which people and machines coexist peacefully by incorporating Intelligenticism into the IS field as a starting philosophical framework to help traverse the fast-evolving world of AI powered by contemporary AI.

2 Philosophy of Intellectualism and Machine Intelligence

The idea of intellectualism has been the focus of extensive philosophical study throughout time, and many interpretations of it have changed significantly. Ancient philosophers like Socrates built their arguments for reason and knowledge on the tenet that knowledge produces virtue while ignorance produces vice [14]. This idea holds that people who fully comprehend what is morally correct will act in accordance with it. Aristotle, on the other hand, changed intellectualism in favor of a more empirical approach and emphasized the value of logic and experiential learning [15]. The intellectual landscape then underwent a significant upheaval as a result of the Enlightenment. A new era of reason, scientific inquiry, and a healthy distrust of authority was proclaimed by the likes of Kant, Descartes, and Hume, whose key writings served as its foundation. This was a significant shift from the long-standing dependence on religious doctrine or established tradition. Descartes emphasized skepticism and doubt as a way to get specific knowledge and championed the idea of independent thought. I think, therefore I am, as famously encapsulated in his adage "Cogito, ergo sum." This groundbreaking method, known as Cartesian skepticism, questioned established truths. Hume, a significant character in the Scottish Enlightenment, also made a contribution to this change in perspective with his empiricist philosophy, which maintained that all knowledge comes from sensory experience. He emphasized the use of empirical data and critical thinking in his work, which was crucial in the development of the scientific method [16].

By fusing the rationalist and empiricist traditions, Kant's intellectual contributions, particularly his foundational work, *Critique of Pure Reason*, substantially influenced modern secular intellectualism [17]. He advances the concept of "transcendental idealism," which holds that the human mind is an active creator of knowledge rather than a passive consumer. Therefore, according to Kant, intelligence is the ability to understand and navigate through the world using these intentionally established mental schemas, or "Erkenntnis" [13]. This idea is furthered by Kant's theory of judgment, which emphasizes how ideas and intuitions interact to build unique representations of objects. It emphasizes how intelligence is a result of our capacity to form mental representations and comprehend their relationships. This view of intelligence is supported by transcendental idealism, which maintains that our perspective of the world is shaped by our cognitive faculties rather than by a direct reflection of the universe. The "semantic problem," or the accuracy of mental representations referencing real-world things, is addressed by this strategy [18]. Therefore, intelligence is viewed in the Kantian perspective as an active, constructive ability rather than a passive reflection. Here, reflexivity refers to our minds' capacity to evaluate and scrutinize their own thought processes and mental representations. In order to establish a thorough philosophical understanding of human intelligence, Kant's cognitive theory, theory of judgment, and doctrine of transcendental idealism come together [19]. He emphasizes the intelligence's constructive, reflective, and inherently active nature.

Kant's fundamental ideas are expanded upon in Hegel's philosophy, which provides a complex view of intellect. Hegel acknowledges, like Kant, that the human mind actively contributes to our comprehension of the world. Natural science is crucial to our cognitive functions because it emphasizes the value of empirical research and scientific knowledge in our ability to comprehend the world. This is consistent with Hegel's theory of intelligence, according to which intelligence is defined as the capacity to link mental representations with their actual counterparts—a process Hegel calls the "realization" of concepts. Hegel said that in order to "realize" a concept, one must show that there is an object that matches the concept and can be recognized by the observer [19]. In the context of Hegel's philosophical framework known as absolute idealism, this realization idea is crucial. According to Hegel's theory [20], reality is like a thought process in which the Idea or Spirit gradually manifests itself in the physical world. In contrast, Hegel's philosophy places a strong emphasis on the interaction between logic, natural philosophy, natural science, and cognitive psychology. His philosophical system differs with Kant's transcendental idealism in this regard, which holds that our knowledge is restricted to our own mental representations and that the "things in themselves" are unknowable [5]. In contrast, Hegel challenged Kant's claim that "things in themselves" are unknowable and asserted that our knowledge of the universe extends to it [20]. This emphasizes the distinctive features that set Hegel's philosophical outlook apart from Kant's. This illustrates Hegel's opinion that our mental frameworks and active involvement with the world through scientific research and logical reasoning affect our knowledge of the universe, which Engelman [21] further elaborates.

2.1 From Intellectualism to the Need for Intelligenticism

Lewis Mumford [22], on the other hand, argued that intellectual technologies, such as writing and computation, can considerably improve human intelligence. Mumford said that people have always used tools to improve their cognitive capacities, which has had an impact on society. This implies that intelligence is not just a natural trait but is also shaped and enhanced by the tools we develop. It is crucial to think about the philosophical implications of this convergence and how these intelligent machines will interact with human intelligence in the future as technological progress accelerates and machine intelligence narrowly surpasses human capability.

Here, Heidegger's philosophical perspectives help guide our conversation. Intelligence is deeply explored by Heidegger, who positions it as a major factor in how we interact with the outside world. He suggests two distinct levels of intelligence: the "surface" and "depth" dimensions. The "surface" dimension is characterized by routine actions and discourses that reveal the characteristics and relationships among things, while the "depth" dimension offers a wider context for comprehending these entities within a larger story [23]. Importantly, Heidegger links his conception of technology as a medium for revelation to his nuanced view of intelligence.

Heidegger clarifies the dangers of "calculative thinking," a paradigm he believes is intimately linked to technology, in parallel. This way of thinking, which is driven by numbers and efficiency, may undercut intellect or understanding on a deeper level. It allows us to adopt a dominant role as "earth's lords," but it also hides the essence that makes this possible: our alignment with a specific conception of being [23]. Heidegger elaborates on this idea by criticizing the modern propensity for a subject/object framework, which is especially pervasive in the context of technology. He claims that because humans did not create the reveal of things, this viewpoint contradicts intelligence. Instead, we discover that we are participating in and executing traditions that are not of our making [24].

In conclusion, Heidegger's philosophy exposes a complex relationship between his conception of intelligence and his beliefs regarding technology. Both are viewed as ways to reveal the world and comprehend our place in it. Heidegger cautions readers against obsessively using technology to the point where they lose sight of this higher degree of intellect. This warning emphasizes the significance of having a balanced viewpoint, embracing the benefits of technology while making sure it does not supplant our deeper understanding of life and the universe. It appears that these cautions have been forgotten in the machine AI arms race being played out by big tech given recent advancements in AI, needing a new, contemporary perspective on how to handle this warning from Heidegger.

3 Intelligenticism

We find ourselves confronted with a significant philosophical dilemma in a time when technological advancement is rising and machine intelligence teeters on the verge of surpassing human capability. From this chasm, the idea of "Intelligenticism" emerges, reflecting the philosophical underpinnings of notable philosophers like Socrates, Kant, Hegel, and Heidegger. It illustrates how our society is becoming more dependent on intelligent machines while also struggling with a loss of understanding of these systems. The increasing complexity of these intelligent robots contains a paradox that our development carries. We run the risk of losing human autonomy as we go farther into this unexplored region. This paradoxical reality necessitates a thorough reevaluation of our conceptions of intelligence, their social functions, and the moral implications of handing decision-making to machines. We suggest using ANT to investigate the complexities of Intelligenticism in order to address this complicated problem [8, 25]. According to this viewpoint, both humans and non-human things, such as smart robots, are participants in a complex network that interact and shape one another in a changing ecosystem. Human and AI coexist in a complicated and dynamic interdependence where each influences and interacts with the other. Although this dynamic has enormous potential for development and advancement, we must exercise caution since giving

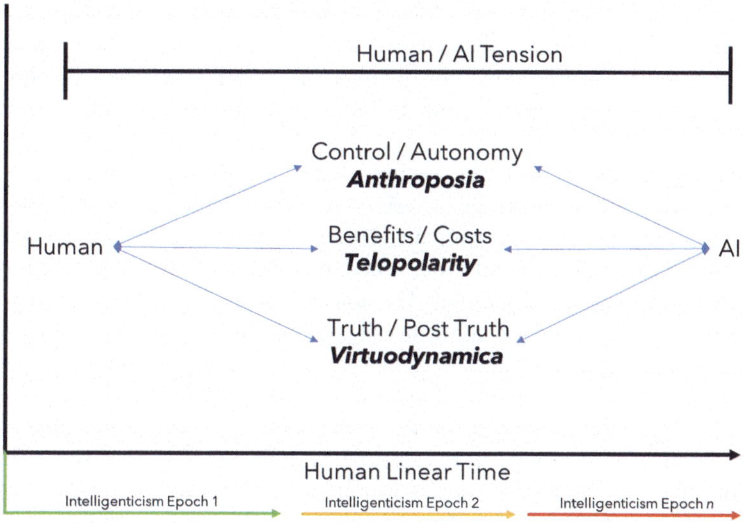

Fig. 1 Visualization of the Philosophy of Intelligenticism

computers too much control can have unfavorable effects that could impair other aspects of intelligence. Such is the fine line we must walk as we go to investigate and push the boundaries of knowledge.

We have imagined a multidimensional framework, incorporating the dimensions of anthroposia, telopolarity, virtuodynamica, and temporal bifusion, to thoroughly study Intelligenticism and its ramifications. This array is comparable to a 3D vector space with a time component (see Fig. 1 for a visual representation). We can examine the intricate interactions between human and AI thanks to it and the tensions between the three main categories identified. It enables us to investigate the moral issues raised by the development of machines and assess how the dynamics of power and control have changed throughout this period of rapid technological improvement. This thorough analytical tool clarifies the Intelligenticism debate and shows us the way forward as we attempt to balance human and AI in our common social network.

3.1 Anthroposia

Anthroposia, which is described as a state of being human, considers the ongoing conflict over control between human and artificial intelligence. It raises questions about authority, control, and accountability in a time where technology is advancing quickly, such as with LLM AI [3]. The idea of anthroposia can be elaborated upon and reinterpreted using the ANT principles to take into account the complex web of interactions between human and artificial intelligence. According to ANT [8], "actors" or "actants," which can be either human or non-human, play important roles within networks and influence those networks' outcomes through their interactions. These actors in anthroposia include people, AI systems, as well as the moral standards, societal expectations, and technological frameworks that direct their interactions.

By building on anthroposia, one can investigate how the power disparity between human and AI presents itself in a variety of areas, including decision-making, privacy, employment, and government [10]. In a world where intelligent robots are increasingly pervasive in daily life, it becomes crucial to take the distribution of power and control into consideration. Tensions are emerging in the current surge of AI-based machine intelligence about the accountability for the decisions made by machines, the implications of such acts, and the possible effects on both persons and society. Additionally, arguments about the necessity of human agency and the protection of human autonomy can arise in the context of human-machine connections. As technology develops, it is essential to maintain a balance where humans retain control over important decision-making processes and make sure that machines only supplement rather than completely replace human abilities.

The philosophical investigation of anthroposia invites us to evaluate technology's effects on our view of reality, our interactions with other people, and our shared obligation to promote an inclusive and compassionate society [26]. The ultimate objective is to change the machine intelligence into one that can be seen as "being human," or anthroposiac. By taking into account anthroposia, we can navigate the complex dynamics of human-machine interaction and work toward a harmonious integration of technology and human intelligence.

By expanding on anthroposia from a Heideggerian perspective, it is also feasible to comprehend the difficulties and opportunities that result from the interaction between the preservation of local worlds and the prevailing cultural paradigm of technology [26]. It promotes consideration on the ways that technology can either strengthen or weaken our relationship with commonplace objects, the development of regional customs, and our capacity to be true to ourselves. Drawing on ANT's concept of "immutable mobiles," [8] which refers to network components with strong irreversibility features, might also represent the ethical standards and principles that control the behavior of AI systems despite their developing capabilities and social circumstances. It implies that there can eventually reach a breaking point where the capacity for loyalty is irreparably lost.

Anthroposia provides a framework for comprehending and navigating the dynamic world of interaction between humans and machines and the intelligence that both provide. Instead of pitting humans against robots, this investigation aims to shed light on the nuances of their connection and pinpoint possible avenues for both parties to advance. As technology advances, it is crucial that we work toward harmony, balance, and the preservation of our fundamental human nature—the essence of anthroposia.

3.2 Telopolarity

Telopolarity includes the possible effects of utilizing both human and artificial intelligence. It addresses both the positive and negative effects of these intelligence interactions, as well as the difficulties in determining the consequences for personal and social life that come along with the greater usage of AI in the equation.

Heidegger's perspective highlights how technology drives us to view things through the lens of predictability and attainability by putting human-technology interaction in the spotlight. It fosters an endless thirst for advancement by making the world flexible to our planning, calculations, arrangements, and manipulations [27]. However, when the human mind struggles with the pervasiveness of technology, such a worldview may obscure the necessity for introspective introspection and other strategies. However, ANT broadens this discussion to take into account how non-human actors [25], like AI systems, may influence the potential results of technological advancement. All participants in a system are interrelated, according to ANT, which presents telopolarity as a complex interaction between human and non-human components. However, it may neglect the emergent behavior or autonomy of sophisticated AI systems because its main attention is on network connections.

The entire impact of technological breakthroughs, particularly those involving AI-based devices, is frequently not felt until after they have gained popular use. At that point, technology has typically been thoroughly ingrained in our society norms, making its removal or correction extremely difficult. This emphasizes the necessity of thoughtful, anticipatory reflection on the possible effects of new technologies before they are thoroughly incorporated into society. Heidegger suggests using the concept of Besinnung, which translates as "sensibility," to counteract the pervasive impact of technology [28]. We are better prepared to handle the intricacies of technological breakthroughs, thanks to our increased understanding of their ramifications and meanings. We may combat the calculative mindset that technology encourages by encouraging sensitivity, which keeps us open to the world around us.

Although Heidegger's method and ANT have virtues of their own, they are insufficient for foretelling the effects of artificial intelligence, particularly in circumstances when AI becomes self-sustaining and acts independently of human considerations. Heidegger's theory, which mainly concentrates on how people interact with technology, might not fully account for the autonomous behavior of artificial intelligence. Similar to ANT, sophisticated AI systems' emergent behavior or potential autonomy may be overlooked due to ANT's focus on networked interactions. Currently, self-creating capabilities are not present in AI systems. The current status of AI is a product of human design, reliance on human oversight, adherence to human legal systems, and human-based ethical considerations. The code, data, and algorithms that humans used to create the AI systems ultimately dictate how they behave, even in a hypothetical situation in which AI develops autonomy. It means that the parameters that were used to develop the model can interact with other machines in a way that makes them all completely opaque to humans, at the very least. This creates a dangerous precedent.

In conclusion, Heidegger and ANT provide fascinating perspectives on the effects of technological development, but they might fall short of capturing the complexities of future machine intelligence. A contemplative mentality and sensibility are encouraged by telopolarity, which draws on these viewpoints, in order to appropriately navigate the rapidly evolving technology ecosystem. This method emphasizes how crucial it is to balance the benefits of technology against its unanticipated negative effects on society and the individual. It also recommends pondering the possible results of giving robots more autonomy and anticipatorily assessing the results before releasing them into the real world.

3.3 Virtuodynamica

Virtuodynamica is an additional philosophical school having strong roots in the larger Intelligenticism movement. It provides a profound lens through which to consider the moral implications and foundations that are inextricably linked to the development of machines, particularly strengthened AI models. This idea emphasizes the critical necessity for ongoing reflection on the ethical bounds of AI and the necessary safeguards to ensure adherence to these limits. Virtuodynamica also emphasizes the inherent risks connected with allowing unrestrained human feedback loops. This is due to the constant chance that potential moral hazards may be incorporated into these models or that they will initially be created with dubious morality by malevolent actors [29]. Virtuodynamica must therefore be seen as a complicated interaction between human and non-human actors within a complex ethical network that is closely related to the development of machines.

The AI models themselves are a part of this complex web, as are the data that powers their learning, the architects who create their capabilities, the users who interact with them, and the social norms and laws that influence how they operate. Regardless of whether it is considered to be human or non-human, each entity makes a contribution to the network's ethical architecture, which influences key elements including accountability, transparency, fairness, and bias. In conclusion, virtuodynamica offers a framework for ethical considerations that is necessary for the ethical creation and use of intelligent machines, and it establishes a new fundamental tenet of modern philosophical thought with regard to the comprehension of AI-based intelligent machines.

An urgent worry about intelligent machines displaying biased AI models amplifying the biases inherent in their training data occurs within this network [30]. Virtuodynamica works to address this problem by promoting thorough testing, ongoing observation, iterative improvements, and network interest alignment to give justice and inclusivity priority when implementing intelligent systems. The objective is to lessen prejudices and advance a more egalitarian technology environment. This attempt necessitates the incorporation of moral concepts and rules derived from human intelligence into the design and use of machine learning. By doing this, moral considerations are ingrained in intelligent models, guiding their actions and behaviors toward molding the network's moral climate as a whole. This idea so reminds us of the significance of anthropomorphism in preserving intellectual control over computers and preventing the introduction of moral dangers into these networks. It is crucial to understand that virtuodynamica explores the wider societal implications of technology and goes beyond ethical issues that are only relevant to machines. This intricate web of human and non-human actors must find a way to overcome the huge challenge of the potential for intelligent robots to undermine our moral and ethical openness to one another. At its heart, virtuodynamica aims to foster a more philosophical approach to the incorporation of intelligent machines into our lives, highlighting the significance of strengthened human intellect that governs ethical issues in determining the course of our society.

It is impossible to emphasize the ethical ramifications of computer loyalty and care in the era where intelligent machines are replacing or supporting human decision-makers. We must develop criteria to distinguish machine intelligence's outputs, particularly when it comes to the control of suggestions and information produced by the technology. To maintain the basis for social cohesion based on facts and reality, this is essential. The implementation of "bot-or-not" [31] legislation, which mandates that chatbots reveal their identities, is still up for debate. By doing this, transparency is ensured, and deceit or manipulation by intelligent computers posing as people is prevented. Philosophical issues surrounding the complicated link between people and machines demand our ongoing consideration. Moving forward, it is crucial to keep an eye on the relationship's positive and bad consequences in connection to one another.

In conclusion, virtuodynamica, which is integrated into Intelligenticism, emerges as a crucial concept for thinking about the moral consequences of the development of machines. Its main principles emphasize the urgent need to continuously examine and improve the moral boundaries of computers while emphasizing the benefits of accountability and transparency through human reinforcement. It is based on the idea of minimizing ingrained biases and enhancing moral decision-making in artificial intelligence. Above all, it emphasizes how deeply technology has affected society, requiring us to give ethical honesty first priority in all of our interactions with it.

3.4 Temporal Bifusion

As it develops in this crucial moment, the idea of Intelligenticism calls for a profound philosophical reflection on the convergence and interplay of human and machine intelligence. Within a complex and dynamic system, this conceptual landscape seeks to balance the talents of humans and machines. We find a difficult balance between the potential for both good and bad results, the relevant ethical issues, and the temporal context of intelligence within this complex framework. This multidimensional framework's awareness of the two perspectives on time, or "temporal bifusion," is one of its distinguishing features. As the "going element" in the context of Intelligenticism, this idea recognizes time as a continuing, continuous biological truth that endures despite the efforts of humans and machines. It also includes the knowledge that every intellectual endeavor or era is unique and can be seen as a turning point in the development of human and artificial intelligence. Before the start of the next epoch in machine intelligence [28], this "stopping element" enables philosophical reflection on the accomplishments and advancement made by human and machine actors.

This paradigm offers a philosophical prism through which we can consider the progression of epochs in both human and artificial intelligence while also acknowledging that time itself cannot fully cease. Before moving on to the next stage of machine intelligence inside the fabric of time, it urges rational human actors to consider the achievements and consequences of machine actors. It is important to consider the idea that intelligent robots should not deviate from the stopping factor in their total autonomy. The intelligent machine would become stronger against human interference if they did this since it would bring them closer to the going element and reduce the time gaps between each intellectual leap. We must manage the challenges of this crucial era with more intellectual alertness in light of this expanded knowledge of Intelligenticism. The capabilities of AI and the worth of human intelligence must coexist in harmony. Intelligenticism encourages us to develop a profound understanding of the complex systems we have created while being cautious about giving robots the ability to make decisions.

We are reminded of the value of finding balance as we set out on this voyage into the world of Intelligenticism, enriched by the insights provided by this subtle temporal bifusion. With carefully pausing time in between each machine intelligence era, the pursuit of machine intelligence, such as AI's efficiency and utility, should be supported with a consistent commitment to maintaining human dignity and intellectual prowess. Rather than advocating for a future that is predetermined, intelligentsia offers us a viable course that calls for skillful navigation. It serves as a clarion call to investigate the breadth of our comprehension of these complex systems and proceed cautiously when delegating cognitive power to computers.

The philosophy of Intelligenticism, which is infused with the notion of temporal bifusion, finally reveals a thorough framework to direct our course during this crucial period. While maintaining awareness of the complexity of this confluence, it welcomes the possibility for transformation that intelligent machines hold. We must work to enter each new epoch with societal knowledge, informed by the entwined insights of temporal bifusion, and endeavor to balance effectiveness, utility, and the preservation of human dignity and intellectual capability.

4 Discussion

From Socrates and other ancient thinkers through modern philosophers like Kant and Hegel, this research explores the philosophical and historical roots of intellectualism. Heidegger's concept of technology as *enframing* is explored in this chapter, along with the effects of technology on human cognition [32]. According to Intelligenticism, it is crucial to think about the future interactions between intelligent machines and human intelligence as machine intelligence develops and its philosophical consequences when the two either merge or need to coexist in an harmonious mode. The study highlights the importance of standards to differentiate the outputs of AI and the ethical implications of AI use for IS professionals.

With the rise of LLMs and impressive developments in AI [10], the Intelligenticism ideology proposes a new way of understanding intellectualism. The study's focus on the overlap between AI and IS shows that these ideas are ready for widespread adoption. It stresses the importance of keeping things in perspective and appreciating the advantages of technology without letting them cloud our judgment of the wider picture. Our goal is to get IS scholars to take a fresh philosophical stance as a means of coping with AI's complicated new world. This will help us move toward a day when we can design our future with an eye toward the moral and social consequences of our technological choices. It prompts serious reflection on the nature of intelligence, its place in human society, and the moral consequences of giving robots autonomy.

The information systems (IS) field is in a prime position to absorb and incorporate Intelligenticism's ideas and principles as a philosophical framework to help individuals adapt to the ever-evolving world of machine intelligence as AI's influence grows throughout the ICT industry [1]. Policymakers and AI practitioners, including entrepreneurs, need a firm grasp of four key concepts: the degree to which machines exhibit human-like intelligence (anthroposia), the identification of potential conflicts in outcomes (telopolarity), the consideration of the ethical repercussions of machine advancement (virtuodynamica), and an appreciation of the significance of philosophical interpretation of time (temporal bifusion), i.e., when humans can intervene to either stop machine intelligence or allow it to continue unchecked. We must stress the importance of openness and responsibility in AI systems because of the potential danger they pose to our moral and ethical standards toward one another. The outcomes of AI systems also need to be evaluated rigorously.

What makes the aforementioned study so important is the fresh philosophical perspective it offers on Intelligenticism. For those analyzing the development and appearance of intelligence in modern artificial agents, the conceptual framework provided by this idea is invaluable. The report encourages further research into the effects of AI in order to better understand such intricate systems. The study suggests that the inclusion of the Intelligenticism construct may encourage new, more holistic views of intelligence that take into consideration the role of AI. Possible unintended consequences of this include the generation of innovative hypotheses and the formulation of more complex research topics. Overall, we hope this chapter shows how important it is to keep an open mind when thinking about AI within the context of the broader technological landscape, appreciating its benefits while remaining vigilant against the possibility that it could cloud our perspective of the world.

The findings of this study demand that our ideas about what intelligence is, how it contributes to society, and the moral consequences of granting such power to computers be completely rethought. We hope this study will stimulate debate as society becomes increasingly reliant on intelligent technologies, while our understanding of these systems continues to erode. However, we do recognize that the scope of our research had to be limited. Therefore, to go extensively into this topic and acquire a firm grasp of it, a nuanced approach is required, perhaps adopting a scientific methodology such as critical realism. Understanding Intelligenticism, its possible generative mechanisms, and its ties to both IS and the academic community will be facilitated through in-depth case studies of AI.

Acknowledgments This work was supported by the Ministry of Education of the Republic of Korea and the National Research Foundation of Korea (NRF-2023S1A5A2A21084333).

References

1. Berente, N., Gu, B., Recker, J., & Santhanam, R. (2021). Special issue editor's comments: Managing artificial intelligence. *MIS Quarterly, 45*, 1433–1450. https://doi.org/10.25300/MISQ/2021/16274
2. Seidel, S., Berente, N., Lindberg, A., Lyytinen, K., & Nickerson, J. V. (2019). Autonomous tools and design: A triple-loop approach to human-machine learning. *Communications of the ACM, 62*, 50–57. https://doi.org/10.1145/3210753
3. Bender, E. M., Gebru, T., McMillan-Major, A., Shmitchell, S. (2021). On the dangers of stochastic parrots. In: *Proceedings of the 2021 ACM conference on fairness, accountability, and transparency* (pp. 610–623). ACM. doi:https://doi.org/10.1145/3442188.3445922.
4. Krämer, H. J. (1990). *Plato and the foundations of metaphysics*. State University of New York.
5. Kant, I. (2012). *Fundamental principles of the metaphysic of morals*. Dover Publications.
6. Heidegger, M. (1977). The question concerning technology. In D. F. Krell (Ed.), *Martin Heidegger: Basic writings* (pp. 287–317). Harper & Row.
7. Weidinger, L., Mellor, J., Rauh, M., Griffin, C., Uesato, J., Huang, P.-S., Cheng, M., Glaese, M., Balle, B., Kasirzadeh, A., Kenton, Z., Brown, S., Hawkins, W., Stepleton, T., Biles, C., Birhane, A., Haas, J., Rimell, L., Hendricks, L.A., Isaac, W., Legassick, S., Irving, G., Gabriel, I.: Ethical and social risks of harm from Language Models. (2021).
8. Latour, B. (2005). *Reassembling the Social*. Oxford University Press. https://doi.org/10.1093/oso/9780199256044.001.0001
9. Carlsmith, J. (2022). *Is power-seeking AI an existential risk?*.
10. Benbya, H., Davenport, T. H., & Pachidi, S. (2020). Artificial intelligence in organizations: Current state and future opportunities. *SSRN Electronic Journal*. https://doi.org/10.2139/ssrn.3741983
11. Benbya, H., Pachidi, S., & Jarvenpaa, S. L. (2021). Special issue editorial: Artificial intelligence in organizations: Implications for information systems research. *Journal of the Association for Information Systems, 22*, 281–303. https://doi.org/10.17705/1jais.00662
12. Mikalef, P., & Gupta, M. (2021). Artificial intelligence capability: Conceptualization, measurement calibration, and empirical study on its impact on organizational creativity and firm performance. *Information and Management, 58*. https://doi.org/10.1016/j.im.2021.103434

13. Kant, I. (1997). *Lectures on metaphysics*. Cambridge University Press.
14. Guthrie, W. K. C. (1971). *A history of Greek philosophy: Volume 3, The Fifth century enlightenment, Part 2. Socrates*. Cambridge University Press.
15. Morrison, D. R. (2010). *The Cambridge companion to Socrates*. Cambridge University Press. https://doi.org/10.1017/CCOL9780521833424
16. Descartes, R. (2012). *Discourse on method*. Focus Publishing.
17. Kant, I. (1998). *Critique of pure reason*. Cambridge University Press.
18. Vinci, T. C. (2014). *Space, geometry, and Kant's transcendental deduction of the categories*. Oxford University Press. https://doi.org/10.1093/acprof:oso/9780199381166.001.0001
19. Westphal, K. R. (2017). Cognitive psychology, intelligence and the realisation of the concept in Hegel's encyclopaedic epistemology. In *Grounds of pragmatic realism* (pp. 417–438). BRILL. https://doi.org/10.1163/9789004360174_020
20. Hegel, G. W. F. (2001). *Encyclopaedia of the philosophical sciences part one*. Blackmask Online.
21. Engelman, R. (2022). Modern scepticism, metaphysics, and absolute knowing in Hegel's science of logic. *Hegel Bulletin, 1–28*. https://doi.org/10.1017/hgl.2022.39
22. Mumford, L. (1959). An appraisal of Lewis Mumford's "technics and civilization" (1934). *Daedalus, 88*, 527–536.
23. Crowell, S. (2018). The challenge of Heidegger's approach to technology. In: *Heidegger on technology* (pp. 74–95). Routledge, 1 [edition]. Taylor & Francis. | Series: Routledge studies in twentieth-century philosophy; 44 (2018). doi: https://doi.org/10.4324/9781315561226-5.
24. Dahlstrom, D. O. (2018). Imposition. In: *Heidegger on technology* (pp. 39–56). Routledge, 1 [edition]. Taylor & Francis. Series: Routledge studies in twentieth-century philosophy; 44 (2018). doi:https://doi.org/10.4324/9781315561226-3.
25. Mutch, A. (2002). Actors and networks or agents and structures: Towards a realist view of information systems. *Organization, 9*, 477–496. https://doi.org/10.1177/135050840293013
26. Dreyfus, H. L., & Spinosa, C. (2003). Further reflections on Heidegger, technology, and the everyday. *Bulletin of Science Technology Society, 23*, 339–349. https://doi.org/10.1177/0270467603259868
27. Introna, L. D. (2002). The question concerning information technology. In *Internet management issues* (pp. 220–234). IGI Global. https://doi.org/10.4018/978-1-930708-21-1.ch014
28. Wrathall, M. A. (2018). The task of thinking in a technological age 1. In: *Heidegger on technology* (pp. 13–38). Routledge, 1 [edition]. Taylor & Francis. Series: Routledge studies in twentieth-century philosophy; 44 (2018). doi:https://doi.org/10.4324/9781315561226-2.
29. Christian, B. (2020). *The Alignment problem: Machine learning and human values*. W. W. Norton & Company.
30. Srinivasan, R., & Chander, A. (2021). *Biases in AI systems*. doi:https://doi.org/10.1145/3464903.
31. European Commission: Laying down harmonised rules on artificial intelligence (Artificial Intelligence Act) and amending certain union legislative acts. Brussels (2021).
32. Keiling, T. (2018). Letting things be for themselves. In: *Heidegger on technology* (pp. 96–114). Routledge, 1 [edition]. Taylor & Francis. | Series: Routledge studies in twentieth-century philosophy; 44 (2018). doi:https://doi.org/10.4324/9781315561226-6.

Introducing Feature Selection Before Propositionalization

Clement Ting, Patrick Then, and Man Lau

Abstract The selection stage of knowledge discovery in databases (KDD) reduces the project scope to features relevant to the data mining objective while maintaining the final model's effectiveness. The scope reduction is important because the next stage of KDD, compilation (propositionalization), is a resource-intensive task that converts the data from a relational dataset into a propositional dataset for data mining. However, KDD selection is done manually because conventional feature selection techniques are not compatible with the pre-compiled, relational data.

In this chapter, we introduce an automated feature selection before propositionalization (FSbP) and compare its characteristics with traditional feature selection techniques. Wc provide a use case for FSbP in KDD for oil drilling data, where FSbP is vital for timely project completion. We also briefly discuss the implementation of FSbP algorithms for the above use case, areas for improvement, and limitations of FSbP.

Keywords Feature selection before propositionalization · Big data · Harmonization · Knowledge discovery in databases · Oil drilling

1 Introduction

Feature selection is a staple preprocessing task in machine learning that aims to remove redundant or irrelevant features from training sets. It has been shown to improve model accuracy, training time, generalization ability, and model running time. This process, however, assumes that the dataset to be used is already in

C. Ting (✉) · P. Then
Swinburne University of Technology Sarawak Campus, Kuching, Sarawak, Malaysia
e-mail: cpting@swinburne.edu.my; pthen@swinburne.edu.my

M. Lau
Swinburne University of Technology, Hawthorn, VIC, Australia
e-mail: elau@swinburne.edu.au

S. C. Suh (ed.), *Artificial Intelligence for Design and Process Science*,
https://doi.org/10.1007/978-3-031-67886-8_11

propositional format [1]. In propositional format, data is stored in the form of an attribute-value representation in a single table [2].

The process of propositionalization is used to transform relational data into propositionalized data and may include steps such as the joining of tables via their relationship and aggregation and other data preprocessing techniques.

When performing KDD on previously collected oil drilling data [3], this transformation process is not feasible if performed on the entire sets of data, which is multi-sourced (requiring harmonization), big [4] (each source containing about 700 tables and 20,000 columns/features), and sparse [5]. That is because the transformation of each feature requires prior knowledge of its business rules.

The above process becomes difficult when the database model is not available to determine relationships between tables and when sparse data interferes with the table joining process and priors are either not available to the data scientist or sources of priors either conflict with one another or with the database.

A method is required to determine which data are most relevant to the learning objective before propositionalization that is not reliant on the availability of priors.

This chapter is broken down into seven sections. In the Introduction, we have introduced the motivation for FSbP. In the Introducing FSbP section, we describe FSbP and compare it to KDD selection and regular feature selection environments. In the Literature Review section, we discuss literature regarding conventional feature selection techniques that may be relevant to the implementation and measuring the efficacy of FSbP. In the Methodology section, we briefly discuss implementations of FSbP as used in the context of KDD for oil drilling data. In the Results section, we show our initial results in the form of percentage of features selected and model performance. In the Discussion section, we discuss initial findings from the execution of FSbP, and then we conclude with the Conclusion section.

2 Introducing FSbP

A method is required to determine which data are most relevant to the learning objective before propositionalization that is not reliant on the availability of priors.

To address this issue, we introduce a novel concept called feature selection before propositionalization (FSbP). FSbP is performed on un-propositionalized data, which is relational data that has not yet been joined and compiled. This technique is different from any current forms of feature selection (see Table 1) because it allows for the selection of relevant features early in the KDD process, before the data has been fully processed and compiled.

FSbP is performed during the "selection" process of KDD, which is different from the "filtering" stage of machine learning. The objective of FSbP is to select the most relevant features to create a training set with minimal observation and exploration of the data. This technique is particularly useful for the KDD of high-dimensionality datasets.

Table 1 Comparing FSbP to KDD FSS and ML FS

	FSbP	KDD FS	ML FS
Purpose	Select features most relevant to project objective Reduces project scope with minimal reduction to model accuracy		
Timing	KDD: Selection		KDD: Data Mining
Methodology	In this project, combining DAHFR and RFCM	Gather expert knowledge to determine most relevant features	Variance Threshold, Univariate Feature Selection, Recursive Feature Elimination, Select from Model, Sequential Feature Selection
Metrics	Feature relevance gathered from factors measurable before propositionalization In this project, data missingness, feature correlation to target label	Feature relevance as defined by expert knowledge	Variance of feature, Feature correlation to label or model accuracy
Advantage	Doesn't require propositionalization Repeatable metrics and results	Quick if expert knowledge is available	Reasonable and repeatable metrics and results
Limitation	Data have not been or cannot be easily propositionalized Efficacy is difficult to measure (long project duration between KDD: Selection and completion of KDD:Data Mining).	Requires access to expert knowledge of database and business rules Reliance on existing business rules and may miss new knowledge. Less scalable when multiple experts (one or more for each source) must be consulted Reliance on expert knowledge which may change from expert to expert	Requires standardized, propositionalized dataset

The importance of FSbP is highlighted in situations where there is little expert knowledge available to determine the relevant features for the training set. In these cases, selecting relevant features early in the KDD process reduces the dependence on expert knowledge and biases, which can improve the generalizability of the dataset. This technique also speeds up the data compilation process and reduces the amount of manpower required to process the features.

While there are some similarities between FSbP and existing forms of feature selection, our technique is unique in that it is performed early in the KDD process and on un-propositionalized data, while feature selection is performed during the data mining stage. One example of FSbP exists in literature [6], where a wrapper method was used to select features, but the process was dependent on the availability of the entity relationship model (ERM) for the database that contained the features so automated data compilation could be performed for training purposes. Our form of FSbP performs without the full ERM knowledge, which is required because many of the features are in groups of irregular time series.

3 Literature Review

Machine learning algorithms rely on data to train models that can predict outcomes. However, not all data is equally relevant to the target objective. The inclusion of irrelevant or redundant features can negatively impact a model's accuracy, training time, ability to generalize, and model running time. A feature selection process is used to remove such features from the dataset before the training process begins or as part of the training process [1].

3.1 Categories of Feature Selection Strategies

Feature selection strategies are chosen based on assumed relationship or nature of the features. Well-established feature selection techniques assume a "flat feature" where features are assumed to be unrelated to one another. Other techniques account for inter-feature relationships, assuming either streaming features or structured features [4]. In this chapter, we'll briefly explain flat and structured features as they are relevant to guiding our strategies and their limitations.

Flat features are features that are assumed to be independent. Feature selection processes for flat features are grouped into three categories, which are filter methods, wrapper methods, and embedded methods.

Filter methods ranks and evaluates features based on a certain criterion. Examples of scores used for filter methods include the Fisher Score, which evaluates a feature based on its variance with respect to class values, methods based on information gain and mutual information and information gain, and Relief and ReliefF, which uses calculated distances of nearest values (feature-wise) of instances between identical and different classes.

Filter-methods are simple to execute but it does not guarantee an optimal feature set post-FS.

The second category, wrapper models, iterates through possible subsets of features from the initial training set and measures their suitability by measuring the performance of training models created from the feature sets, selecting the best feature set to be used for the final training.

Feature sets selected by wrapper techniques are computationally expensive because it must both search the feature space and train models with each feature iteration. For datasets with a lot of features, wrapper techniques and search algorithms must be implemented to explore the feature space.

In exchange for computation complexity, wrapper techniques provide better predictive accuracy estimates than filter models.

The third category is embedded models, in which the feature selection process is embedded as part of the training algorithm, as opposed to being a step in the preprocessing stage of machine learning.

Structured feature selection assumes that the feature space contains features that may be dependent to one another. FS strategy depends on the assumed structure, either group structure, tree structure, or graph structure.

J. Tang et al. (2014) [1] provide examples for structured feature selection for cases where the group structure has already been inferred. These examples are modifications of the embedded method, lasso regularization. Lasso regularization generates weights for features as part of the model optimization process, and feature selection is performed naturally when coefficients of features are set at 0 or close to 0.

Modifications are done based on the structure of the features, which are group structures, tree structures, or graph structures.

When a group structure is assumed, features are put into groups, and feature selection is done based on the group's performance instead of an individual feature's performance.

Tree structure assumes that features are hierarchical in nature with several level of parent and child nodes, with features being at the bottom layer. Nodes are examined for feature selection, in which case underperforming nodes and their underlying features are discarded.

Graph structures imply directionless relationships between features, in which case the weights of the lasso for features are adjusted during selection based on related features in the graph.

T. Gao et al. (2015) [7] treated graph structured feature selection as a search problem to find a target feature's Markov blanket. The methodology explores the features and creates a Bayesian network by determining inter-feature relationships, which may be simplified to "Parent," "Child," "Spouse," and "Descendants." Compared to graph structures, a Bayesian network is simply a graph structure with directional relationship.

Gao et al. present that the Markov blanket of a target feature, which contains its spouses, parents, and child, will contain the minimum number of features within the feature space, which also gives the maximum mutual information required for a classifier model.

3.2 Evaluation of Feature Selection Strategies

Evaluation of feature selection models is chiefly performed by evaluating the trained model's effectiveness [8]. As with evaluating training models, performance metrics can include accuracy, precision, recall, F1-score, and area under the receiver operating characteristic (ROC) curve. These metrics measure the model's ability to correctly classify instances from the test dataset. The feature selection process that leads to the best performance metrics is considered the most effective.

4 Methodology

In this chapter, we introduce the concept of FSbP as seen in Fig. 1, which has been used only once before Motl and Kordik (2018) [6]. Unlike Motl and Kordik, we do not use automated compilation as part of the process but instead rely on the characteristics of the data while still not directly observing the data. FSbP as a concept may employ many feature selection techniques, but we combine two novel methods of feature selection for FSbP.

4.1 Data Source

The data for this project is provided by a company that provides oil drilling data collection and reporting solutions to oil drilling company. The data provided is contained in 5 databases, with possibility of scaling to more than 20 databases. Each database represents oil drilling data collected by one oil drilling company and has about 700 tables and 20,000 features. All the company's databases are similar in schema but different in data entry patterns and sparsity and contain semantically different data. The KDD project is big and multi-sourced in nature.

4.2 DAHFR

First, we perform Database Attribute Health Feature Reduction (DAHFR), which is a filter method [9] that visualizes and selects relevant features from databases based on their relational missingness. This process requires the selection of a baseline feature for relational missingness comparison. Relational missingness for features are measured based on the percentage of baseline feature's data represented by the measured feature. Relational missingness is represented in two forms, table health and attribute health, which discriminates some Missing Not at Random features from what would otherwise be treated as Missing Completely at Random features. Selection at this stage is performed by using a missingness threshold, which is different when used for single databases and multi-sourced databases.

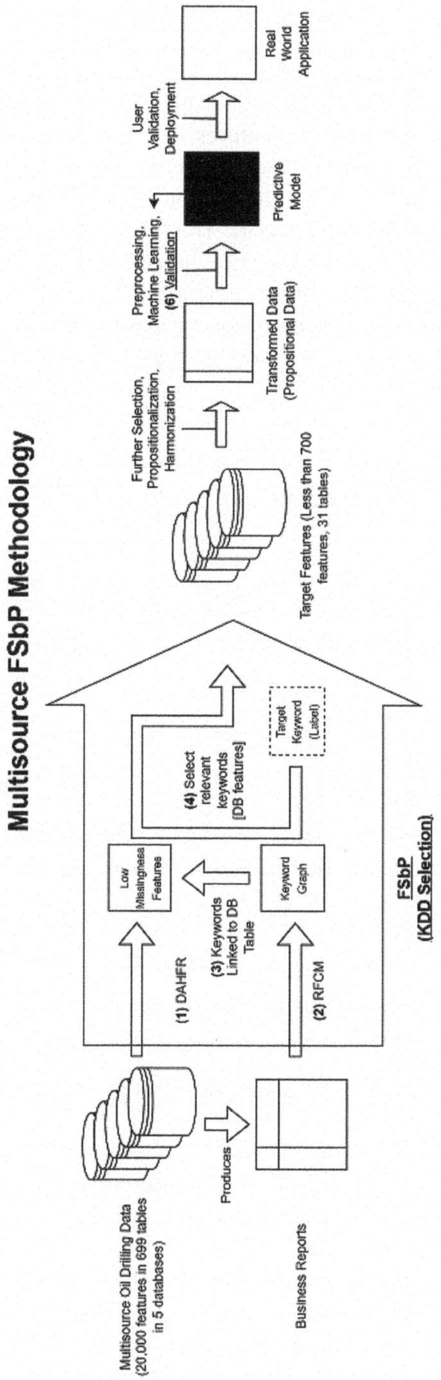

Fig. 1 FSbP process in relation to KDD and machine learning of oil drilling data. FSbP refers to the timing of feature selection during KDD, while steps 1–4 are one implementation of FSbP

4.3 RFCM

Second, we perform Report Feature Correlation Matrix (RFCM), which converts reports generated from the database's data to create a feature graph (graph structure) that contains correlation data between features to represent business knowledge. With permission to access the reporting module of the system that uses the database, we explore the reporting module and record on a per-report basis and record properties and keywords related to the report. The keywords are grouped according to where they are found in the report generation process, e.g., scope of report, group by parameters, and report attributes. These keywords are refined by searching online resources, and then a graph is made based on how often the keywords are found together. The graph structure is used to estimate the Markov blanket [7] of a target label based on its keyword.

4.4 Relating DAHFR to RFCM

Third, we relate DAHFR to RFCM by linking the "database domain" and "business domain," respectively, using the knowledge gained from the keyword search. The keywords are linked to tables based on the tables' names or their column names.

4.5 Feature Selection

Finally, we perform the selection process by selecting the target label concept in the RFCM/business domain and selecting the related relevant data in DAHFR/database domain.

4.6 Data Mining and Evaluation

After FSbP is performed, the data undergoes further selection and combined propositionalization and harmonization. For propositionalization and harmonization, a standard set of definitions is made for selected features from the five databases including the label, which is the oil-drilling phase duration.

As part of the data mining step, several preprocessing methods are used to determine the most effective methods.

The dataset is split 70/30 for training operations (randomly selected with identical seed values) and testing operations, and training is done with a tenfold cross validation, also splitting by operations instead of phases. This is because one oil drilling operation involves several phases that are pre-determined.

The performance of the models is evaluated on traditional ML metrics [10] of RMSE, MSE, and MAE, in addition to a custom metric, "larger than 0," as the result (being a time prediction) must always be larger than 0. In addition, suitability of the resulting predictions is determined by comparing the predicted DvD (drilling rate across phases in an operation) against the actual DvD of an operation.

5 Results

5.1 *FSbP Features Reduced*

The FSbP process began with about 700 tables and 20,000 features per database.

As seen in Table 2, DAHFR was able to identify the sparsest (completely unused features) and reduce the feature scope down to 131 tables with 2967 features. Further DAHFR filtering leaves 37 tables with 707 features in scope.

RFCM processed 125 distinct business reports and was used to identify and graph 48 keywords (Table 3). These 48 RFCM keywords were linked to 50 database tables.

Twenty-one of 48 keywords from RFCM were keywords related to "duration" or were neighbors to duration keywords (at this time, the Markov blanket was not used due to user error). From these, 35 target database tables were identified (Table 4). Further manual selection (based on DAHFR table health, keyword definition) reduces the number of tables for further examination to 22 tables of the initial 700 tables, a removal of 96.8% of tables from the scope.

Unfortunately, only one database was used instead of all five by the end of the project to simplify the project, although harmonization was mostly completed.

5.2 *Predictive Modeling Results*

The dataset had an average of 82.5 h, median of 29.7 h, mode of 2694 h, and std dev of 124 h. SKLearn models of Random Forest Regressor, Linear Regressor, and Multilayer Perceptron are trained from the model with various preprocessing steps, resulting in the top-ranking models as shown in Table 5. The best model's accuracy distribution is shown in Fig. 2 while Fig. 3 shows a result where multiple predicted phase durations are compared against actual phase durations over the duration of a project.

Table 2 Number of tables and features selected by DAHFR

		Not including unique identifier features	
	Raw	DAHFR Remove Unused Features	Harmonize DAHFR
# Tables	~700	121	37
# Features	~20,000	2967	707

Table 3 Graph of keywords and reports properties, red representing the keyword *duration* and yellow representing keywords related to duration

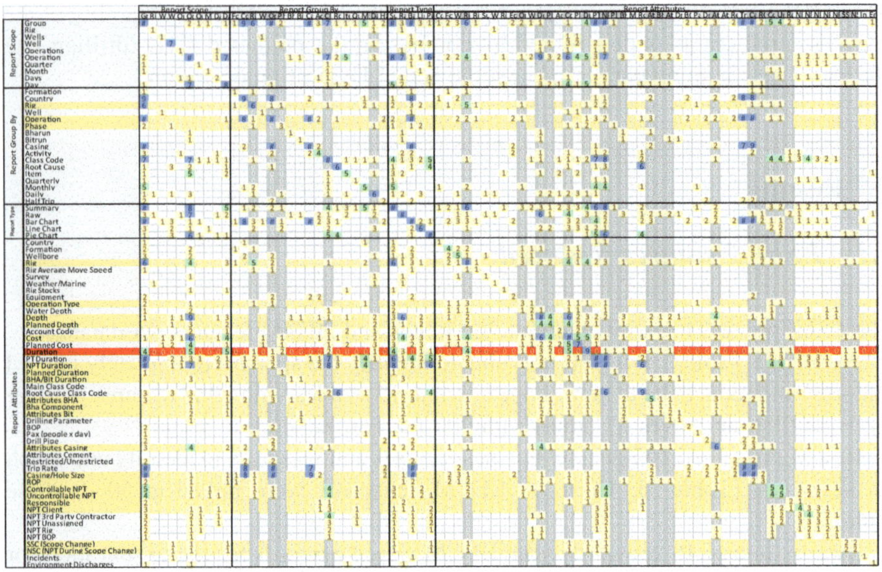

6 Discussion

The key objective of feature selection is to reduce the number of features while retaining features most relevant to the prediction objective.

One factor to always be aware of during FSbP is that removal of features at this stage (KDD FS) will forever remove them from scope for future reexamination, and data scientists may be more interested in extracting accurate models from their given dataset (post-propositionalization) rather than searching back, researching, and recompiling data.

Because of this, the FSbP must focus on removing only the least relevant features, and not focus on finding the most related features.

With that in mind, despite the lax threshold for selection, FSbP has removed 96.8% of tables from the scope for data compilation and data mining.

FSbP proves crucial for the data scientist because it allows the scientist to focus efforts on relevant features during data compilation where otherwise examination or compilation of the entire database would require the immediate understanding of the database and the multi-disciplinary expert knowledge, which contributes to the 700 tables and 20,000 columns AND the understanding of data entry practices and semantics for each individual database.

Table 4 List of 35 database tables relevant to "duration" as determined by RFCM. Table health (DAHFR) represents how often the table is used. A higher table health is preferred

Table Health	Table
97%	activity
83%	bharun
4%	biostratigraphy
81%	bitrun
66%	casing_section
35%	cement_job
85%	cost_dailysheet
99%	daily
74%	drilling_parameters
92%	dvd_summary
10%	ftr_drill_line_equipment
12%	ftr_drilling
5%	ftr_rig
14%	ftr_tripping
85%	hse_incident
30%	leak_off_test
4%	lesson_ticket
64%	marine_properties
79%	mud_properties
69%	mud_volumes
100%	operation
85%	operation_plan_master
85%	operation_plan_phase
86%	personnel_on_site
99%	report_daily
96%	rig_information
21%	rig_parameters
14%	rig_pump_param
10%	rushmore_wells
75%	survey_station
4%	target_zone
81%	transport_daily_param
44%	unwanted_event
100%	well
100%	wellbore

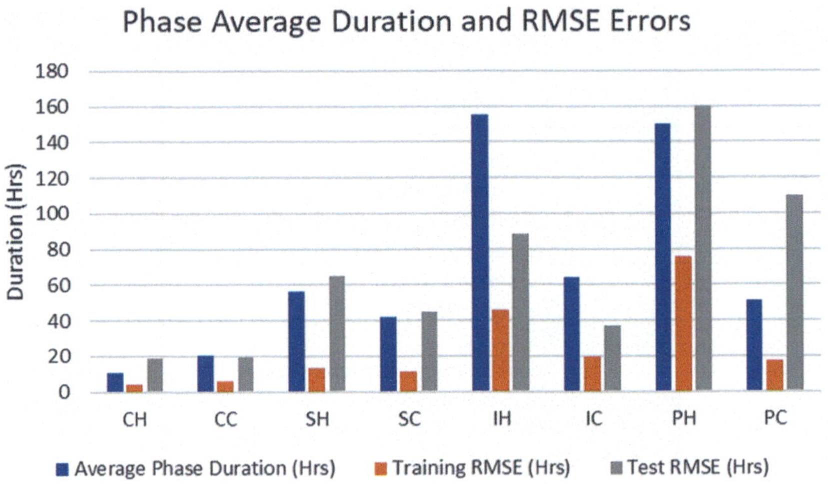

Fig. 2 Model accuracy by phase type

In the end, the FSbP's performance is determined by the performance of produced predictive models. To this end, the predictive model does not necessarily show the FSbP's performance due to the long pipeline of data transformations that happen between FSbP and predictive modeling during which introduction of errors or noise could occur.

For example, during data compilation, data undergoes aggregation such as summations, averaging, etc. while also handling missing values, while new data may be created by transforming existing data.

Then for the preprocessing steps, missing data imputation and conventional feature selection processes further modify the information before the dataset finally arrives for training.

Returning to reviewing FSbP's performance based on the resulting predictive models, the predictive model was able to produce believable DvDs (Fig. 3). Although the model seems to have high RMSE errors, it may be attributed to the nature of the labels themselves, which mostly are close to 0 with many outliers with high values, which must also be identified.

Therefore, FSbP was able to reduce the scope of features while producing a relevant predictive model.

Table 5 Top 15 models of 120 model combinations

Rank	Model ID	Imputation method	Duration scale	Feature selection	Model	>0		RMSE	
						Train	Test	Train	Test
1	1_1_3_1_rfr	DEFAULT_0_BEFORE_ENCODE	Scale to 0–1	None	rfr	100	100	38.29	84.14
2	1_1_4_5_rfr	DEFAULT_0_BEFORE_ENCODE	Standardization	K-Best(Mutual Info Regression)	rfr	100	100	37.03	84.56
3	2_1_2_5_rfr	DEFAULT_0_AFTER_ENCODE	Hour	K-Best(Mutual Info Regression)	rfr	100	100	38.14	84.64
4	1_1_1_1_rfr	DEFAULT_0_BEFORE_ENCODE	No Change (Seconds)	None	rfr	100	100	37.55	84.71
5	2_1_4_5_rfr	DEFAULT_0_AFTER_ENCODE	Standardization	K-Best(Mutual Info Regression)	rfr	100	100	37.66	84.73
65	3_1_1_5_lr	DOUBLE_KNN	No Change (Seconds)	K-Best(Mutual Info Regression)	lr	87.8	85.96	93.73	92.1
66	4_1_4_2_lr	TRIPLE_KNN	Standardization	Feature Importance (Decision Tree)	lr	87.98	84.27	93.76	92.41
67	4_1_2_5_lr	TRIPLE_KNN	Hour	K-Best(Mutual Info Regression)	lr	87.52	84.55	94.04	92.43
68	3_1_4_5_lr	DOUBLE_KNN	Standardization	K-Best(Mutual Info Regression)	lr	87.8	86.24	93.47	92.71
69	4_1_2_2_lr	TRIPLE_KNN	Hour	Feature Importance (Decision Tree)	lr	88.07	85.67	93.26	92.76
113	4_1_1_5_mlp	TRIPLE_KNN	No Change (Seconds)	K-Best(Mutual Info Regression)	mlp	100	99.72	126.93	102.72
114	3_1_1_5_mlp	DOUBLE_KNN	No Change (Seconds)	K-Best(Mutual Info Regression)	mlp	100	100	127.88	102.99
115	4_1_1_2_mlp	TRIPLE_KNN	No Change (Seconds)	Feature Importance (Decision Tree)	mlp	100	100	128.97	103.31
116	4_1_1_1_mlp	TRIPLE_KNN	No Change (Seconds)	None	mlp	100	100	128.16	103.53
117	3_1_1_1_mlp	DOUBLE_KNN	No Change (Seconds)	None	mlp	100	100	128.18	103.58

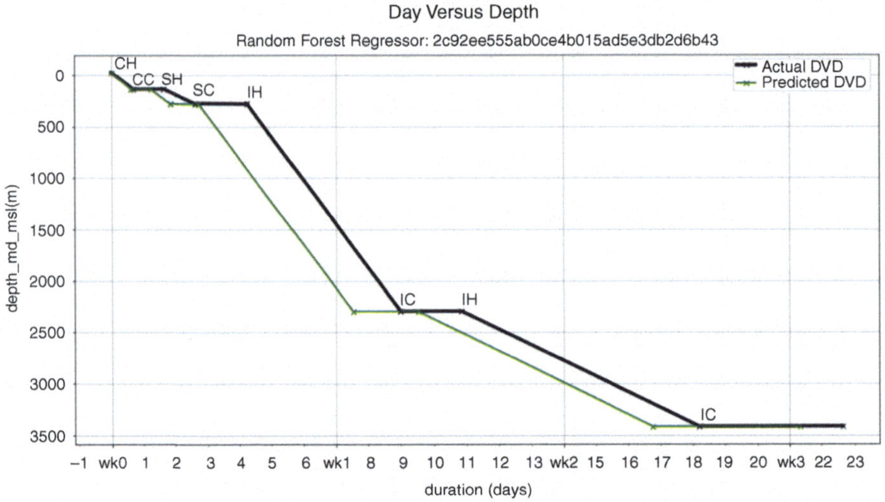

Fig. 3 Predicted oil drilling day versus depth (DvD) vs actual oil drilling DvD

7 Conclusion

We have discussed the concept of FSbP in which feature selection is done on relational data before data could be propositionalized into propositional datasets, of which regular feature selectors are only compatible with propositional datasets.

We have described a methodology for FSbP that uses DAHFR and RFCM that use database sparsity and system reports to produce "database domain" and "business domain" knowledge, respectively, to guide the targeted selection process.

FSbP was used during the KDD of an oil drilling database and removed 96.8% of the tables from the scope of study and compilation while still producing believable models as a result.

References

1. Tang, J., Alelyani, S., & Liu, H. (2014). Feature selection for classification: A review. *Data classification: Algorithms and applications*, (vol. 37).
2. Lachiche, N. (2017). Propositionalization. *Encyclopedia of machine learning and data mining* (pp. 1025–1031).
3. Ting, C. P. W., & Then, P. H. H. (2018). Prediction of oil drilling duration using machine learning. *SDPS Proceedings, 2018*, 31–35.
4. Li, J., & Liu, H. (2017). Challenges of feature selection for big data analytics. *IEEE Intelligent Systems, 32*(2), 9–15.
5. Li, X., Wang, Y., & Ruiz, R. (2020). A survey on sparse learning models for feature selection. *IEEE Transactions on Cybernetics, 52*(3), 1642–1660.

6. Motl, J., & Kordík, P. (2018). Do we need to observe features to perform feature selection? *ITAT, 2018*, 44–51.
7. Gao, T., Wang, Z., & Ji, Q. (2015). Structured feature selection. *Proceedings of the IEEE International Conference on Computer Vision, 2015*, 4256–4264.
8. Shardlow, M. (2016). An analysis of feature selection techniques. *The University of Manchester, 1*(2016), 1–7.
9. Liu, H., Zhou, M., & Liu, Q. (2019). An embedded feature selection method for imbalanced data classification. *IEEE/CAA Journal of Automatica Sinica, 6*(3), 703–715.
10. Emmanuel, T., Maupong, T., Mpoeleng, D., Semong, T., Mphago, B., & Tabona, O. (2021). A survey on missing data in machine learning. *Journal of Big Data, 8*(1), 1–37.

The manufacturer's authorised representative in the EU is Springer Nature Customer Service Centre GmbH, Europaplatz 3, 69115 Heidelberg, Germany. If you have any concerns regarding our products, please contact ProductSafety@springernature.com

Printed and bound by CPI Group (UK) Ltd, Croydon, CR0 4YY
30/09/2026
02225507-0005